My good friend Gene Getz has done it again . . . lifting the biblical essence of the Church and planting it squarely on the front lines of contemporary life. In a day when churches are floundering in stagnant mediocrity and uncertainty, *Elders and Leaders* bursts through with the brilliant and transforming biblical model.

> Bruce Wilkinson, Author: *Prayer of Jabez*

How refreshing to read a book dealing with church that is historically biblical yet contemporarily relevant. Both biblical accuracy and a lifetime of wisdom merge on a subject filled with controversial issues. I applaud Gene for providing such clarity on a very misunderstood subject. This book should be read by all who are in leadership of God's church.

> Randy Pope, Pastor, Perimeter Church, Atlanta, Georgia

Houses of worship dot the American landscape, places where people come to gain inner strength for the tough game of everyday life. But we the people seem to post a low spiritual batting average, largely because gaping holes exist in our leadership. Most church leaders sincerely want to represent their Lord well, but often fail because the job is much harder than it looks—a daunting mix of business, education, soul care and social life. *Elders and Leaders* points the way toward building an effective leadership team. Not merely a "my-story" account, this clearly-written and well-researched manual explains the way a church should work. Gene Getz, professionally-competent and biblically-astute pastor of long experience, has written a superb tool which should be required for reading and discussion in every church which hopes to make a permanent impact for Jesus Christ in its community.

> Howard G. Hendricks, Distinguished Professor and Chairman,
> Center for Christian Leadership
> Dallas Theological Seminary

Whatever your denominational orientation might happen to be, this book is a "must read." Our dear friend, teacher, leader, and scholar, Gene Getz, has given us his Magnum Opus in this carefully researched and written book on *Elders and Leaders*. The crisis in leadership in our churches today is at an all-time high. What the Bible and especially the New Testament has to say on this subject is clearly, comprehensively, and convincingly spelled out with supporting exegesis and Scriptural references. Not everyone will agree with everything presented, but all will find biblical, practical, and helpful teaching on leadership. We warmly and urgently commend this book to pastors and serious students of God's Word.

Stephen F. Olford and David L. Olford
Stephen Olford Center for Biblical Preaching

ELDERS
and
LEADERS

GOD'S PLAN FOR LEADING THE CHURCH

*A Biblical, Historical
and Cultural Perspective*

Gene A. Getz

MOODY PUBLISHERS
CHICAGO

All Scripture quotations, unless otherwise indicated, are taken from the *Holy Bible, New International Version®*. NIV®. Copyright © 1973, 1978, 1984 by International Bible Society. Used by permission of Zondervan Publishing House. All rights reserved.

Scripture quotations marked NASB are taken from the *New American Standard Bible®*, © Copyright The Lockman Foundation 1960, 1962, 1963, 1968, 1971, 1972, 1973, 1975, 1977, 1995. Used by permission.

Editor: Jim Vincent
Interior Design: Ragont Design
Cover Design: Smartt Guys design
Cover Photo: Dale Sanders/Masterfile

Library of Congress Cataloging-in-Publication Data

Getz, Gene A.
    Elders and leaders : God's plan for leading the church / Gene A. Getz.
       p. cm.
    Includes bibliographical references and index.
    ISBN 978-0-8024-1057-3
       1. Christian leadership—Biblical teaching. 2. Leadership—Religious aspects—Christianity.
    I. Title.

    BS680.L4G48 2003
    262'.1—dc21

                                                                        2003007611

We hope you enjoy this book from Moody Publishers. Our goal is to provide high-quality, thought-provoking books and products that connect truth to your real needs and challenges. For more information on other books and products written and produced from a biblical perspective, go to www.moodypublishers.com or write to:

Moody Publishers
820 N. LaSalle Boulevard
Chicago, IL 60610

9 10

Printed in the United States of America

CONTENTS

ILLUSTRATIONS

Figures

Maps

FOREWORD

A couple of years ago, we were having dinner with Gene Getz and a question surfaced that we've heard more than a few times before: "I am at a stage in my life where I have more opportunities than time. What is the most important thing I can do with the rest of my life?"

Neither of us hesitated, didn't slow down to confer, didn't even reflect, pray, or ponder. It was that obvious. It's not often that a man with such a rare treasure asks you to help him spend it. Perhaps the flailing arms and unbridled enthusiasm of our answer explains why the waiter started moving people away from nearby tables.

Our answer? "Gene, you have one of the best church models in the world that displays healthy eldership. You have years of experience and understanding of how a church board works with godliness, effectiveness, and joy. Additionally, you are practicing one of the healthiest and intentional processes of succession that we've seen: replacing yourself and having each member of your governing board replace themselves. We've seen thousands of the most effective churches in North America. Most have lost hope that church governance can actually be spiritual, effective, and enjoyable. You have a proven story that repudiates that loss of hope. This is rare. This is valuable. You need to share this gold."

Gene went back and prayed, waited, talked to his elders, his staff team, and his wife. They agreed with the same enthusiasm. The die was cast. Over the next year, this book was written.

What has resulted is characteristically Gene Getz. It is steeped in biblical scholarship, the reality of experience and the keen scrutiny of accountable relationships far beyond the average standard for any book. Biblical governance is a serious issue. This book takes it seriously. This book explores the biblical teaching of eldership and church leadership with intensity like no other.

While comprehensive, this book is also written to be a solution starter, not a simple "right answer" book. Reading this book, you may have questions such as:

☐ How many people should be on our governing board?

☐ How should we make decisions—consensus, majority, three-fourth vote?

☐ What is the role of the board versus the role of the staff—especially as the church grows and we rely more and more on professionally trained staff?

☐ Who leads the governing board—the senior pastor? A lay person? How are ordained pastors held accountable to the board?

☐ How is governance different in ecclesiastical systems with bishops?

☐ How does a governing board work in a church that requires congregational votes?

☐ How do we set vision, exercise church discipline, and test theology?

☐ How do we deal with conflict, late night meetings, too much business and too little spiritual discernment, and the dearth of qualified leaders?

The answers to these questions and more are in this book, but they are not packaged in a three-easy-steps format. We don't want to spoil the punch line of this book, but the bottom line is that the Bible does not provide a specific template for the exact right way to do governance for your church. However, the Bible *is* very specific about the *character* of those who serve as church leaders. The Bible is clear that their big picture role is to "prepare God's people for works of service, so that the body of Christ [grows to maturity]" (Ephesians 4:12 NASB). Beyond that, the Bible says very little about structure, policies, titles, organizational charts, parking places, and capital campaigns.

Gene is in a church that has no direct denominational connections, although there are approximately three hundred "Fellowship Bible Churches" that have grown out of his original vision in Dallas thirty years ago. Some readers have the same opportunity and danger of being non-denominational. They can read the biblical record and build their governance system on an empty lot based upon the blueprints of the first-century church—no bishops, no denominational rule book, no precedence. This book can help these "new construction" churches avoid the myriad of potential problems—and there have been many mistakes made in the last few decades creating enormous pain in many congregations. Furthermore, it will help those leaders who live in ecclesiastical systems that on some days they describe as steeped in rich God-directed history and theology, and other days they describe as straight-jacket bureaucracies. This book will take your faith to the Source to evaluate why you do what you do.

Finally, a warning: This is not a book that should be read alone. A key theme is that governing boards were established to make decisions in community, learn in community, trust God in community, and have fun as a community. Make the time as an elder board to read this book together with regular bouts of an hour set aside at the beginning of board meetings to discuss what you are learning. Also, the type of elder camaraderie that you see in the stories of this book didn't happen just because people in Texas are friendlier or have more time to sit in rocking chairs and visit. Gene made huge sacrifices in his time and work to prioritize time with his elders. As a result, they responded by making significant career and life decisions to do the same.

Gene, his elders, and his staff have participated in Leadership Network events for years. In a variety of forums they have the "E. F. Hutton" effect—when they talk, people listen, and take notes, and chase them to lunch to ask more. Gene is also a friend, pastor, and mentor to both of us. He is the real thing. It is our privilege and honor to know we've served even a small part of his sharing the treasure of these life experiences with you.

BRAD SMITH
CEO, International Center for
   Theological Urban Studies
BOB BUFORD
Chairman, Leadership Network

ACKNOWLEDGMENTS

I would like to express deep appreciation to my fellow elders at Fellowship Bible Church North. As often as their business commitments allowed, they met with me for many weeks to study together what the New Testament teaches about local church leadership. They've also read and evaluated great sections of this manuscript as it has evolved, giving very helpful feedback. So, here's a special thanks to: Eddie Burford, Jack Cole, Mike Cornwall, John Craig, Dan Debenport, Vince Ellwood, Dirk Hansen, Jeff Jones, Earl Lindgren, Don Logue, and Dwight Saffel.

I would also like to thank the following special people who served faithfully in helping to bring this manuscript into being:

☐ Bob Buford, Brad Smith, and my associate pastor, Jeff Jones, who first challenged me to take on this project.

☐ Iva Morelli, my executive assistant and a constant encourager, who coordinated this team effort and spent

countless hours formatting this manuscript and helping me with
the editing process.

☐ Mark Chalemin, my research assistant, who helped me discover
and evaluate a number of resources.

In addition, I am grateful to Sue Mitchell, Iva's administrative assistant, who spent many hours at the computer typing revision after revision, as well as Miriam Durham and the other staff who helped in many
ways in order for this effort to be accomplished.

I also want to express appreciation to the church body at Fellowship
Bible Church North where I serve as senior pastor. Many of these faithful
people prayed diligently for me as I wrote this book.

Finally, I want to thank my wife, Elaine, who has served as my faithful companion in the ministry. She has been a constant encouragement as
I've worked on this manuscript. Humanly speaking, I could not have completed this project without her consistent loving support.

"WHO LEADS THE CHURCH?"

The year was 1968. Little did I realize how my move to Dallas would reshape my life and ministry. I had served on the faculty of Moody Bible Institute in Chicago for thirteen years prior to accepting a professorship at Dallas Theological Seminary.

I'd always been committed to the local church and particularly to the area of Christian education. But as I faced the "winds of change" that were whirling and swirling across our nation in the late 1960s and early 1970s, my students challenged me to take a fresh look at what God intended the church to be. For the first time in twenty years as a professor, I laid aside my syllabus in the middle of the semester. My students were asking questions I wasn't prepared to answer. Together, we immersed ourselves in the book of Acts and the epistles to see just how Jesus Christ intended for us to carry out the Great Commission. It became a great adventure, and I certainly didn't anticipate that this new direction would eventually lead me out of the "sacred halls of learning" into a church-planting ministry.

One of the great principles that grabbed my attention during this process was "plurality in leadership." I'd always enjoyed working with a "team," but as I ventured into church planting, I became even more committed to this concept. I saw no other "plan" in the New Testament story —and still don't. To be perfectly honest, I have always been very disappointed with what I've perceived to be ministries built around the personality and abilities of a single leader.

Let me be perfectly honest. I was initially so committed to the principle of plurality in leadership that I, at times, downplayed and, in some respects, denied how important it is to have a strong primary leader. When I was asked, "Who leads the church?" I would always say, "The elders." In essence, that was a very true statement. And when I was then asked, "Who leads the elders?" I'd answer, "*We* lead the church, together." Again, this was a true response, but I didn't answer the question adequately. The facts are that "*I* led the elders" and *together* "we led the church." I was then, and always have been, the primary leader in the Fellowship churches where I've served as senior pastor. Unfortunately, in those early years, I communicated a "model of leadership" I was not in actuality practicing.

It didn't take me long to discover I was overreacting to what I still believe is a distortion of what God intended in the realm of local church leadership. I needed to discover a balance. Personally, I believe we see this balance in the section of this book we call "The Biblical Story," and, hopefully, you'll see this balance in "our own story" as elders, as I share aspects of our own personal journey.

The first part of this book describes the process my fellow elders and I have been involved in at Fellowship Bible Church North where I serve as senior pastor. The second part is the biblical story—what happened during the first century as recorded in the New Testament. Part 3 outlines the observations we've made as we analyzed the biblical story. The culminating section outlines the supracultural principles we've formulated based on this biblical, historical, and cultural study.

In this final section, I've shared our own experiences as we've attempted to apply these principles—particularly as they relate to "forms" we've developed and reshaped over the years. Our hope is that what we've learned will motivate anyone who reads "our story," to evaluate their own leadership model in the light of the "biblical story" and the "supracultural principles" that emerge from this study. Though I rejoice at those things we've done well, perhaps the most helpful illustrations are those things we could have done better.

GENE A. GETZ

FOUNDATIONS

This introductory section describes the learning process I've been involved in with my fellow elders at Fellowship Bible Church North. You'll be introduced to our basic research paradigm as well as our "frame of reference"—our "basic assumptions" and the way we "defined our terms."

To help you evaluate the final results of our study, we'll explain "up front" the guidelines we've used to determine and formulate supracultural principles—those biblical truths regarding local church leaders that we believe are normative for local churches in every culture and at any moment in history.

FLYING IN FORMATION: A COMMUNITY PROJECT

Hopefully, the cover design team at Moody Publishers captured your attention as they did mine when they chose a flock of geese to illustrate the contents of this book as well as the process that brought the book into existence. Perhaps you even asked yourself, *What does a flock of birds have to do with leadership?* That's a valid question, especially for those of us who haven't studied their instincts and behavior.

So consider the following rather startling facts about a flock flying in formation:

☐ As each goose flaps its wings, it creates an "uplift" for the birds that follow. By flying in a "V" formation, the flock adds 71 percent greater flying range than if each bird flew alone.

☐ When a goose falls out of formation, it suddenly feels the drag and resistance of flying alone. It quickly moves back into formation to take advantage of the lifting power of the bird immediately in front of him.

☐ When the lead bird tires, it rotates back into the formation to take advantage of the lifting power of the bird immediately in front of it.

☐ The geese flying in formation honk to encourage those up front to keep up their speed.

☐ When a bird gets sick, wounded, or shot down, two geese drop out of formation and follow it down to help and protect it. They stay with it until it dies or is able to fly again. Then they launch out with another formation or catch up with the flock.

LEADERSHIP LESSONS FROM GEESE

"Look at the birds of the air," Jesus said while teaching a group of disciples on a hillside in Galilee (Matthew 6:26). When we look at the geese that fly in formation, we can learn much about leadership. This marvelous metaphor from nature offers several obvious lessons about teamwork and leadership—lessons that hardly need to be explained. However, because I've experienced some very significant lessons in a specific way serving with my fellow elders at Fellowship Bible Church North (FBCN) in Plano, Texas, I want to clarify why these facts about geese flying in formation are so important to me personally.

First, over the years, my fellow elders and I have had the wonderful opportunity to serve together, moving in a common direction. We've all felt the "uplift" that has enabled all of us to continue our journey and to achieve far more than if I or any one of them had been "flying alone."

Second, we've all felt the "drag" of falling out of formation and how refreshing it is to once again join the team and feel the "lifting power" of a community effort.

Third, as I reflect back on our ministry together, there have been times when I as the primary leader have needed a break. In short, I've gotten weary and even discouraged. How refreshing it is to have one or more fellow leaders temporarily share the lead, particularly during times when "the winds of resistance" are rather overpowering and exhausting.

Fourth, the leaders I have served with have given positive feedback— not just to encourage me, but also to encourage one another. Just recently, one of these men penned a letter to me personally that has motivated me to continue to lead out strongly—particularly during a rather difficult challenge in our ministry.

Fifth, one of the great benefits of serving together is to have leaders who bear each other's burdens, especially when we face difficulties, not only in our ministries, but also in our lives generally. Over the years, we've experienced family challenges—illnesses and even deaths. In fact, one of our most faithful men suffered deeply from cancer and eventually entered heaven's gates to receive his reward. How encouraging to see our leaders and their families encourage this man and his own family as they faced this traumatic event in their lives.

So, what can we learn from a flock of geese? Perhaps the most striking lesson of leadership to take from a "flock of birds" is that they carry out their purpose on earth as God designed them. But this distinct species can only operate with God-created instincts. Those of us who are made in God's image have far greater potential to practice these lessons consistently and creatively. We are uniquely designed and if we know Christ personally as Lord and Savior, we have the capacity to be empowered by the Holy Spirit to function as one, as Jesus Christ was one with the Father. This, of course, was Jesus' prayer for the apostles as well as for all of us who have come to believe in the Lord Jesus Christ "through their message" (John 17:20–23).

DOING THEOLOGY IN COMMUNITY

What you're about to read is the product of an exciting group effort— "flying in formation" if you will. It has been, and continues to be, a community project. I've had the privilege of guiding this research and putting thoughts on paper. In this sense, I feel we have been involved in a process that Stanley Grenz described in his very thought-provoking treatise *Renewing the Center*. In this postmodern world, he challenges Christian leaders at all levels—in academic centers and particularly in local churches—to be in-volved in theological study and dialogue in the context of community.[1]

Personally, as a former Bible college and seminary professor for twenty years and a church-planting pastor for the past three decades, I agree with this challenge. I've been involved in both learning environments. Though the academic community has always been very intellectually stimulating and personally rewarding, it's the local church setting that provides the grassroots context for doing theological studies that relate to the total person—mind, emotions, and will. Furthermore, it's in this unique God-designed environment that we as leaders particularly can "all reach unity in the faith and in the knowledge of the Son of God and become mature, attaining to the whole measure of the fullness of Christ" (Ephesians 4:13). As the *total* body of Christ "grows and builds itself up in love, as each part does its work" (v. 16), so a body of spiritual leaders can experience the same community dynamic.

Twelve of us who serve as elders at FBCN accepted the challenge to do "theology in community"—namely, studying carefully God's plan for local church leadership. Some of us have ministered together in this role for more than twenty years, and all of these men have been active in the business world except two of us—yours truly and my associate pastor—who will, Lord willing, eventually become my successor as senior pastor.

FINDING ANSWERS

To carry out this stimulating process, we met regularly for a number of months to ask and answer the following questions:

1. What does the New Testament teach us about local church leaders?

☐ Who were they?

☐ How were they identified?

☐ What did they do?

☐ How were they selected?

☐ What were their qualifications?

    ☐ How long did they serve?

    ☐ How did they function as a team?

2. How did local church leaders in the New Testament churches relate to those who were identified as apostles, prophets, and teachers?
3. What can we learn from church history, particularly during the centuries following the New Testament era?
4. What have we learned in our journey together as local church leaders?

In answering these questions, we've used a very basic research paradigm involving three perspectives. Though serious students of the Scriptures describe this design in various ways, we've used the three-lens metaphor (depicted in figure 1).

A BIBLICAL PERSPECTIVE

To answer the questions we've outlined earlier, our first step was to look through *the lens of Scripture,* looking carefully at everything the Bible says about local church leaders. This narrowed our focus primarily, but not exclusively, to the book of Acts and the New Testament letters. It's here we encounter local churches and two groups of leaders: elders or overseers (two titles that are used interchangeably) and deacons, including both men and women.

This "focus," of course, also includes those leaders who were called and gifted to have an *itinerant* church-planting ministry (apostles, prophets, evangelists, pastors, and teachers), who were often involved in planting local churches and appointing leaders—men like Peter, John, Paul, Barnabas, Silas, Luke, Timothy, and Titus. As we've looked through the lens of Scripture, we've been able to make observations that have enabled us to formulate supracultural principles—principles that endure in all cultures and that we believe are foundational to help in carrying out local church leadership functions today.

To quote Grenz, the Bible must be the "primary voice" in any "theological conversation" in order to be true to our evangelical heritage.[2] We must not look first and foremost to the systematic outlines and categories

Figure 1
A Biblical and Pragmatic Perspective on Eldership
(Research Paradigm)

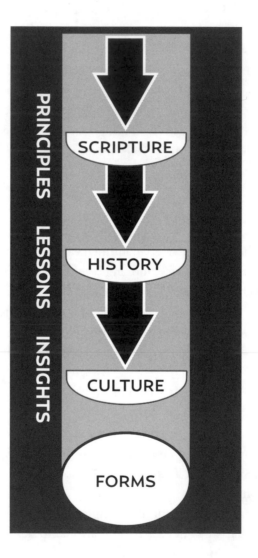

made by theologians—no matter how astute they may be. Rather, we must take a fresh look at what God has said in the pages of Scripture. This has been our goal in this study.

AN HISTORICAL PERSPECTIVE

Scriptural history flows naturally into extrabiblical church history, which helps us understand what happened in local churches following the New Testament era. From the early church fathers we've learned valuable lessons that gave us important glimpses into what transpired beyond the period described in the sacred text of Scripture.

We look through *the lens of history* to consult those who have gone before us, realizing, as Grenz states, that "we are not the first generation since the early church to seek to be formed into the community of Christ in the world." We must understand that our theological heritage provides a reference point for us today. "This heritage offers examples of previous attempts to fulfill the theological mandate, from which we can learn."[3]

Perhaps one of the greatest benefits of studying history is to eliminate those things in our present approach to leadership that are out of harmony with biblical functions and directives and to accentuate those approaches that have been in harmony with scriptural principles. Again Grenz says it well—"Looking at the past alerts us to some of the pitfalls we should avoid, some of the land mines that could trip us up, and some of the cul-de-sacs and blind alleys that are not worth our exploration."[4]

A CULTURAL PERSPECTIVE

Gaining insights from the third lens—*the lens of culture*—is absolutely essential. Without an ongoing understanding of the way people think, feel, and function in a given culture, it's impossible to both interpret Scripture properly and to apply biblical principles in various cultures of the world. Jesus, of course, understood this notion perfectly in His ministry to people from various cultural backgrounds. And Paul stands out as our most dynamic example in becoming "all things to all men so that by all possible means [he] might save some" (1 Corinthians 9:22). Paul understood culture and used cultural insights without compromising divine absolutes. So should we!

Here Grenz offers a word of caution—with which we agree wholeheartedly. We must never look to what we think is the "Spirit's voice in culture" when it contradicts the text of Scripture. Rather, we must evaluate cultural insights against the backdrop of biblical truth—not the other way around. Though insights from culture may challenge us to evaluate historic interpretations of Scripture, these insights must not drive the process. If they do, we're in danger of making judgments that are out of harmony with God's revealed will in the Word of God.

A Pragmatic Perspective

No leader can *function* without some kind of *form*. For example, we cannot "teach" and "preach" (functions) without some kind of methodology (forms). In fact, we cannot carry out *any* God-ordained function without developing ways to do it (see figure 1).

It's here that the Scriptures are basically silent—and by divine design. If the Holy Spirit had designated specific forms for carrying out specific functions, we would be severely limited in practicing biblical Christianity in other cultures of the world and at different moments in history.

This leads us to the essence of this study. If we, as local church leaders, are to develop the best possible forms for implementing biblical functions, we must first of all clearly comprehend these functions and understand how they span history and culture. This means we must see clearly the supracultural principles that emerge from this kind of biblical study. Once we are able to state these principles clearly and understand them, we are ready to evaluate current forms and to create new patterns in our own local churches that are in harmony with God's plan that unfolded during the first century—no matter where we are located in the world and regardless of the nature of our community, the size of our church, and/or other socioeconomic dynamics. If they are indeed supracultural, these principles will work in communities that are rural or urban, primitive or modern. More specifically, they'll work in the heart of a large city or in a small Indian village in the heart of the Brazilian jungle.

If they do not work in such diverse communities, either they are *not* truly supracultural or we simply don't know how to apply them. It's possible that we can be so influenced by our own culture that we have difficulty thinking and functioning beyond those parameters. That's why it's so important to have a total perspective when doing ministry—biblically, historically, and culturally.

REVIEWING FUNCTIONS AND RESHAPING FORMS

Let me say that this study includes the biblical story and our own story at FBCN. Though I've recorded the results of our process thus far, we are continuing to discuss implications for our church—even though what we've learned has grown out of our own believing community. We firmly believe that learning to do effective ministry is an ongoing experience. Together, we want to continue to study the biblical story, review our observations, and refine the supracultural principles we believe have grown out of this study. Pragmatically, our goal is to continue to develop and reshape "forms" to be in harmony with biblical principles. Not only must we continue to evaluate our conclusions regarding principles through fresh biblical, historical, and cultural studies, we must always make sure that our forms *never* become ends in themselves, but only a means to achieve the divine ends that were revealed by God Himself.

NOTES

1. Stanley J. Grenz, *Renewing the Center: Evangelical Theology in a Post-Theological Era* (Grand Rapids: Baker, 2000), 206–11.

2. Ibid., 206.

3. Ibid., 208–9.

4. Ibid, 209.

OUR FRAME
OF REFERENCE

On one occasion during our study together, one of my fellow
elders made a very important statement. "Gene," he said, "we
need to make sure we define our terms." He was right!

Terms are important. One editorial in *Christianity Today* (CT)
affirmed this conclusion—particularly as we attempt to communicate our thoughts to a variety of people from various ecclesio-
logical and cultural backgrounds in a postmodern world. CT
stated: "As Christianity sees a rise in cultural and ethnic contex-
tualizations, defining our terms and core principles will become of
prime importance."[1]

In order to enable you to grasp rather quickly our own frame
of reference, this chapter includes some of the basic *assumptions*
and *definitions* that have affected the way we have perceived and
interpreted *biblical*, *historical*, and *cultural* data. Considering the
wide range of viewpoints many Christians have regarding local
church leadership functions and forms, as well as how to study and
interpret the Bible, we certainly anticipate questions and even

disagreements. We are simply inviting you to evaluate carefully what we believe are valid observations and conclusions.

Basic Assumptions

Regarding the Scriptures

We believe that the Bible in its entirety—including both the Old and New Testaments—is God's Word and, to quote the apostle Paul, "is useful for teaching, rebuking, correcting and training in righteousness, so that" all Christians "may be thoroughly equipped for every good work" (2 Timothy 3:16–17).

In this study, our elders looked particularly at the New Testament in order to be *taught* and *trained* by what God says about local church leadership and to be *rebuked* and *corrected* when our conclusions were inadequate or in error and our applications were out of harmony with the Word of God. This, we believe, is a divine learning experience that will enable us to be *"thoroughly equipped"* to fulfill our leadership roles in a more effective way.

Since we believe the Holy Spirit inspired the authors of Scripture to record God's Word, we also believe the Holy Spirit can enlighten our minds to understand what He has written. Furthermore, we are continuing to ask God's Spirit to help us develop proper methodologies in order to apply what we've learned from Scripture in creative ways.

Regarding the Process

We believe that the Holy Spirit uses the group process to enable believers to arrive at correct biblical insights and conclusions. This is the nature of the "body of Christ." We are a community living in a particular culture. Paul made it clear that it is as "each part does its work" and as "every supporting ligament" functions that we will grow in our relationship with God and one another (Ephesians 4:16). This dynamic is vital in keeping any one of us from drawing erroneous conclusions from the Scriptures and any other source of truth because of subjective tendencies—

which all of us are prone to do because of our humanness. Unfortunately, age does not protect us from engaging in unclear thinking. Learning is an ongoing process—no matter the number of years in ministry.

Regarding Truth

As stated already, we believe the Bible is the ultimate source for discovering God's truth. However, we also believe that "all truth is God's truth." Numerous researchers and practitioners have accumulated knowledge, gained insights, and learned significant skills about effective leadership through sociological research as well as experience generally.

For example, while engaging in this research, I had the unique privilege of interviewing Ken Blanchard, author of *The One Minute Manager*—a book that made the *New York Times* best-selling list two years running. Interestingly, Ken wrote this book prior to becoming a Christian, and no one who reads it can deny that it is filled with very practical wisdom on how to be a good manager. Furthermore, much of this wisdom correlates and amplifies what we learn from the Scriptures.

There are, then, significant bodies of literature—including secular—that "contain" truth. *Our challenge is to discover what is true.* To do so, we must carefully use God's revealed truth in Scripture to serve as criteria for evaluating what appears to be extrabiblical truth. And once we discover truth—both biblically and extrabiblically—we must carefully consider that truth and act on what we know (Philippians 4:8).

BASIC DEFINITIONS

Following are some of the terms we used during our study. In fact, you've already encountered these words in the introductory chapter.

History: A narrative of events related to the church and the larger culture that are extrabiblical which we identify as church history.

In this study, we've looked particularly at what we can learn from the history of local church leaders' functions and forms that developed immediately following the first century. One example is Ignatius, writing at some point at the end of the first century or at the beginning of the second to promote a three-tier pattern for local church leadership.

Culture: The way people in given locations and communities think, feel, and act, including the forms and structures they have developed to meet their needs and to perpetuate their values.

Fortunately, many of our elders have had opportunities to minister cross-culturally over the last several years—in Russia, the Ukraine, Africa, Pakistan, Romania, Burma, and Mexico. These experiences are invaluable when attempting to discover and apply timeless supracultural principles from the New Testament.

Functions: Activities that believers engage in to meet certain spiritual needs and to reach certain goals in order to carry out biblical commands and directives.

For example, when Paul and Barnabas could not resolve the circumcision controversy in Antioch, they went to Jerusalem to meet with the *"apostles and elders"* (Acts 15:2, italics added; all italics added to Scripture hereafter is that of the author). Together they reported, dialogued, and consulted the Old Testament and eventually composed a letter to be read to churches where this was an issue (Acts 15:1–29).

Directives: Teachings, exhortations, and commands that appear in Scripture in order to carry out local church leadership functions.

One example of a directive appears in Peter's first epistle to believers scattered "throughout Pontus, Galatia, Cappadocia, Asia and Bithynia" (1 Peter 1:1). In this epistle, he exhorted the elders in these churches to *"be shepherds of God's flock,"* to be *"eager to serve,"* and to be *"examples to the flock"* (5:2–3).

Forms: Patterns, methodologies, means, and techniques that are created to carry out biblical functions and directives.

Supracultural principles: Doctrinal guidelines that grow out of biblical functions and directives and which can be applied in any culture of the world and at any moment in history.

INTERACTION BETWEEN FUNCTIONS AND FORMS

In conclusion, one very important construct has grown out of our study of Scripture and, in turn, has continued to guide our thinking as we evaluate our biblical observations and conclusions. In essence, this concept is as follows:

It's possible to describe functions and directives without describing forms, but it's impossible to carry out directives and engage in functions without creating forms.

For example, Christian leaders in the first-century world were to preach and teach (1 Timothy 5:17). However, New Testament authors often described these directives and functions without describing the "forms" used in "preaching" and "teaching." However, anyone who engages in this kind of communication is aware that it's impossible to do so without using some type of form and methodology.

To be able to differentiate between "functions" and "forms" is to be able to distinguish between what should never change and what should change in order to carry out the Great Commission of our Lord Jesus Christ.

NOTE

1. "CT Predicts: More of the Same" *Christianity Today,* 6 December 1999, 37.

DISCOVERING
SUPRACULTURAL
PRINCIPLES

On one occasion, a group of spiritual leaders and I met in our church to look carefully at everything the Bible teaches about how to use our material possessions. After six months of intensive study, we outlined 126 principles to guide Christians wherever they live in the world—whether in a primitive village in Nigeria, Africa, or in an affluent city like Dallas, Texas.

In many respects, the more recent biblical study on local church leadership has been a very similar group process and community effort. We've utilized the same basic guidelines in discovering supracultural principles for leading a local church.

GUIDELINES

We formulated four guidelines by which to develop supracultural principles.

GUIDELINE 1: *To formulate biblical principles, we must look at the totality of Scripture on a particular subject.*

Our elders' team did an in-depth study of church leadership as detailed in the Scriptures. As we studied together, we looked particularly at both *functions* (activities) as well as *directives* (exhortations, instructions, etc.). These *functions* appear most frequently in the book of Acts. This is logical since Luke recorded the acts (or activities) of church leaders during the time the church came into existence in Jerusalem and as it expanded throughout the Roman world. For example, when Paul and Barnabas founded churches in Lystra, Iconium, and Antioch on their first missionary journey into the Gentile world, they eventually returned to these cities and "*appointed elders* . . . in each church" (Acts 14:23). This illustrates a "function" or "activity" Paul and Barnabas carried out in their itinerant ministry.

Directives, or "exhortations," appear most frequently in the epistles—the letters that were written either to local churches or to men like Timothy and Titus who were helping to establish these churches. For example, when Paul wrote to Titus after leaving him in Crete to "appoint elders in every town," he gave him very specific instructions on what qualities he should look for in appointing elders (Titus 1:5–9). First and foremost, "an elder must be blameless"(1:6). This illustrates a "directive."

In a sense, *functions* and *directives* are like "two sides of a coin." Luke's story in Acts is primarily a description of the *functions* of church leaders as they were used of God to bring local churches into existence. The epistles include *directives* to these local churches as well as to the leaders of these local churches to instruct them regarding how to function. This is why we see functions primarily in the narratives of Scripture and directives primarily in the didactic sections.

GUIDELINE 2: *As we study a particular subject in Scripture, we must follow God's unfolding revelation.*

To determine accurate supracultural principles relative to any aspect of the church and how it should function, we must study God's Word as it was revealed. To do this in relationship to local church leadership, our elders began the leadership study in the book of Acts. At the same time, we consulted sections in the epistles as they were written chronologically in harmony with events in the book of Acts (see figure 2). In order to make this study more meaningful, we suggest you print out the Scriptures recorded in figure 2 and study them carefully on your own.

GUIDELINE 3: *We must be sure to interpret Scripture accurately.*

As we study scriptural revelation chronologically, we must always look at the text in the larger context of Scripture. Fortunately, we have many helpful tools to help us in this process—interlinear translations, Greek and English concordances, a variety of Bible translations, word studies, commentaries, journals, and historical studies.

Our research team devoted itself to this process week after week. After each interactive session, I wrote cumulative summaries of our observations, which we used in subsequent sessions to review and to maintain continuity in the process.

Unfortunately, when we study the scriptural events and injunctions out of context, we can arrive at false conclusions regarding the responsibilities of local church leaders. For example, there are groups that call themselves "New Testament churches" who have developed a view of church leadership that creates an authoritarian and secretive system that actually manipulates and abuses their followers—and all in the name of Christianity. This is tragic and completely violates what Jesus taught the apostles in the Upper Room when He washed their feet—he that is greatest is to be servant (John 13:12–17; cf. Luke 22:24).

GUIDELINE 4: *We must make general observations that summa-*
rize our more specific discoveries.

After we looked carefully at every reference to church leadership as these passages unfolded chronologically, we began to make more general observations. After looking at the "trees," we looked at the "forest." In other words, when making observations on the biblical story, we need to see the specifics in relationship to the whole.

Figure 2
Timeline Regarding Local Church Leadership

DATE	THE BOOK OF ACTS AND THE EPISTLES	EVENTS
A.D. 45	Acts 11:30	Elders in Judea
A.D. 45–47	James 5:13–16	Elders' prayer and healing ministry
A.D. 47	Acts 14:21–23	Paul and Barnabas appointing elders
A.D. 48–49	Galatians 6:6	Material support for spiritual leaders
A.D. 49	Acts 15:1–32	Apostles and elders in Jerusalem
A.D. 49–50	Acts 16:4	Delivering the letter composed by the apostles and elders
A.D. 51	1 Thessalonians 5:12–13	Respecting and honoring overseers
A.D. 58	Acts 20:17–38	Paul's directives to the Ephesian elders and overseers
A.D. 58	Acts 21:17–26	Paul met with James and the elders in Jerusalem
A.D. 61	Philippians 1:1	Paul greets the overseers and deacons in Philippi
A.D. 63	1 Timothy 3:1–13	Qualifications for elders and deacons
A.D. 63	1 Timothy 4:13–14	Paul, the body of elders, and Timothy's gift (2 Timothy 1:6)
A.D. 63	1 Timothy 5:17–18	Material support for some elders
A.D. 63	1 Timothy 5:19–20	Both protecting and disciplining elders
A.D. 63	1 Peter 5:1–4	Peter's directives to elders and overseers
A.D. 65	Titus 1:5–16	Qualifications for elders and overseers
A.D. 64–68	Hebrews 13:7, 17, 24	Directives to imitate spiritual leaders

The following questions helped us in making these observations:

- ☐ What have we learned from each reference?
- ☐ Who is mentioned?
- ☐ Why are they mentioned?
- ☐ What functions and directives are mentioned?
- ☐ What functions and directives are repeated?
- ☐ What are the leaders called?
- ☐ How were they appointed?
- ☐ What were their qualifications?
- ☐ When did each event happen?
- ☐ What were the cultural dynamics?
- ☐ What were the specific needs of each church?

During this process, we were able to begin to forge out supracultural principles, remembering that if they are indeed supracultural, they can be applied in every culture of the world and at any moment in history. If it's not possible to create a relevant form that is in harmony with a particular principle, chances are we have not stated the principle accurately. If this happens, we need to go back and take a closer look. In other words, the more carefully and comprehensively we look at Scripture, utilizing the lenses of history and culture, the more we will be able to clarify our observations and conclusions and the more we'll be able to refine the principles we see emerging from our study of the Word of God.

SOUND DOCTRINE

In this study, we've used the term "supracultural principle" to describe a biblical truth that is normative and transferrable. If these "principles" we've outlined from studying the biblical story are indeed a true reflection of what Scripture teaches, they can be aligned with what the New Testament calls "sound doctrine" (see 1 Timothy 1:10; 2 Timothy 1:13; 4:3; Titus 1:9).

Biblical truth and teaching (*didache*) is indeed content we can trust. It's reliable. Consequently, supracultural principles that relate to how to function as local church leaders are certainly a part of God's "trustworthy message" (Titus 1:9). However, we must recognize that these principles may not be on the same level as other biblical doctrines.

For example, if we fail to understand and believe that we are "by grace . . . saved, through faith—and . . . not by works," we may miss eternal life (Ephesians 2:8–9). This doctrine is foundational and essential in becoming children of God (John 1:10–13). On the other hand, if we fail to understand and apply biblical principles regarding "local church leadership," the church members we lead will simply not become all that God intended them to become as believers—to "become mature, attaining to the whole measure of the fullness of Christ" (Ephesians 4:13). We'll not experience God's greatest blessings in our ministry. True, this may affect the eternal rewards that God gives us for faithful leadership, but it will *not* affect our eternal salvation (see 1 Corinthians 3:10–16).

Having made this differentiation, we must never consider understanding and applying local church leadership principles as unimportant and something we should give careful attention to only when it's convenient. This process should be a priority!

PART TWO

THE
BIBLICAL
STORY

The following chapters tell the "biblical story" of local church leadership. We begin with a foundational chapter that explores what New Testament writers meant when they referred to the "church" (*ekklesia*).

From that point, we'll look at what we can learn from the "elders" in the church in Jerusalem. As we follow this unfolding story regarding the expansion of the church, we'll journey with Paul on his missionary travels and, at the same time, consult the letters he wrote that correlate with his church-planting efforts. We'll also look at other New Testament epistles that address the subject of local church leadership.

FOUR

THE *EKKLESIA* OF GOD
(A.D. 33)

BACK TO THE SOURCE

*Before proceeding, study appendix A, which profiles every text
in the book of Acts and the epistles where the Greek term translated "church" or "churches" is used.*

This biblical study on leadership must begin with the story of the
church that came into existence on the Day of Pentecost. The term
ekklesia is used more than one hundred times in the New Testament. In fact, it's virtually impossible to understand God's will for
our lives as believers without comprehending this wonderful
"mystery of Christ" that has "been revealed by the Spirit to God's
holy apostles and prophets" (Ephesians 3:4–5).

Beyond the Gospels, most of the New Testament is the story
of "local churches" and how God intended them to function.
True, Jesus Christ came to lay the foundation and to build His

ekklesia (Matthew 16:18) and when He said to Peter, "I will build my *church*," He was certainly thinking more broadly than establishing a "local church" in Caesarea Philippi where this conversation took place (Matthew 16:13–20). Without question, He was referring to that great company of the redeemed—His bride that will be finally united to Him at the Wedding Supper of the Lamb (Revelation 19:6–8).

On the other hand, Jesus was also anticipating the multitude of *local churches* that would be established in Judea and Samaria and throughout the Roman Empire—and eventually all over the world as we know it today. This story begins in the book of Acts and spans a significant period during the first century (approximately from A.D. 33 to A.D. 63). Furthermore, during this time frame, most of the New Testament letters were written to these local churches—or to men like Timothy and Titus who were helping to establish these churches.

THE UNIVERSAL CHURCH

Before we continue to look at the New Testament focus on *local churches*, let's examine more closely the *universal church* that Jesus came to build. The apostle Paul often used the term *ekklesia* in this broader sense. This is especially true in his letter to the Ephesians (see appendix A). Throughout this epistle, he described believers who become a part of the body of Christ anytime from Pentecost to that moment when the church will be "face-to-face" with the Savior (see Ephesians 1:22–23; 3:10–11, 20–21; 5:23–25, 27, 29, 32).

However, Paul also used the term *ekklesia* in a universal sense to refer to all first-century believers scattered throughout the Roman world. For example, when he wrote to the Galatians and Corinthians, he confessed that as an unbeliever he had "persecuted the *church* of God" (Galatians 1:13; see also 1 Corinthians 15:9; Philippians 3:6). Paul was obviously thinking of the believers in Jerusalem where he began his attack on the church but also of all followers of Christ throughout Judea—and even as far as Damascus in Syria. In his later testimony before King Agrippa, he said that he "even went to foreign cities to persecute" those who had accepted Jesus Christ as the true Messiah (Acts 26:11).

THE LOCAL CHURCH

Although biblical writers definitely used the term *ekklesia* in a universal sense, in most instances—eighty-two times to be exact—they used this word to refer to believers who lived in specific geographical areas. In other words, approximately 80 percent of the time when these authors penned the word "church" or "churches," they were referring to what we call "local churches" (they referred to a *group of local churches* thirty-five times and to *specific local churches* forty-eight times).

We must not, however, view these "local churches" through the lens of our twenty-first century structural models. In most instances, New Testament writers were referring to all professing believers in a particular *city* or *community*. Luke cited "the church at *Jerusalem*" (Acts 8:1) and "the church at *Antioch*" (13:1). Describing Paul's first missionary journey, Luke referenced "each church" in "*Lystra, Iconium* and *Antioch* [Pisidia]" (14:21–23).

In defining the "church," we tend to focus on the literal definition of the word *ekklesia,* which actually means an "assembly" or "congregation" of people. However, this definition is too narrow when we observe the way believers functioned in the New Testament world. Biblical writers used the word to describe Christians whether they were gathered for worship and practicing certain rituals or scattered throughout a particular community —in their homes, at work, shopping, visiting relatives, or recreating at the local spa. Furthermore, each believing family in a given community, ideally speaking, was to be the "church in miniature" and the father the primary spiritual leader (1 Timothy 3:4–5).

PEOPLE IN COMMUNITY

In order to understand the scriptural meaning of the local church, we must think in terms of people in relationship—not structures, not meeting places, not buildings. New Testament writers used three basic concepts almost exclusively to *describe the church as God's people in community*. They were called disciples, brothers, and saints.

Disciples

The term "disciple" literally means both "a learner" and "a follower." It was a common concept in the first-century world. The Gospel According to John refers to the "disciples" of John the Baptist (1:35) and the "disciples" of Moses (9:28). Those who followed Christ were also identified as His "disciples," many of whom eventually no longer followed Jesus (6:66).

When we encounter this term in the book of Acts—which is used thirty times—we meet "disciples" who understood much more fully that Jesus Christ was the promised Messiah and the Savior of the world. They were not just "learners" and "followers," but believers who had been baptized by the Holy Spirit into the body of Jesus Christ. They were all born-again Christians, though clearly at various levels of Christian maturity.

When Luke identified these believers as "disciples," he did so *only* in the context of local churches—not the universal church. In fact, Luke used the terms "disciples" and "churches" interchangeably. For example, when Paul left on his second missionary journey, "he went through *Syria* and *Cilicia, strengthening the churches*" (Acts 15:41). However, when he left on his third journey, he "traveled from place to place throughout the region of *Galatia* and *Phrygia, strengthening all the disciples*" (18:23).

Brothers

Biblical authors used the term "brothers" more frequently than any other word to refer to people who embodied the local church. For example, James penned this basic word in his epistle eighteen times. And overall, we encounter this concept more than two hundred times throughout the book of Acts and the epistles.

Note, however, that the Greek word *adelphoi*, which is translated as "brothers" or "brethren," is often used generically to refer to both brothers and sisters in Christ. This is true in various languages. For example, in Spanish the term *hermanos* can be used to refer exclusively to men (brothers), or it can be used to refer to both men and women (brothers and sisters). Unfortunately, we have no equivalent word in the English language that describes both men and women. Consequently, when we read our Bibles, it's easy to interpret "brothers"—a literal translation—as masculine. In some instances, it is used in a masculine sense, but many times it is used to refer to both men and women who are believers in Jesus Christ—members of the family of God. And, as we'll see, apparently the term "brothers" was also sometimes used more narrowly to refer to local church leaders (see Acts 12:17; 16:2; 21:17).

Predictably, *adelphoi* is used extensively to describe intimate family of God relationships within *local churches*—not the universal church. This, of course, makes sense, since it was impossible for the great majority of New Testament Christians to relate to people in other geographical areas.

Saints

Hagios ("saints") is another word New Testament writers used frequently to describe born again people in a local church. This term appears nearly fifty times in the New Testament, almost always in the context of local churches.

For example, Paul addressed the Corinthian believers as *saints* (2 Corinthians 1:1), even though most of them were living anything but godly lives (1 Corinthian 3:1–3). Yet, because of their faith in Jesus Christ and their true salvation experience, God viewed them through Christ's death and resurrection as perfectly *hagios,* or holy.

This is the way God sees all of us in local churches who are truly saved. If He did not, no one could inherit eternal life. This is why the doctrine of salvation by grace through faith and not by works is so important. None of us by our own strength can live a perfect life, nor can anyone qualify on his own to gain entrance into God's eternal kingdom.

However, even though we cannot reach God's standard of holiness in this life, both individually and as a church body, it is still His will that all of us become holy, as He is holy (1 Peter 1:15–16). As participating members in local churches, we are to renew our minds—not to "conform any longer to the pattern of this world," but to "be transformed" (Romans 12:2). Put another way, as Christ's disciples and as brothers and sisters in Christ, we are to become more and more conformed to the image of Christ, reflecting the fruit of the Holy (*hagios*) Spirit in all of our relationships with one another (Galatians 5:16–26).[1]

The Same Plan Today

This is primarily a biblical study about *local church leadership*. When we discover God's plan for the first century, we'll discover God's plan for us today. This plan, of course, began when Jesus Christ chose and prepared twelve men who were first called "disciples" and later identified as "apostles" (Matthew 10:2; Mark 6:30; Luke 6:13). And just prior to His return to heaven, He charged eleven of them to "make disciples of all nations" and to baptize and teach these disciples to obey everything He had taught them (Matthew 28:19–20).

As we move into the book of Acts, Luke described what happened when Jesus returned to heaven and sent the Holy Spirit. A local church was born in Jerusalem that would eventually multiply many times throughout the Roman world. And, as in Jerusalem, these local communities of believers would be led by a group of godly leaders.

NOTE

1. For a careful analysis regarding the way the terms "disciples," "brothers," and "saints" were used to describe those who comprised a local church, see Gene A. Getz, *The Measure of a Church* (Ventura, Calif.: Regal, 2001), appendix B, 249–64.

THE ELDERS IN
JERUSALEM (A.D. 45)

BACK TO THE SOURCE

Before reading further, take time to read the first eleven chapters of the book of Acts. Consider the following question: What can we learn about leadership selection and appointments?

It may surprise you that Luke never mentioned local church leaders (elders) until approximately twelve years after Pentecost. However, this doesn't mean that he didn't consider this a very important subject.

The setting is the church in Antioch of Syria. For some unstated reason, some believers in Jerusalem who had the gift of prophecy traveled to this city. One of them was Agabus, who "stood up and through the Spirit predicted that a severe famine would spread over the entire Roman world" (Acts 11:28a). As prophesied, it happened—and when it did, Luke reported what happened in Antioch: "The disciples, each according to his ability, decided to provide help for the brothers living in Judea. This they did, sending their gift to the *elders* by Barnabas and Saul" (vv. 29–30).

THE LARGER SCENE

Stephen's martyrdom precipitated an intense persecution against the believers in Jerusalem. Luke wrote, "*All except the apostles* were scattered throughout Judea and Samaria" (Acts 8:1). It may appear that he was referring to "all" believers in Jerusalem, but a careful look at the context indicates he may have been referring specifically to the other six men (other than Stephen) who were appointed to serve the Grecian widows (6:1–7).

Stephen's stirring and stinging message before the Sanhedrin caused intense anger and led to his martyrdom as Saul consented to his death (7:1–8:1). This tragic event precipitated a great persecution against the church. In the midst of this turmoil, Luke reported good news. Philip went down to Samaria to proclaim Christ. There he met the Ethiopian eunuch, led him to faith, and then continued his journey throughout Judea until he reached Caesarea, his home city (8:40; 21:8).

What happened to the other five dedicated and Spirit-filled men who had been chosen to wait tables in Jerusalem? It appears that along with Philip, they were "scattered throughout Judea and Samaria" (8:1). However, Luke picked up the story later, stating that "those who had been scattered by the persecution in connection with Stephen traveled as far as Phoenicia, Cyprus and Antioch" (11:19). Initially, they preached the Gospel only to the Jews, but several of these men who had grown up in Cyprus and Cyrene broke rank and went on to Antioch and preached Christ to the Greeks (11:20–21). Consequently, a church was born in this predominantly Gentile city.

Remember, too, that one of these seven men—Nicholas—was actually a Gentile "*from Antioch,* a convert to Judaism" (6:5). It's likely he convinced several of these men—perhaps Procorus, Nicanor, Timon, or Parmenas—to come with him to his home city to preach the Gospel to his fellow Gentiles.

The Church in Antioch

Regardless of who these men were, a strategic church was born in this huge pagan city, which then numbered approximately a half million people. At some point in time, Agabus and some fellow prophets from Jerusalem appeared on the scene and predicted the famine that would create serious needs in the churches in Judea. As stated earlier, the believers in Antioch decided to help their fellow believers in Judea. Receiving a special offering, they sent "their gift to the *elders* by Barnabas and Saul" (Acts 11:30).

Notably, this is Luke's first reference to local church leaders in the book of Acts. They're called *elders*—and since Agabus and his fellow prophets had come from Jerusalem, we can assume he was referring to the "elders" in the Jerusalem church.

Some Significant Questions

Two Key Questions

Luke's rather brief but descriptive reference to "elders" raises two very important questions:

1. *Since approximately twelve years had passed since Pentecost, when were these elders appointed in Jerusalem?* There is no way to answer this question definitively. We can only speculate that it happened after the seven men were appointed to care for the Grecian widows who were being neglected in the daily distribution of food—which would have been early in the history of the church (Acts 6:1–2). This conclusion is based on the fact that the apostles were still directly involved in overseeing the ministry. If there had been elders already functioning at this point in time, it seems the apostles would have involved them in solving this problem.

2. *Who selected and appointed the elders in Jerusalem?* Again, we can only speculate as we attempt to answer this question. Contextually,

we do have some possible clues, found in the choosing of Matthias
and of the seven Grecian Jews.

Choosing Matthias

Just prior to the birth of the church, we have one example when the
apostles selected and appointed a spiritual leader to replace Judas. Peter
outlined the qualifications. He had to be a man who had traveled with the
apostles from the time John had baptized Jesus until He ascended. This
meant, of course, that he had to have witnessed Christ's death and resurrection (Acts 1:21–22).

Joseph Barsabbas and Matthias qualified, but we're not told how the
apostles narrowed their choice to these two men. In order to determine
God's will as to which man should join the apostolic team, they prayed
specifically and then "cast lots"—which meant they probably wrote the
names of these men on two stones, placed them in a jar and the stone that
fell out first indicated who should succeed Judas. Matthias was chosen and
joined the other apostles.

This approach involved both human and divine elements. On the human side, apparently the apostles themselves chose two men as candidates
based on predetermined qualifications for an apostle—eyewitnesses of
Christ's ministry, death, and resurrection. On the divine side, they then
asked God specifically for direct guidance in choosing one of the two.

Though there are certainly elements in this approach that are important, such as establishing certain spiritual qualifications and then asking
God for guidance, the "method" is certainly not presented in Scripture as
a model for selecting and appointing spiritual leaders. As far as we know,
it was never used again.[1]

The Seven Grecian Jews

Appointing seven men to care for the Grecian–Jewish widows gives us
another illustration involving leadership selection. The process was primarily based on human consensus. They instructed the Grecian contingency who brought the complaint to "choose seven men" who were also

Grecian–Jewish believers who had certain qualifications. They were to be men who were "known to be full of the Spirit and wisdom" (Acts 6:3). Pleased with the suggestion, Grecian representatives made the selection and then brought them "to the apostles, who prayed and laid their hands on them" (6:6), confirming that the Grecians had made a proper selection. They then prayed for them as they faced this rather tedious task.

It's feasible that the apostles used a similar approach in selecting "elders" in Jerusalem, only this time choosing qualified Jewish believers who were "Hebraic Jews"   those men who lived in Jerusalem or its vicinity.

A Third Important Question

Here's a third important question about these first elders: *What qualifications would the apostles have looked for in selecting and appointing elders?*

It would be at least another thirty years before Paul outlined in writing the qualifications for elders/overseers. Consequently, we cannot be certain regarding any particular maturity profile. However, we mustn't forget what the apostles had learned about spiritual maturity just a short time before Christ's death and resurrection—which would have definitely helped them formulate criteria for selecting men who were to "manage" and "shepherd" a local church.

THE FINAL DAYS WITH CHRIST

Jesus had spent the last couple years preparing these twelve men for the birth of the church. However, just a few days before the Crucifixion, they were still woefully immature. Even while Jesus passed the cup at the Passover meal and announced the betrayal by Judas, "a dispute arose among them as to which of them was considered to be the greatest" (Luke 22:24).

It was during this final experience together that Jesus taught them their greatest lesson in character development. He took the place of a servant and washed their feet. Unknown to them at this moment, Jesus was simply illustrating "the full extent of his love" (John 13:1)—His death on the cross (Philippians 2:5–8). Furthermore, they had no clue they would all forsake Him in His "hour of death." Even Peter who said he would lay down his own life for Jesus denied he ever knew Him.

The Holy Spirit's Arrival

But all of this was destined to change when the Holy Spirit descended on these men on the Day of Pentecost. This dramatic event marked their ultimate transformation. Gone was their prideful jealousies, their desire for power and prestige! And James, the very man who strategized with his brother and mother to sit on Jesus' right hand in the kingdom, demonstrated the ultimate act of love when he literally shed his own blood in martyrdom. His brother, John, initially described by Jesus as one of the "sons of thunder," became known as the "apostle of love" and years later put in writing what Jesus really meant when He told them "to love one another" as He had loved them. No doubt, deeply moved as he reflected on his brother's death at the hands of Herod (12:1–2), he penned these particular words: "This is how we know what love is: Jesus Christ laid down his life for us. And we ought to lay down our lives for our brothers" (1 John 3:16).

The Great Commandment

Though the apostles continued to mature in Christ following the birth of the church, they were definitely different men after the Holy Spirit descended. They became servants of God and of one another. Motivated by the Great Commandment (Matthew 22:37–39, to love God and one another), they began to carry out the Great Commission (28:18–20). In essence, they had learned the most important lesson in character development. Though the apostle Paul would not spell out the specific manifestations of this foundational quality until he outlined the qualifications for spiritual leaders in the Pastoral Epistles, love for God and for one another formed the foundation of what it means to follow Christ's example of servanthood.

We can certainly assume then that the Great Commandment formed the foundation for leadership appointments in the early days of the church.

Though we're not told how the elders/overseers were selected in the church in Jerusalem, we can be certain that the apostles were very directly involved and that they looked for men who shared their commitment to this "new commandment." Though the Holy Spirit may have revealed in a supernatural way who these individuals should be, more than likely, the apostles simply looked for men who had been God-fearing Jews who very quickly began to reflect the fruit of the Holy Spirit in their lives once they became believers. After all, out of the thousands who responded to the Gospel, there were probably many like Barnabas, Stephen, and Philip who would soon qualify to give oversight to the church as servant leaders.

A DYNAMIC STORY

As we continue to unfold this biblical leadership story, we'll gain more insight as to how local church leadership functioned in the New Testament churches that will enable us to see rather clearly how leaders should function in the twenty-first century—in the Middle East where it all began, in America, in Europe, in Africa, in South America—and in all parts of the world. Though we'll still have unanswered questions when we reach the end of the story, particularly regarding methodological details, we'll discover principles that will guide us in all cultural situations. In fact, we'll discover that these omissions are by divine design. So, stay with us as we continue to unfold this dynamic biblical story.

NOTE

1. There are some who believe the apostles made a mistake when they chose Matthias. They point to the fact that the apostle Paul was God's choice to be an apostle, and he was the one who should have replaced Judas—even though this came later in early church history. Though the apostles were certainly not above being guilty of human error, it's difficult to prove they made a mistake in this case. It's true that Paul was indeed called to be an apostle by Jesus Christ Himself on the road to Damascus. However, it certainly seems to be pure speculation to say that the apostles were out of the will of God when they chose Matthias. See Stanley D. Toussaint, *The Bible Knowledge Commentary: An Exposition of the Scriptures*, eds. John F. Walvoord and Roy B. Zuck, New Testament edition (Wheaton, Ill.: Victor, 1985), 357.

A PRAYER AND HEALING
MINISTRY (A.D. 45–47)

BACK TO THE SOURCE

Before reading this chapter, take time to read James' epistle.
Consider the following question: What would have caused physi-
cal, psychological, and spiritual infirmities for these believers?

James, the half brother of Jesus, was the primary leader of the
elders in Jerusalem.[1] This will become increasingly clear as we
continue to unfold this biblical story. We're not told when he began to occupy this position, but we do know that the "other"
James, John's brother and an apostle, was killed by King Herod
about the same time as the church in Antioch sent their gift of
money to Jerusalem (Acts 12:1). Peter was also taken into cus-
tody and was headed for the same fate when he was miraculously
delivered from prison.

James not only served as the primary leader in the church in

Jerusalem, but he penned a significant letter "to the twelve tribes scattered among the nations" (James 1:1b)—which no doubt refers to his fellow God-fearing Jews who had come to Jerusalem from all over the New Testament world to celebrate the Feast of Pentecost (Acts 2:5–11). Many of these believers were certainly among the first three thousand who had received Jesus Christ as the Messiah and Savior following Peter's message (2:41). But, at some point in time, they returned to their homes, sharing this messianic message primarily with their Jewish neighbors and friends.

Inspired by the Holy Spirit, James addressed these believing Jews in his letter. Based on the content, he may have written this epistle about the same time the famine spread throughout the Roman world (A.D. 45–47). This would give particular meaning to his concerns when he wrote:

> What good is it, my brothers, if a man claims to have faith but has no deeds? Can such faith save him? Suppose a brother or sister is without clothes and daily food. If one of you says to him, "Go, I wish you well; keep warm and well fed," but does nothing about his physical needs, what good is it? In the same way, faith by itself, if it is not accompanied by action, is dead. [James 2:14–17]

Though James was very concerned about meeting physical needs, when he closed out this letter, he shared another significant concern which gives us the next specific reference to local church leaders. Once again they are called "elders."

A PRIMARY RESPONSIBILITY

James introduced us to the first major responsibility for elders that is described in Scripture—a prayer and healing ministry:

> Is any one of you in trouble? He should pray. Is anyone happy? Let him sing songs of praise. Is any one of you sick? He should call the *elders of the church* to pray over him and anoint him with oil in the name of the Lord. And the prayer offered in faith will make the sick person well; the Lord will raise him up. If he has sinned, he will be forgiven. Therefore confess

your sins to each other and pray for each other so that you may be healed. The prayer of a righteous man is powerful and effective. [James 5:13–16]

When James wrote this letter to believers scattered throughout the Gentile world, there were Jewish churches in those areas led by "elders." However, we are never told how or when these leaders were appointed.

MORE SIGNIFICANT QUESTIONS

James' directive to believers to "call the elders of the church" raises some very specific questions which I've attempted to answer more definitively in appendix B. However, the following are some brief responses:

1. *What kind of sickness was James addressing?* James did not limit prayer requests to certain kinds of illnesses. Whether the sickness was rooted in the physical, the psychological, or the spiritual, believers were to be free to ask for prayer from the elders of the church.
2. *How did the sickness James was referring to relate to what these Jewish believers were experiencing in terms of persecution?* It's clear from the context that James was addressing issues he referred to throughout this letter—"trials of many kinds" (1:2, 12), as well as the "suffering" that often accompanies trial (5:10). In this respect, these believers were facing the physical, psychological, and spiritual results of stress: weariness, discouragement, and doubt.
3. *How did these sicknesses James referred to relate to sinful attitudes and actions?* James addressed this issue as well throughout his letter— inappropriate use of the tongue (1:26; 3:1–12), showing favoritism and creating feelings of rejection (2:1–12), fights, quarrels, and slander (4:1–2, 11). This is why James exhorted these believers to "confess" their "sins to each other" and to "pray for each other so that" they might "be healed" (5:16).
4. *Does James guarantee healing for all diseases if elders pray in faith for people?* Nowhere in Scripture are we guaranteed that we'll always be healed of every sickness. If this were true, we could stop the aging process. Even the apostle Paul was not healed from his "thorn"

in the flesh. Though we are never told what this "thorn" was, it was causing a difficult illness of some kind. Even though Paul pleaded with God to take away this "thorn," God did not remove the ailment. However, He did provide grace to bear the pain—emotionally and physically (2 Corinthians 12:8–10).

5. *How did the healing ministry by elders in local churches compare with the healing ministry of Jesus and the apostles, including Paul?* For a detailed answer to this question, please see the in-depth presentation in appendix B. However, one thing is clear in this letter: James' focus was on the welfare of all believers. Prayer for healing was not to affirm the elders' calling and position or to verify the Gospel, but to minister to every member of the body of Christ who desires prayer for healing.

6. *What about "anointing with oil"? How does this relate to this prayer process?* We believe that oil was actually used in the New Testament days as a healing balm. However, we believe this practice is very appropriate today as a symbol of our concern and of God's healing touch.

A FINAL WORD

In conclusion, it's clear from even a simple reading of James' letter that when believers are not doing well physically, emotionally, and spiritually, they should feel free to ask the spiritual leaders in their churches to pray for them. It goes without saying, of course, that these leaders should communicate this opportunity and then be available to honor these requests. It's not an accident that James' directive appears so early in the biblical story of local church leadership. Praying for the sick was to be a priority function.

NOTE

1. During the very time my fellow elders and I were engaging in this study, a remarkable report appeared in the *Biblical Archeology Review*. According to Andre Lemaire, "A limestone bone box (called an 'ossuary') has surfaced in Israel that may once have contained the bones of James, the brother of Jesus. We know this because the extraordinary inscriptions incised on one side of the ossuary reads in clear Aramaic letters: 'James, son of Joseph, brother of Jesus.'" Lemaire, himself a well-known and competent epigrapher (a specialist in ancient inscriptions), further states that in his opinion, this discovery "is genuinely ancient and not a fake." See Andre Lemaire, "Burial Box of James, The Brother of Jesus," *Biblical Archeology Review* 28 (November/December 2002): 25–33.

THE FIRST
CHURCH-PLANTING
MISSION (A.D. 47)

 ## BACK TO THE SOURCE

Before proceeding, read Luke's account in Acts 13:1–14:28.
Note particularly the appointment of elders. Since these churches
were probably no more than a year or two old, where did Paul
and Barnabas discover men who were mature enough to be spiri-
tual leaders?

Luke's next reference to "elders" allows us to witness for the
first time the actual appointment of elders. It happened on the first
missionary journey into the Gentile world. After starting churches in four significant cities in southern Galatian, Paul and Barnabas "returned to Lystra, Iconium and Antioch [of Pisidia]" (Acts
14:21) to establish these new believers in their faith. Luke has
recorded: "*Paul and Barnabas appointed elders for them in each*
church and, with prayer and fasting, committed them to the Lord,
in whom they had put their trust" (14:23).

Again, we're left with some unanswered questions. But before we explore these questions and possible answers, let's once again set the stage.

THE LARGER SCENE

As the biblical story on leadership unfolds in the book of Acts, Luke opened a window on a remarkable scene. After Barnabas and Paul finished their benevolent mission to Jerusalem, they returned to Antioch and were worshiping the Lord and fasting with three other men who were "prophets and teachers" (Acts 13:1). This was definitely not a strategy meeting where these five men were brainstorming and discussing how to reach the Gentile world. At this moment in history, they suddenly and unexpectedly received a very direct message from God: "The Holy Spirit *said*, 'Set apart for me Barnabas and Saul for the work to which I have called them'" (13:2).

Since it appears that all five of these men were "prophets and teachers," they may have received this revelation simultaneously. If so, this added unquestionable verification that this message was indeed from God.

This was a unique moment in biblical history. This divine directive launched an outreach to Gentiles that had been in the mind of God since He spoke directly to Abraham in Ur and promised that through him "all peoples on earth will be blessed" (Genesis 12:3). This prophetic promise to Abraham millennia earlier now would be realized as these five men received a very specific message from the Lord—one that charged Barnabas and Saul to carry the saving message of salvation through Jesus Christ to both Jews and Gentiles. Centuries earlier, God had spoken to a lone pagan idolater, assuring him he would be a channel to introduce the whole world to the Savior. Now the Lord spoke to five dedicated and spiritually gifted men in the church in Antioch who would be part of making this promise a reality.

Apparently, at this time, there were still no elders in Antioch. Rather, these five "prophets and teachers" helped give overall direction to this church. Responding to this precise message from the Holy Spirit, Simeon, Lucius, and Manaen took charge. They placed their hands on Barnabas and Paul and "sent them off." With Barnabas in charge, these two men chose

John Mark to be their assistant, and from this point forward, they followed the direction of the Holy Spirit as they "went down to Seleucia and sailed from there to Cyprus" (Acts 13:4).

A Shift in Leadership:
Paul's First Missionary Journey

When this missionary team reached the island of Cyprus, there was a noticeable shift in leadership. After Paul encountered a false prophet and struck him temporarily blind, Barnabas, who was definitely the leader when they left Antioch, recognized Paul's unique apostolic calling and voluntarily became second in command. With few exceptions, Luke reversed their names from this point forward. As these men moved on, Luke recorded—"From Paphos, Paul and his companions sailed to Perga in Pamphylia" (13:13).

Antioch of Pisidia

They arrived on this fertile coastal plain, where stories abounded regarding the bandits that roamed the Taurus Mountains. John Mark soon got cold feet and returned to Jerusalem as Paul and Barnabas continued on a very torturous path up the mountains. One hundred miles later, they reached another city called Antioch in the province of Pisidia (see map 1). Occupying about 150 acres, it dominated the region. There Paul and Barnabas discovered a strong contingency of Jews and "devout converts to Judaism" (Acts 13:43).

On the Sabbath, the two entered the synagogue and when Paul was invited to speak, he presented the gospel of Jesus Christ from the Old Testament. As a result of this ministry, there were a number of both Jews and Gentiles who accepted their message. On one Sabbath day, there was such spiritual interest that "almost the whole city gathered to hear the word of the Lord" (13:44). In spite of persecution from the nonbelieving Jews, many believed and came to faith in Christ (13:48).

THE FIRST MISSIONARY JOURNEY

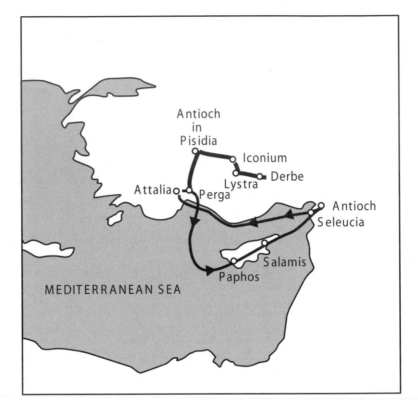

Iconium

The same dynamic happened in Iconium. Paul and Barnabas entered the Jewish synagogue and "spoke so effectively that a great number of Jews and Gentiles believed" (14:1). Again they faced persecution. This time, both unbelieving Jews and Gentiles fought against them, and they had to flee to the Lycaonian region.

Lystra

Initially, these brave missionaries were well received in Lystra—but for the wrong reasons. The Holy Spirit enabled Paul to miraculously heal a crippled man who had been born lame. Amazed and elated, these people concluded that Paul and Barnabas were Greek gods that had come to earth, and they wanted to worship them. But their popularity ended when irate Jews from Antioch and Iconium turned the crowds against them. No doubt because Paul had performed the healing, the very people who wanted to worship him actually stoned him and dragged him out of the city.

Though Paul was left for dead, God miraculously raised him, and he and Barnabas turned east to Derbe. There they also "won a large number of disciples" (14:21).

APPOINTING ELDERS

After planting a church in Derbe, Paul and Barnabas retraced their steps and "returned to Lystra, Iconium and Antioch"—called by historians the Pisidian Triangle. Luke made their purpose clear—to *strengthen* these disciples and to *encourage* them "to remain true to the faith" (14:22). But before they left each city, they *"appointed elders for them in each church"* (14:23).[1]

This was a somber moment—just as it had been in Antioch of Syria when the Holy Spirit had called Paul and Barnabas to make this trip. They appointed these individuals to their local church leadership positions and "committ[ed] them to the Lord" in the context of "prayer and fasting"—warning all of these believers that they would continue to face persecution and hardships on their spiritual journey.

Paul and Barnabas, then, wound their way back down to the coast and eventually returned to their home base in Syria. They had been away approximately three years. When they arrived, they called the church together and reported what God had done, particularly among the Gentiles. This, of course, was a very encouraging report since most of the Christians in Antioch were also Gentile converts.

MORE SIGNIFICANT QUESTIONS

As we reflect on the "appointment of elders" in these churches, we are once again faced with some very intriguing questions:

1. *How were Paul and Barnabas able to discover leaders who were qualified after such a brief time—probably a year or so after the churches were founded?* Since there were a number of committed Jews and devout Gentiles in these cities, these men who responded to the Gospel would have grown quickly in their faith. And when Paul and Barnabas returned to these churches, we can be sure they looked for these men.

2. *Did Paul and Barnabas use their prophetic gifts in making this determination?* Based on the limited information Luke recorded about their ministry in these three cities, we cannot answer this question with certainty. Since the Holy Spirit spoke directly through five "prophets and teachers" in Antioch to commission Paul and Barnabas, it's certainly feasible that He would also have spoken through these men to determine who among these converts to Christ were ready to be spiritual leaders. However, it's also possible that Paul and Barnabas simply made judgments based on the reputation these men had already developed in their respective communities.

3. *Did the disciples in each church have a "say" in recommending these leaders?* As we'll see in a future chapter, when Paul returned to Lystra on the second missionary journey, he chose Timothy to join his missionary team. The key factor in making this choice was that "the *brothers* at Lystra and Iconium *spoke well* of him" (Acts 16:2). It would not be surprising that this was also an important factor in selecting and appointing elders in these cities in the first place. As we'll see in this unfolding biblical story, a "good reputation" among believers becomes more and more important in choosing spiritual leaders.

NOTE

1. Note that when Paul and Barnabas appointed elders in Lystra, Iconium, and Antioch, these "communities of faith" were called "churches" before they had elders. This was also true in Antioch of Syria and probably numerous other churches throughout the New Testament world. In other words, it is not necessary to have official elders in order to "be a church." Wherever you have a community of believers, you have an *ekklesia*.

THE LAW-GRACE CONTROVERSY (A.D. 49)

BACK TO THE SOURCE

Before proceeding, read Acts 15:1–35. Note carefully both the human and divine process involved as the "apostles and elders" in Jerusalem resolved this law-grace controversy.

After Paul and Barnabas returned from their first mission to the Gentile world, they faced a serious theological problem in their home-based church. Some men came to Antioch from Judea and were teaching Gentile believers that they couldn't be saved unless they were circumcised. Imagine the confusion, insecurity, and resentment this created. Both Paul and Barnabas took on this challenge in heated public debates—but to no avail. Consequently, they "were appointed, along with some other believers, to go up to Jerusalem to see the *apostles* and *elders* about this question" (Acts 15:2).

This was not a matter of public debate with those Jews who rejected Jesus Christ as the Messiah and Savior. Rather, this was a disagreement among believers as to what was necessary for Gentiles to be saved. Consequently, when the meeting took place in Jerusalem, we read that "some of the *believers* who belonged to the party of the Pharisees stood up and said, 'The Gentiles must be circumcised and required to obey the law of Moses'" (15:5).

This was a question that could not be solved by just any group of local church leaders—or even by Paul and Barnabas who were under direct and specific orders from the Holy Spirit to carry the Gospel to the Gentile world (13:1–3). This was the first time—as far as we know—since the beginning of the church over fifteen years earlier that the "apostles and elders" in the birthplace of Christianity had to work together to answer the most important theological question in all of Christian history.

A DYNAMIC PROCESS

It's intriguing to analyze what happened when these men tackled this issue—especially in view of some of the special revelations we've encountered thus far in this leadership story. Even Paul and Barnabas, who were "prophets and teachers," were not able to clarify this theological issue based on an immediate and direct revelation from God. Rather, after having a lengthy "discussion," Peter—representing the apostles—shared a previous *revelatory experience* he had on a rooftop in Joppa and subsequently, how Cornelius (a Gentile) was saved by the grace of the Lord Jesus Christ—and nothing more (10:1–11:18; 15:7–11). Paul and Barnabas then confirmed Peter's experience by reporting what they had experienced on their first missionary journey—how God had done "miraculous signs and wonders" and how many of the Gentiles had been saved by grace through faith (15:12).

James, the half brother of Christ and the lead elder in Jerusalem, followed next and verified Peter's testimony regarding Gentile conversion by quoting the prophet Amos. Even then James did not claim to have a direct revelation at that moment, but simply shared his opinion—his "judgment" —regarding how to solve the problem (15:13–21).

However, once these men had engaged in this lengthy process involving debate, reports, dialogue, and discussion, it appears that the Holy Spirit directly confirmed their conclusions through Judas and Silas, "two men who were leaders among the brothers" (v. 22) and whom Luke identified as prophets (v. 32). These men were also chosen by the apostles and elders and the "whole church" to help Paul and Barnabas deliver the letter. Note especially the highlighted sections below in their little epistle:

> The *apostles* and *elders,* your *brothers,* To the Gentile believers in Antioch, Syria and Cilicia: Greetings. We have heard that some went out from us without our authorization and disturbed you, troubling your minds by what they said. So we all agreed to choose some men and send them to you with our dear friends Barnabas and Paul—men who have risked their lives for the name of our Lord Jesus Christ. *Therefore we are sending Judas and Silas ["prophets," v. 32] to confirm by word of mouth what we are writing. It seemed good to the Holy Spirit and to us not to burden you with anything beyond the following requirements:* You are to abstain from food sacrificed to idols, from blood, from the meat of strangled animals and from sexual immorality. You will do well to avoid these things. [15:23–29]

When this missionary team arrived in Antioch, they shared this letter with the whole church. And once again the Holy Spirit spoke directly and enabled Judas and Silas to deliver some prophetic and encouraging messages, confirming the content in this letter.

MORE SIGNIFICANT QUESTIONS

The process and decision made at the Jerusalem counsel raises more questions about the leadership of the church. For instance . . .

1. Since Paul and Barnabas were both "prophets and teachers," why didn't the Holy Spirit speak directly through them in Antioch in order to silence these false teachers?
2. In view of the spiritual stature of Peter and James, their calling as leaders, and their spiritual giftedness, why didn't they receive a

direct revelation from the Holy Spirit at that moment so they could pass it on to the other "apostles and elders" as they met in session?

3. Who was actually involved when the "apostles and elders, *with the whole church*, decided to choose some of their own men and send them to Antioch with Paul and Barnabas" (Acts 15:22)?

In contemplating answers to these questions, we must understand that something unique was happening. A gradual transition was taking place as God gave more and more responsibility to Christian leaders to make decisions based on previous revelations and experience. God did not always step in and tell believers exactly what to do and say—even during the early years of the church before the Scriptures were recorded as we have them today.

Something else is very apparent. In the early years of the church, *the Holy Spirit decided when to speak directly* through men and women and when to be a "silent" *encourager* so believers could make decisions based on what He had already revealed.

HAVING A DIALOGUE IN COMMUNITY

With access to so much information about God's divine work in history, it shouldn't surprise us that God has given all of us an awesome responsibility. This is why we believe this study on local church leadership is so important and strategic. God wants us to clearly understand His will—but He hasn't promised to make the process simple or easy. Like the "apostles and elders" in Jerusalem, we too need to dialogue "in community" —asking God for wisdom and guidance from the Holy Spirit so that we can understand God's marvelous revelation in the Scriptures and learn how to apply what we learn from the Bible in our churches today.

This is why this study has been so exciting for me personally—and my fellow elders. It has involved a group of twelve men who have studied the Word of God together and have with one mind asked God for wisdom through the Holy Spirit so that we might accurately understand the biblical story and comprehend God's will for us as a group of elders who are committed to being faithful shepherds of God's flock in our own local church.

CHARACTER-BASED JUDGMENTS (A.D. 49–50)

BACK TO THE SOURCE

Before proceeding, read Acts 15:36–16:5. What are the human elements in these two stories of young proteges, John Mark and Timothy?

In recording the next two events in this unfolding story, Luke affirmed the God-designed transition that was taking place in terms of giving believers more responsibility in making wise decisions. The focus was on selecting two young, potential leaders, John Mark and Timothy, to assist in planting and growing local churches.

Imagine the relief Paul and Barnabas must have felt once the "apostles and elders" in Jerusalem had resolved this law-grace controversy—at least on parchment. They had in their hands a written document signed and sealed by the "apostles and elders" in Jerusalem. Paul particularly must have felt affirmed.

But at this point, Paul and Barnabas faced a new challenge—to communicate the content of this powerful little letter, not only to the church in Antioch but to other Gentile believers in Syria and Cilicia (Acts 15:23). Though Luke did not record how the other churches in these areas were started, they definitely existed—and they needed this encouraging message of clarification.

PAUL'S BROADER CONCERNS

Paul's concerns soon extended beyond the Syrian and Cilician borders. One day, he shared his burden with Barnabas: "Let us go back and visit the brothers in all the towns where we preached the word of the Lord and see how they are doing" (15:36). Here, of course, Paul was referring primarily to the churches in the Galatian region—in Derbe, Lystra, Iconium, and Antioch of Pisidia. By now, he had probably written the Galatian letter, which would have been delivered. Since Paul had spoken very directly about their confusion regarding "law and grace," he would have been very concerned about how well these believers had received his message. After all, he didn't hide the fact that he was angry and perturbed at those who had attempted "to pervert the gospel of Christ" (Galatians 1:6–7)—the very issues the "apostles and elders" in Jerusalem had clarified in their letter. How had the Galatian believers responded to his tough love? Clearly, this would have been heavy on Paul's heart when he proposed this return trip.

AN UNEXPECTED ARGUMENT

Barnabas concurred with Paul's proposal, but he wanted to once again take John Mark. But Paul immediately opposed the idea. This young man had "deserted them" on the first journey, and Paul didn't want to take a chance on it happening again.

Luke's report on what happened next leaves nothing to the imagination. These two devoted missionaries had an intense argument—literally "a sharp disagreement" (Acts 15:39). Both men stood toe-to-toe and wouldn't budge! Consequently, "they parted company." Barnabas stood by John Mark and they "sailed for Cyprus," but Paul chose Silas to accompany him on his second missionary journey.

This disagreement was definitely about whether John Mark should have another chance. Initially, they needed an assistant, and this young man was available. However, in retrospect, Paul firmly believed they had made a mistake in selecting Mark. Based on this young man's performance, Paul didn't believe he had the spiritual fiber to serve in this capacity. But it's just as clear that Barnabas wanted to give his cousin another opportunity to prove himself. However, they couldn't agree—and they decided to go their separate ways.

PAUL'S SECOND MISSION

While Paul and Barnabas and the two prophets (Silas and Judas) were in Antioch ministering together, Paul must have already publicly shared his concern about revisiting the churches he and Barnabas had launched on the first journey. Apparently, he had developed a close relationship with Silas and perhaps had suggested that he accompany him and Barnabas through Syria and Cilicia and then on to the Galatian region. Evidently, Silas felt he needed to return to Jerusalem first—but consented to join the team when they reached Lystra. In the meantime, Paul and Barnabas had their disagreement regarding John Mark. Consequently, with the Jerusalem letter in hand, Paul set out alone going "through Syria and Cilicia, strengthening the churches" (15:41).[1]

Leaving Cilicia, Paul crossed the Pisidian border and probably returned to Derbe—the last church he and Barnabas started on the first journey (see his route in "The Second Missionary Journey," map 2). From there he returned to Lystra, where, on the first journey, he had been stoned and left for dead but had miraculously recovered (14:19–20).

THE SECOND MISSIONARY JOURNEY

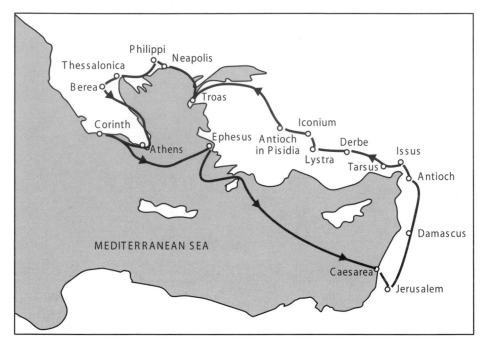

Timothy's Conversion

A young man named Timothy no doubt had stood with these disciples, observing Paul's supernatural healing (Acts 14:19–20). After he heard Paul share that Jesus Christ was the promised Messiah, Timothy apparently received the Lord Jesus Christ as his personal Savior. Perhaps this was the moment Paul later referred to in his second letter to this young man when he reminded him that he had become "wise for salvation through faith in Christ Jesus" (2 Timothy 3:15).

Timothy's Spiritual Growth

When Paul arrived in Lystra on the second mission, he met Timothy personally—perhaps for the first time. This young man had continued to grow in his Christian faith—so much so—that "the *brothers* at Lystra and Iconium *spoke well* of him" (Acts 16:2). Apparently, these men were the "elders" Paul and Barnabas had appointed in these two churches on their first journey—just as Peter may have been referring to the elders in Jerusalem when he told the believers to "tell James and the *brothers*" about his miraculous escape from prison (12:17). This conclusion is also based on Paul's reference in his first letter to "the body of elders" who had "laid their hands" on Timothy (1 Timothy 4:14). It's logical that in this instance Paul was referring to the same men   "the *brothers* at Lystra and Iconium [who] spoke well" of Timothy.

If this is a correct assumption, this recommendation from the local church leaders, not only in Timothy's hometown but in neighboring Iconium twenty miles north, would have carried a lot of influence in Paul's mind. Clearly, he was more cautious this time around in choosing an assistant. He didn't want to make the same mistake twice.

Timothy's Family Background

At this point, we can certainly read between the lines. Paul must have pursued this "generalized" report in more depth, getting to know Timothy's parents and his mother in particular. He discovered that Eunice was a Jewish believer, probably accepting her Messiah at the same time as her son Timothy. However, Paul also discovered that Timothy's father was a Gentile, probably not a Christian (Acts 16:1).

Paul also found that Eunice had taught Timothy "from infancy the holy Scriptures. . . ." Furthermore, Timothy was deeply influenced by the "sincere faith" of both his mother and grandmother (2 Timothy 1:5; 3:14–15). As God-fearing Jews, they were great models of godliness—regardless of Timothy's pagan father.

The point is this: Paul became very intentional in checking out Timothy's home background and his reputation as a dedicated Christian. And again, it's apparent that God gave Paul freedom to choose Timothy to be his traveling companion—just as he and Barnabas had the freedom to choose John Mark to accompany them on their first mission trip.

By this time, Silas had arrived from Jerusalem, and together these three men "traveled from town to town" and delivered the decisions reached by the apostles and elders in Jerusalem (Acts 16:4). As a result of this encouraging letter, the churches continued to grow both spiritually and numerically (16:5).

A FINAL WORD

These two stories involving John Mark and Timothy demonstrate that God was putting more and more responsibility on New Testament leaders to discern whether or not spiritual leaders were qualified. When we read Paul's letters to Timothy and Titus outlining the qualifications for elders/overseers, we'll see how important it is to select leaders based on character.

NOTE

1. Following Luke's statement indicating that Judas and Silas returned to Jerusalem (Acts 15:33), some Greek manuscripts contain the statement: "But it seemed good to Silas to remain there" (15:34). Personally, I have concluded that some copyist may have added this explanation to clarify why Silas was able to join Paul on the second journey. However, the context seems to indicate that Paul began the second journey alone and Silas eventually joined him in Lystra. (Note the singular pronouns in 15:41 and 16:1.)

RESPECT AND ESTEEM (A.D. 51)

BACK TO THE SOURCE

Before proceeding, read Acts 17:1–9 as well as 1 and 2 Thessa-lonians. What clues can you find in the overall context that explain why Paul mentioned these leaders' "hard work" as well as their responsibility to "admonish" believers?

During Paul's second missionary journey, he wrote his second letter—this time to a church that he, Silas, and Timothy launched in Thessalonica. In the closing section of the epistle, rather than addressing the spiritual leaders directly, he exhorted all believers to love, respect, and esteem them, because of their position and God-given responsibility as well as their hard work. This is the first time in this biblical story that we get a "view from the pew": "Now we ask you, brothers, to respect those who *work hard* among you, who are *over you*[1] in the Lord and who *admonish* you. Hold them in the *highest regard in love* because of their work (1 Thessalonians 5:12–13a).

Paul did not identify these leaders with a specific title. Rather, he described their overall functions—to "manage" and "oversee" the church and, in this case, to admonish believers.

ENTERING NEW TERRITORY

After visiting the churches in the Galatian region and sharing the letter composed by the "apostles and elders," Paul and his companions ventured into virgin territory. Once again, the Holy Spirit spoke directly, this time giving them specific geographical directions. As far as we know, they had not been this way before, and they knew very few people who had. Satellite guidance systems were two thousand years into the future. However, when God so willed, these men had access to a divine guidance system. Consequently, they were "*kept by the Holy Spirit* from preaching the word in the province of Asia" (Acts 16:6). God had another plan for reaching this territory, which He unfolded during the third missionary journey (16:8–10).

Traveling on, Paul and his companions "came to the border of Mysia" (map 2). There "they tried to enter [the province of] Bithynia, but *the Spirit of Jesus*" once again stopped them (16:7). We're not told specifically how the Holy Spirit communicated to these two missionaries, but we can assume He spoke to Paul and/or Silas directly (13:1–3).

Traveling farther west, these ambassadors for Christ arrived in Troas, a city on the coast of the Aegean Sea. Evidently, Luke met them there and joined the team (note how Luke used the personal pronoun "we" in Acts 16:10–11 compared with "they" in Acts 16:7–8). It was here that Paul had one of his most dramatic revelations to date in terms of where they were to preach the Gospel. He "had a vision of a man of Macedonia standing and begging him, 'Come over to Macedonia and help us'" (16:9). Following God's specific directions, Paul, Silas, Timothy, and now Luke entered the European territory where they had a very successful ministry planting churches—first in Philippi, and then in Thessalonica, Berea, Athens, and Corinth.

A Serious Concern

After Paul and his companions left Thessalonica because of intense persecution, they became very concerned about these relatively new believers. Had they withstood their trials or had they reverted to idolatry? To get an answer to this question, Paul and Silas agreed to stay in Athens while Timothy returned to Thessalonica to assess the situation. When Timothy returned, he brought a very positive report. The Thessalonian Christians were "standing firm in the Lord" (1 Thessalonians 3:6–8).

Paul wasted no time in penning his first letter, thanking God for their "work produced by faith," their "labor prompted by love," and their "endurance inspired by hope in our Lord Jesus Christ" (1 Thessalonians 1:3). However, he had a serious concern that he had already addressed while ministering among them (2 Thessalonians 3:10). Some of these new believers were still slothful—shirking their responsibility to earn a living. Instead, they were mooching on others to meet their physical needs. Apparently, some of these believers—perhaps using the promise of the second coming of Christ as an excuse to be lazy—were neglecting their domestic responsibilities.

Once again, Paul addressed this issue: "Make it your ambition to lead a quiet life, to mind your own business and *to work with your hands,* just as we told you, so that your daily life may win the respect of outsiders and so that you will *not be dependent on anybody*" (1 Thessalonians 4:11–12).

A Challenging Task

Apparently, the spiritual leaders in Thessalonica had picked up where Paul left off—to *admonish* those who were not working to earn a living. Predictably, their message would not be well received—at least by some of these slothful and carnal believers. Consequently, Paul exhorted them *not* to resist their leaders' exhortations regarding this tendency to be lazy. Rather, they were to "respect" them and to "esteem" them, to "hold them in highest regard in love because of their work." After all, this *is* a difficult task—to admonish Christians who are not living in the will of God and then to face their resistance and criticism.

"Who are you?" some no doubt asked. "What authority do you have over us? What right do you have to reprove us?" Paul answered questions like these by explaining that their leaders were appointed to oversee this church "in the Lord." In other words, they were representing Jesus Christ who taught believers that they are "the salt of the earth" and "the light of the world" (Matthew 5:13–16). As Christians, we are to "win the respect of outsiders" (1 Thessalonians 4:12)—not to be a negative witness among unbelieving neighbors.

At this point, Paul appealed to all the believers in Thessalonica to support their leaders by admonishing one another. Tasks such as this are the responsibility of the whole church—not just its leadership. Thus, Paul wrote: "And we urge you, brothers, *warn those who are idle*" (5:14).

MORE SIGNIFICANT QUESTIONS

As with most events we've encountered thus far regarding local church leadership, we are left with some very thought-provoking questions:

1. *Who appointed the spiritual leaders in the church in Thessalonica?*
   We're not sure when and if Paul appointed these leaders. It's possible that Luke carried out this function in the Macedonian churches (Philippi, Berea, and Thessalonica), since he stayed on in Philippi to establish this new church.

   From Luke's own historical record, we know he was with Paul, Silas, and Timothy when they crossed the Aegean Sea and arrived in Philippi. This is why he wrote that "from Troas *we* put out to sea" and "*we* traveled to Philippi" (Acts 16:11–12). And when his fellow missionaries left Philippi, Luke stated that "*they* left" and "*they* came to Thessalonica"—indicating that he stayed behind (16:40; 17:1).

   We don't meet Luke again as a traveling companion with Paul until seven or eight years later when they left Philippi together after the third journey was coming to a close.[2] Luke once again included himself in this historical record when he wrote, "*We* sailed from Philippi after the Feast of Unleavened Bread" (20:6). It's logical to conclude then that during this time, Luke may have served as a "general overseer" in the Macedonian churches—eventually appointing spiritual leaders in each town just as Titus did in Crete (Titus 1:5).

2. *What were the spiritual leaders called in the church in Thessalonica?* We're not given a specific answer to this question, but it may have been *overseers* and *deacons*, the same terms used to address the church leaders in Phillipi. We can speculate based on at least three factors: the mix of Jewish and Gentile believers in this church, Luke's own background as a believing Gentile, and his church-planting influence in the Macedonian region.

During Paul's first imprisonment in Rome, he would write a letter to the church in Philippi, greeting "the *overseers* [or bishops] and *deacons*" in this church (Philippians 1:1). Since Luke stayed on in Philippi after Paul, Silas, and Timothy left for Thessalonica, it makes sense that he eventually became involved in appointing spiritual leaders in the Philippian church.

Further, as we've already noted, it's logical to conclude that Luke may have also traveled to Berea and Thessalonica and helped appoint spiritual leaders in these towns as well. If so, it would not be surprising that the leaders in Thessalonica were also called *overseers* rather than *elders*.

3. *Why would Luke choose the term "overseer"* (episkopos) *rather than "elder"* (presbuteros)? Since the Macedonian churches were composed of many Gentile believers who had "turned to God from idols" (1 Thessalonians 1:9), and since Luke himself was a Gentile Christian, it's logical to conclude that he would have also been very culturally sensitive to the needs of these churches. After all, these cities were Roman colonies (see Acts 16:12), and the term *episkopos* (overseer) was used to identify a leader or superintendent of each colony.

Consequently, the term for "overseer" would be far more prevalent and familiar than the term for elder. As we'll see, Paul began to use these terms "elders" and "overseers" interchangeably to identify spiritual leaders in local churches. From this point forward in the biblical story, we'll note how often this happened.

NOTES

1. From the Greek *proistamenous*. The Greek participle Paul used is the same basic word he used later when writing to Timothy regarding spiritual leaders (see 1 Timothy 3:5; 5:17).

2. Paul's second journey lasted approximately three years, and the third journey up to six years. Consequently, Luke may have stayed in Philippi for seven or eight years.

THE EPHESIAN
ELDERS (A.D. 58)

BACK TO THE SOURCE

*Before proceeding, read Acts 19:1–20:1; 10:17–38. What can
we learn from Paul's ministry model?*

The next episode in this biblical story is the most descriptive and
comprehensive scene thus far. It's a very touching exposure of
the depths of Paul's heart. The once tough-minded, task-oriented
Pharisee who had approved Stephen's death had become a sensitive and compassionate shepherd of shepherds.

READY TO "SAIL PAST EPHESUS"

Paul was headed for Jerusalem—even though the Holy Spirit
kept informing him through various disciples he was heading for
serious resistance to the message of grace (Acts 21:4, 10–11).

Knowing that he would be delayed if he entered the province of Asia, Paul decided "to sail past Ephesus"—but could not ignore some deep concerns he wanted to share with the Ephesian elders/overseers. Motivated by his deep love for these fellow pastors, he disembarked at Miletus, a coastal village, and sent someone to ask them to make the day's journey to join him there (see Ephesus on map, next page).

When these men arrived, Paul reflected on his own three-year ministry in Ephesus and then charged them and warned them very specifically:

> Keep watch over yourselves and all the flock of which the Holy Spirit has made you *overseers*. Be *shepherds* of the church of God, which he bought with his own blood. I know that after I leave, savage wolves will come in among you and will not spare the flock. Even from your own number men will arise and distort the truth in order to draw away disciples after them. So be on your guard! Remember that for three years I never stopped warning each of you night and day with tears. [Acts 20:28–31]

PAUL'S FIRST VISIT TO EPHESUS

Paul's first experience in Ephesus went back to the closing days of his second mission. He had "set sail" to return to Antioch of Syria. However, he decided to stop over in this city, the capital of the Roman province of Asia (see map, page 78). Superseded in size and importance only by Rome and Antioch, Ephesus was a thriving metropolis and a central place for pagan worship. People came from all over the province to pay homage to the pagan goddess Artemis. However, as in many places in the Roman world, there were Jews living in Ephesus who still followed Jehovah.

As Paul often did, he began his witness in the synagogue—"reason-[ing] with the Jews" regarding the promised Messiah. Even though he encountered openness to the Gospel and an invitation to stay longer, "he declined" and promised them he would return, if God so willed (Acts 18:18–21).

THE THIRD MISSIONARY JOURNEY

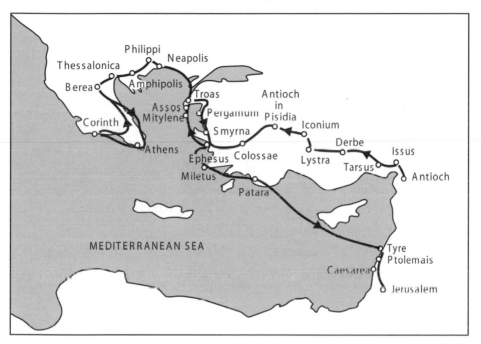

A SECOND JERUSALEM

Paul *did* return and spent three years in Ephesus. In many respects, this city became a "second Jerusalem" in terms of being an influential center for the Gospel. When Paul arrived, he found *twelve men* who believed in Jesus but had only been exposed to the teachings of John the Baptist (19:1–7). They hadn't even heard about the third person of the Trinity. But when Paul placed his hands on them, "the Holy Spirit came on them" (19:6) just as He had done on the Day of Pentecost when the church was born in Jerusalem. Like the apostles, these twelve men also "spoke in tongues and prophesied"—no doubt miraculously speaking various languages and dialects that were spoken in this region of Asia (19:1–6; compare with 2:5–11).

Paul was encouraged, and intensified his ministry in the synagogue, but eventually he faced serious resistance. He then moved his base of operation to a lecture hall where he continued to explain the Scriptures, not just on the Sabbath, but day after day. He faithfully continued this evangelistic, apologetic ministry "for two years, so that all the Jews and Greeks who lived in the province of Asia heard the word of the Lord" (19:10).[1]

RESUMING THE THIRD JOURNEY

After a three-year ministry in Ephesus, Paul continued on into the provinces of Macedonia and Achaia, visiting the churches he, Silas, and Timothy had started on the second missionary journey (see map 3). Eventually, he came to Philippi, where Luke once again joined him and they began their journey toward Jerusalem. It was then they stopped in Miletus and Paul sent for the leaders in Ephesus (Acts 20:17).

Paul's Example to Leaders

As Paul reunited and fellowshipped with these men, he reminded them of the way he lived when he ministered among them. As a powerful example to other leaders, he had shown:

□ *Humility and compassion.* In spite of the persecution from his Jewish brothers, Paul had "served the Lord with great humility and with tears" (20:19). No one could question his dedication to the Lord and to them. It's impossible to make this kind of claim unless it's absolutely true.

□ *Faithful teaching and preaching.* Paul spoke publicly in the lecture hall of Tyrannus, sharing everything that would help them grow in their Christian faith. However, he also taught them "from house to house," apparently spending time with each leader's family (20:20).

□ *An evangelistic ministry.* Paul preached the gospel of God's grace to everyone who would listen—both Jews and Gentiles— encouraging them to turn from their sins and put their faith in the Lord Jesus Christ (20:21).

☐ *A discipleship ministry.* Paul not only preached the gospel of God's grace, but also once people responded in repentance and faith, he taught these new believers how to live the Christian life (20:27).

☐ *Pure motives.* Paul never took advantage of these believers materially. In this sense, he was a great example to these Ephesian elders/overseers. At times, he actually supplied his own needs and the needs of his fellow missionaries (20:33–35).

Paul's Exhortations

Before he left, Paul exhorted the leaders of the Ephesian church to remain diligent in their various tasks:

☐ *Accountability.* Paul urged these men to "keep watch over" themselves—to be "overseers" to one another, both in their Christian lifestyle and in their ministry, holding each other accountable (Acts 20:28).

☐ *Oversight.* Paul urged them to "keep watch over . . . all the flock"—to manage the whole church well (20:28a).

☐ *Shepherding.* Paul urged the elders to "be shepherds of the church of God"—to care for these believers and to make sure they were not led astray by false teachers and deceptive prophets, which he called "savage wolves." He warned them that some from their own group would "arise and distort the truth" in order to gain followers (20:28b–30).

☐ *Faithfulness.* Paul urged these leaders to never let their guard down but to follow his example by warning believers consistently with sincere compassion and deep concern (20:31).

Paul's Doxology

Paul culminated his stay in Miletus by committing all of these spiritual leaders to God's grace. As they were about to conclude their time together, they knelt and prayed, and when they rose from their knees, all of them "wept as they embraced" Paul and "kissed him"—believing they would probably never see their apostolic mentor again on this side of heaven. In fact, Paul and Luke literally had to pull themselves away from these elders in order to board the ship and continue toward Jerusalem.

NOTE

1. Luke often used the word "all"—not in an absolute sense, but in this case, the large number who visited Ephesus from all over Asia.

LEADERSHIP
QUALIFICATIONS
(A.D. 63)

BACK TO THE SOURCE

Before proceeding, read Acts 20:17–28:30 and Paul's first letter to Timothy. As you read this pastoral letter, remember that Paul had been released from prison and was somewhere in Macedonia, and Timothy was in Ephesus dealing with certain men who were teaching false doctrine and were causing controversy and divisions in the church (1 Timothy 1:3).

More than fifteen years after Paul and Barnabas first appointed elders on the first missionary journey—in Lystra, Iconium, and Antioch of Pisidia—Paul wrote a letter to Timothy outlining criteria for determining whether a man was qualified to be a spiritual leader in the church.

Paul had left Timothy in Ephesus to handle a leadership crisis. Apparently, what Paul warned against at Miletus had happened.

"Certain men," particularly Jewish believers, were teaching "false doctrine" and devoting "themselves to myths and endless genealogies" creating "controversies" and divisions among God's people (1 Timothy 1:3–4; see Acts 20:30). But it's also obvious that the current elders/overseers were not the only cause of the problem. There were others who wanted to become leaders and were not qualified. Consequently, Paul outlined (1 Timothy 3:1–7) a standard for selecting and appointing these men.

Before we look specifically at these qualifications, let's trace Paul's activities after he said farewell to the Ephesian elders in Miletus, leading up to his first imprisonment in Rome approximately three years later.

GAINING PERSPECTIVE

When Paul arrived in Jerusalem, he and his traveling companions met with *"James and all the elders."* By this time, the apostles must have begun their ministry beyond "Judea and Samaria" and were proclaiming the Gospel to what they perceived as "the ends of the earth" (Acts 1:8). We can be quite confident that Peter ended up in Rome. Beyond that, we can only rely on tradition and speculation. Regardless of what happened to these men as their names disappeared from the pages of New Testament history, we know for certain their ministries changed the course of history.[1]

When Paul met with the Jerusalem elders, he gave a complete report of his ministry, culminating in a time of praise regarding what God had done among the Gentiles. However, this positive time of worship was dampened by the news that thousands of believing Jews in Jerusalem were still mixing law and grace. Ironically, many Jewish believers were still confused about the very issue that had been clarified and put in writing in Jerusalem more than ten years earlier (Acts 20:20–25).

Persecution and Imprisonment

As predicted along the way by various prophets as Paul traveled toward Jerusalem, the atmosphere quickly turned hostile when some Jews from Asia (who were obviously not believers) saw Paul in the temple. Earlier they had seen Trophimus who was from Ephesus, with Paul. Assuming the worst, they reported that he had taken this Gentile into the temple area that was off limits to non-Jews. Obviously aware of his three-year ministry in Ephesus and the number of Jews that had accepted the Messiah, they stirred up the whole city against Paul (Acts 21:27–31).

This was no minor disturbance. The hostility was so intense that some actually plotted to kill Paul (Acts 23:12–15)—ironically, a replay of what he had done years before as an unsaved Jewish leader when he approved of Stephen's death and began to persecute the church. To save Paul's life, the Romans transported him to Caesarea, where he was incarcerated for two years. Though men came from Jerusalem to accuse him before various Roman officials, they had no accusations to warrant Paul's imprisonment—let alone a death sentence.

As a Roman citizen, Paul finally appealed to Caesar, which resulted in his house arrest in Rome, the final chapter in Luke's historical account. During this two-year period, Paul wrote his letters to Philemon, the Philippians, the Colossians, and the Ephesians. The only specific reference to local church leaders in these epistles is his greeting to the *"overseers and deacons"* in Philippi (Philippians 1:1) and possibly to Philemon who may have served as a spiritual leader of the church that met in his home along with Archippus (Philemon 2).[2]

Another Missionary Journey

At the end of two years, Paul was released and apparently made a fourth missionary journey. He and Timothy traveled once again into the province of Asia and visited Ephesus. Paul then traveled on into Macedonia, leaving Timothy behind to deal with a leadership crisis. Concerned that his young companion be able to follow through on a very challenging task, Paul at some point penned a letter to this young man, giving him very specific directions in terms of the qualifications for those who were to manage and shepherd the church. (In that letter, Paul also outlined the qualifications for "deacons," which we'll look at in chapter 13.)

A Noble Task

Paul viewed the position of being an "elder/overseer" as a very significant role, and anyone who had a desire to serve in this way would be pursuing a valuable, upright, and responsible ministry. However, Paul also made it unmistakably clear that a man who served in this position should demonstrate character qualities that reflect Christlike maturity. Apparently, some of the men who were already "elders/overseers"—perhaps some that Paul had exhorted in Miletus—were distorting "the truth in order to draw away disciples after them" (Acts 20:30). However, there were obviously other men in Ephesus who also wanted to be spiritual leaders but who were definitely not demonstrating "noble character," disqualifying them from being involved in this "noble task" (1 Timothy 3:1).[3] Consequently, Paul outlined fifteen qualities for measuring Christlike character.

Before looking at these qualities specifically, here are two important observations. First, Paul implied that any Christian man could seek this role. There was no special, divine calling associated with this task. Second, the primary criterion for selection and approval was maturity in Jesus Christ.

The Maturity Profile

Here are the fifteen qualities Paul specified in 1 Timothy 3:1–7 for a qualified elder/overseer. Again, they are measures of maturity in Christ.

QUALITY 1: *"Above reproach"*

Paul began the list with an overarching quality: "Now the *overseer* must be *above reproach*" (3:2a; see also Titus 1:6). In essence, this means a spiritual leader should have a "good reputation" among believers as well as unbelievers. This is why Paul concluded this list by saying that anyone who served in this role "must also have a good reputation with outsiders" (3:7), that is, unbelievers.

QUALITY 2: *"The husband of but one wife"*

This requirement has yielded various interpretations (described in chapter 20). We believe Paul was dealing primarily with moral purity, which is why he lists this quality immediately, stating that an elder/overseer must be "above reproach." There is nothing that builds a man's reputation more significantly than being faithful to one woman—his wife. However, nothing destroys trust more rapidly than immorality. In essence, Paul was saying that if you couldn't trust a man to be loyal to his wife, you couldn't trust him in other areas of his life, particularly in the area of honesty and integrity.

QUALITY 3: *"Temperate"*

With this word (from the Greek *nephalios*), Paul was describing a man who had a clear focus on life. He was stable and steadfast, and his thinking was clear, reflecting faith, hope, and love (1 Thessalonians 5:8).

QUALITY 4: *"Self-controlled"*

The translators of *The New American Standard Bible* chose the word "prudent." The Greek term (*sophron*) literally means to be "sound in mind." In fact, the word can be translated in various ways—to be "discrete," "sober," "sensible."

QUALITY 5: *"Respectable"*

The most descriptive use of the word for "respectable" (*kosmios*) appears in Paul's letter to Titus when he urged slaves "to *adorn* [*kosmeo*] the doctrine of God our Savior in every respect" (Titus 2:10, NASB). Our English word "cosmetics" comes from the same basic word (*kosmios*). In essence, Paul was teaching that our lives are to be like "cosmetics to the Gospel"—to make the Gospel attractive by the way we live our lives.

QUALITY 6: *"Hospitable"*

Generally speaking, "being hospitable" refers to the way we use our material possessions—particularly the homes we live in and the food we eat. All Christians are to be hospitable—but this is a quality that should characterize every spiritual leader, no matter what his resources.

QUALITY 7: *"Able to teach"*

Paul used *didaktikos,* the basic Greek for "able to teach," only twice in his letters. The second time he used it was in his second letter to Timothy to describe how this young man should relate to those who disagreed with him (2 Timothy 2:23–25). Those who have developed this character quality are able to communicate in a nonargumentative, nondefensive, and nonthreatening way.

QUALITY 8: *"Not given to drunkenness"*

Most scholars agree that most references to wine in both the Old and New Testaments refer to fermented grape juice; thus Paul wrote that a spiritual leader should not be *"addicted* to much wine" (Titus 2:3)—since it's impossible to be addicted to a nonalcoholic beverage. From a larger biblical perspective, Paul was saying that spiritual leaders should (1) never overindulge and over drink (Proverbs 23:29–30); (2) never cause others to sin by using their freedom in Christ (Romans 14:21); and (3) never become addicted to anything, including food (Proverbs 23:20–21)

QUALITY 9: *"Not violent"*

Paul warned leaders to avoid having anger out of control—physically and verbally. Such a violent person (*plektes*) is literally a "bruiser," one who is "ready with a blow," a "pugnacious, contentious, quarrelsome person."

QUALITY 10: *"Gentle"*

Being "gentle" is in contrast to being "violent." There are several Greek words that are translated "gentle," and here Paul chose *epieikes,* a word that describes a person who is "forbearing," "equitable," "fair," and "reasonable."

QUALITY 11: *"Not quarrelsome"*

The *New American Standard Bible* uses the word "peaceable"—a person who avoids debates and arguments. This is a very basic character quality that describes a leader who is "able to teach."

QUALITY 12: *"Not a lover of money"*

The Scriptures do not teach that "money" per se is evil. Nor do they teach that it is wrong to have money in abundance. This is why Paul stated that those who are selected for leadership positions should be "free"—not from money—but "from the *love* of money" (NASB). They must model generosity and nonmaterialistic attitudes and actions to those they shepherd.

QUALITY 13: *"Manage his own family well"*

If a man is married and has children, a basic criterion for determining whether he is ready for a key leadership role in the church is how well he is functioning as a spiritual leader in his home. Paul viewed a well-ordered family as the true test of a man's maturity and ability to lead other Christians. However, there are many misunderstandings regarding what Paul meant by this requirement. We often set a standard that Paul did not have in mind. Clearly, he was thinking of grown children who were probably already married and how "wild and disobedient" behavior was affecting their father's reputation both in the church and the nonbelieving community. (See chapter 20 for a fuller discussion.)

QUALITY 14: *"Not a recent convert"*

Paul warned against appointing men to leadership who were new Christians. If we do, we are setting that person up for a direct attack from Satan—and that point of attack will be pridefulness.

QUALITY 15: *"A good reputation"*

Finally, the overseer needed to have a good reputation in the local community. Just as a spiritual leader must have a good reputation with believers by being "above reproach" (the first quality), his reputation with outsiders must be above question.

This is the first of two very detailed maturity profiles outlined by Paul for selecting and appointing elders/overseers. When Paul left Titus in Crete to establish the church, he outlined a second list of qualifications (Titus 1:5–9). In chapter 19, we'll compare these two criteria and look carefully at the "similarities" and the "differences."[4]

NOTES

1. For an in-depth study on each apostle, see Gene A. Getz, *The Apostles: Becoming Unified Through Diversity* (Nashville: Broadman & Holman, 1998), 1–2.

2. Some believe Paul was referring to "elders" or "overseers" in his letter to the Ephesians when he referred to gifted individuals who were "pastors and teachers" (see Ephesians 4:11–12). For another point of view, see the section "Observation 5" in chapter 22 and appendix C.

3. The Greek word translated "noble" in the NIV *is kalos.* This word is often used to describe "works" that please God.

4. For a detailed description and application of these qualities outlined in 1 Timothy 3:1–7 and Titus 1:5–9, see Gene A. Getz, *The Measure of a Man*, rev. ed. (Ventura, Calif.: Regal, 1995).

ASSISTANTS TO ELDERS/OVERSEERS: DEACONS (A.D. 63)

 BACK TO THE SOURCE

Before proceeding, read 1 Timothy 3:1–13 and Titus 1:1–9. Why did Paul instruct Timothy to appoint both elders/overseers and deacons in Ephesus but only elders/overseers in the churches in Crete?

When under house arrest in Rome, Paul wrote to the Philippians and greeted not only the *"overseers"* but also those he identified as *"deacons"* (1:1). This is the first time the term "deacons" (*diakonoi*) is used in the biblical story to designate a group of people who were to serve in this kind of official capacity. During the six to eight years Luke ministered as an apostolic representative in the church in Philippi, he apparently appointed not only those who were to "shepherd the flock" but also those who would assist the overseers (or these shepherds) in their ministry.

A couple of years after Paul was released from prison, he once

again used this terminology when he wrote his first letter to Timothy, listing not only the qualifications for elders/overseers, but also for deacons
(1 Timothy 3:8–13).

WORKS OF SERVICE

Before looking at these character qualities, note that biblical writers
used the basic terms *diakoneo* (to serve), *diakonia* (service), and *diakonos*
(servant) to describe *the ministry all believers* should have within the body
of Christ. For example, when Paul wrote to the Ephesians, he stated that it's
God's plan that all believers are to be equipped "for works of service [*diakonia*]" (Ephesians 4:12). Though there are those who are to serve the
body of Christ in a special way, every believer is to be a "deacon" or "servant" (*diakonos*) who participates in building up the body of Christ (v. 16).

THE ACTS 6 MEN

The first illustration of this kind of special "service" (*diakonia*) happened in the church in Jerusalem when the apostles asked the Grecian Jews
to select seven qualified men from among their number who could care
for the Grecian widows. Their service enabled the apostles to continue to
concentrate on their primary God-given responsibilities—to give their
"attention to *prayer* and the ministry of the *word*" (Acts 6:4).

Though these "Acts 6" men are not identified as "deacons," this
unique event serves as a model in clarifying why official leaders with this
title were appointed in various churches. As the seven men in Jerusalem *assisted the apostles* in meeting a unique cultural need at that time, just so
"deacons" were later commissioned in the churches to *assist elders/over-
seers in carrying out their shepherding responsibilities,* which included helping them to meet unique cultural needs.

A SUPRACULTURAL AND CULTURAL SEQUENCE

When Paul and Barnabas returned to Lystra, Iconium, and Antioch
of Pisidia on the first missionary journey, they first of all "appointed *elders*

... in each church" (Acts 14:23). There is no reference to "deacons." And when Paul left Titus in Crete, he was to "straighten out what was left unfinished and appoint *elders* in every town" (Titus 1:5). Again, "deacons" are not mentioned.

Does this mean that "deacons" were never appointed in these churches? Not at all. They simply were appointed at a later time. Elders/overseers were appointed first for two reasons. First, all believers need qualified shepherds who will first of all feed them the Word of God. This is a spiritual need that crosses culture and is always necessary if believers are going to grow and mature in Jesus Christ.

Second, Paul and Barnabas appointed elders/overseers in these towns and not deacons for pragmatic and cultural reasons. Initially, these churches were relatively small and the elders/overseers did not need deacons to assist them in overseeing in the church. However, as the churches increased in numbers, so did special needs, and the elders/overseers faced the same challenge as the apostles faced in Jerusalem—to meet those needs and, at the same time, to maintain their shepherding priorities.

This overall perspective also helps clarify why Paul and Peter listed and described specific "functions" for elders/overseers. These are *supracultural responsibilities* (see "A Comparison of Elders/Overseers and Deacons," figure 3). God's people in "every tribe and language and people and nation" (Revelation 5:9) and at any period in history need oversight, teaching, admonishing, and prayer. However, the specific "functions" for deacons are never spelled out in detail—except the one that is inherent in their title—to "serve" (*diakoneo*). This generic "function" must be fleshed out in various ways from place to place at different points in time and history. For example, "waiting tables" in Jerusalem was directly related to a cultural need at that time. When the church was scattered, the seven men who were caring for the needs of widows discontinued carrying out this responsibility.

Against this backdrop, we can also conclude that "titles" are not the most important issue when it comes to this kind of service and ministry. These men and women could very well be called "assistants," "helpers," "servants," or "ministers"—depending upon the cultural setting. This harmonizes with what we've already observed about those who are to manage and shepherd the flock. In some cases, they were called "elders" and

in other instances, they were called "overseers"—depending again on the
cultural dynamics.

Figure 3
A Comparison of Elders/Overseers and Deacons

TERMS	QUALIFICATIONS	FUNCTIONS
Elders/Overseers		
First to be appointed; permanent positions	Described in detail (1 Timothy 3:1–7; Titus 1:5–9)	Manage/shepherd in ways that are *supraculturally defined*; e.g., overseeing, teaching, admonishing, praying, delegating
Deacons		
Appointed only when necessary; position may be temporary	Described in detail (1 Timothy 3:8–13)	Serve in various ways that are often *culturally defined*

WOMEN DEACONS

One Interpretation of 1 Timothy 3:11

When outlining the qualifications for selecting men to serve as "deacons," Paul inserted a paragraph that is puzzling, even for Bible translators.
He mentioned four qualifications for women, using the Greek word *gu-
naikas* that can be used to describe any adult woman who is married, who
has never been married, or who is widowed or divorced (1 Timothy 3:11).
This, of course, poses a challenge to translators since they have to determine what Paul meant based on the overall context.[1]

Most Christian leaders over the centuries have not accepted the interpretation that Paul was referring to "deacons' wives." Rather, the most
common understanding is that he was addressing the qualifications for
"women" who also serve as deacons. This is why Williams in his trans-

lation coined the word "deaconesses." This interpretation indeed seems to fit the context better, especially since Paul did not outline qualifications for the "wives" of elders/overseers—an even more strategic role in the church.

However, church leaders have taken this one step further and concluded that Paul was referring to three "offices" in his letter to Timothy—elders/overseers, male deacons, and female deacons. This is interesting, as the term "office" is never used in the New Testament either to describe the position of elders/overseers or deacons.[2]

An Alternate Interpretation

Though the "three office" approach has often been practiced in church history, we believe there is another interpretation that is more logical when we consider other textual, contextual, and cultural factors. When we look at the total biblical story, it appears there is only one primary leadership role in the church; namely, elders/overseers who are responsible to manage and shepherd God's people, just as fathers are primarily responsible to lead their families. Deacons, on the other hand, are qualified men and women who *are to assist* the elders/overseers in their pastoral ministries.

This interpretation includes unmarried women, as well as married women, who may be able to serve as "deacons" in assisting elders/overseers without neglecting their family responsibilities. This would include women like Priscilla who certainly served as an assistant to the apostle Paul, along with her husband Aquila (Acts 18:1–3, 18; Romans 16:3). It would also include women like Phoebe, a servant (or deacon) of the church in Cenchrea (Romans 16:1).[3]

QUALIFICATIONS OF DEACONS

Against this backdrop, we can now look at the specific character qualities Paul outlined in 1 Timothy 3:8–13 for both men and women who serve as deacons.

QUALIFICATION 1: *"Worthy of respect"*

Paul used the basic Greek word *semnos* to describe an overarching quality for both men and women (1 Timothy 3:8a, 11a). The *New American Standard Bible* reads: "Deacons likewise must be men of *dignity*" (3:8) and "women [in deacon's roles] must likewise be *dignified*" (3:11).

QUALIFICATION 2: *"Sincere"*

This quality of sincerity (from the Greek *dilogos*) demonstrates honesty and integrity in communication. The NASB translates *dilogos* "not double tongued," i.e., not speaking out of two sides of one's mouth.

QUALIFICATION 3: *"Not indulging in much wine"*

This is the same basic quality Paul required of elders/overseers (see "The Maturity Profile," chapter 12). In essence, no elder/overseer or deacon should serve in the church who is "addicted to much wine" (1 Timothy 3:8 NASB).

QUALIFICATION 4: *"Not pursuing dishonest gain"*

Paul probably zeroed in on this requirement in a specific way for deacons because they are often entrusted with the task of handling money in the church (1 Corinthians 16:3–4). They were never to "dip their hand in the till."

QUALIFICATION 5: *"Keep hold of the deep truths of the faith with a clear conscience"*

There were leaders emerging in the New Testament churches who used biblical truth to "pursue dishonest gain"—to manipulate people to give money that was used selfishly. Paul taught and modeled that this kind of behavior was unconscionable (1 Thessalonians 2:5).

QUALIFICATION 6: *"They must first be tested"*

Paul does not mention in verse 10 any particular method for conducting this test—which once again introduces us to "freedom in form" in order to carry out important "biblical functions."

QUALIFICATION 7: *"Not malicious talkers"*

At this point in the list, it appears Paul shifted his thoughts to women who were also being considered to serve as deacons (1 Timothy 3:11). We've already noted that both men and women serving in this role are to "be worthy of respect." However, Paul mentioned three very specific additional requirements for women. The first is that a woman deacon is not to be a "malicious talker."

This was obviously a problem among women in the New Testament culture since Paul addressed the same issue in his letter to Titus, who was to "teach the older women to be reverent in the way they live, *not to be slanderers*" (Titus 2:3). Paul was not teaching that men do not have a problem with "slander" and "malicious talk." However, when we compare the overarching qualifications for men serving as elders/overseers with the overarching qualities for women in serving and teaching roles, we see an interesting emphasis. Notice the comparisons in figure 4.

This literary pattern does not seem to be accidental but, rather, reflects a reality. Normally, a man's area of vulnerability is sexual—which relates to the qualification of being a "man of one woman." On the other hand, a woman's area of vulnerability is often verbal—an inappropriate use of the tongue. Again, this does not mean that a woman is not tempted to be immoral but her temptation focuses more on inappropriate communication.

QUALIFICATION 8: *"Temperate"*

Here Paul mentioned the same characteristic he had already outlined for elders/overseers (1 Timothy 3:2). Broadly speaking, a "temperate" (from the Greek word *nephaleos*) person has a clear focus on life.

Figure 4
A Comparison of Qualifications for Elders and Women Deacons

MEN (ELDERS)	WOMEN DEACONS
In 1 Timothy:	In 1 Timothy:
"Above reproach" (3:2a)	"Worthy of respect" (3:11a)
"The husband of but one wife" (3:2b)	"Not malicious talkers" (3:11b)
In Titus:	In Titus:
"Blameless" (1:6a)	"Reverent in the way they live" (2:3a)
"The husband of but one wife" (1:6b)	"Not to be slanderers" (2:3b)

QUALIFICATION 9: *"Trustworthy"*

This Greek word for "trustworthy," *pistos,* can also be translated "faithful." In other words, a woman who exhibits this quality is "trustworthy in *everything*." Obviously, this applies to men as well, but for some unstated reason, Paul believed he should emphasize this character trait for women who are being considered to serve as deacons.

QUALIFICATION 10: *"Husband of but one wife"*

In verse 12, Paul once again addressed men, emphasizing moral purity. (This phrase is discussed in detail in chapter 20.)

QUALIFICATION 11: *"Manage his children and household well"*

Here Paul repeated the qualification he had already outlined for elders/ overseers. If a "family man" is going to serve the church in either role, he'll not be able to function as he should if he is unable to serve as a faithful husband and a successful father (see chapter 20).

MALE AND FEMALE ASSISTANTS

In essence, men and women who serve as assistants to elders/overseers in the church should be just as qualified as those they serve. This makes sense since in both lists, Paul was outlining qualities that reflect maturity in Jesus Christ. In other words, these character traits should be goals for every Christian who desires to live in the will of God by reflecting the "fruit of the Spirit."

NOTES

1. For instance, the translators of the *New American Standard Bible* used the word "women"; the *Williams New Testament* translated the word "deaconesses." The *New International Version* translated the word "wives."

2. The translators of the King James Version used the phrase "office of a bishop" (1 Timothy 3:1) and "office of a deacon" (3:10, 13) when they translated the basic Greek terms *episkopos* and *diakonos*. However, the term "office" is not used in the Greek text. Consequently, those who worked on the *New King James Version*, in order to be more accurate, omitted the term "office" when referring to deacons and used the term "position" when referring to the role of elders/bishops. The translators of the *New American Standard Bible* used the term "office" when referring to the "overseer," but for some reason, omitted the term "office" when they came to the basic term for "deacons." In other words, the original translators of the KJV helped create the "three-office" concept that is so prevalent today, which doesn't seem to reflect what the authors of the New Testament's story had in mind.

3. Robert Lewis in a very helpful article poses the idea that the "women" Paul had in mind were "single" and were to be assistants to men who serve as deacons. He also helps us to understand various positions on this passage of Scripture. Robert M. Lewis, "The 'Women' of 1 Timothy 3:11," *Bibliotheca Sacra* 136 (April 1979): 167.

A WOMAN'S ROLE
IN MINISTRY
(A.D. 63)

BACK TO THE SOURCE

*Before proceeding, compare Paul's restrictions on women in
1 Timothy 2:11–14 with what he wrote in Galatians 3:27–29
and Colossians 3:16. How do we reconcile "male and female"
equality "in Christ" with Paul's leadership restrictions?*

When Paul addressed the qualifications for both elders/over-
seers and deacons in his first letter to Timothy, he introduced us to
the subject of women and their leadership roles in New Testament churches. This leads to a very relevant question, particularly
in today's world: How should first-century practices determine
leadership roles for women in twenty-first century churches?

Most church historians agree that among Christian leaders,
this matter has been considered settled—that a woman should not
occupy an elder/overseer position. However, this is no longer

true, both within denominational and nondenominational settings. There are new voices challenging traditional views.[1]

This is why it's important for all of us who hold to biblical authority to take a fresh look at this subject through the lenses of Scripture, history, and culture. Though some of us may not agree with certain new trends in biblical interpretation and application, these challenges can and should help all of us evaluate our theological perspectives and to refine those perspectives if indeed our conclusions are out of harmony with biblical truth. With this in mind, let's look at what seems nondebatable in the biblical story.

The Body of Christ

When it comes to defining the church and how it functions, the apostle Paul carried the banner for a unified, functioning *body*. As a biblical writer, he alone used this metaphor to illustrate that the church, like the human body, "is a unit" and "each member belongs to all the others" (1 Corinthians 12:12; Romans 12:5). When he wrote to the Galatians, he made it very clear that there are no gender differences when it comes to our personal relationship with God: "There is neither Jew nor Greek, slave nor free, *male nor female,* for you are *all one in Christ Jesus*" (Galatians 3:28).

Paul also made it unmistakably clear that this truth involves more than our personal and corporate relationship with Christ. We must be functionally involved in one another's lives in the here and now. In his letter to the Ephesians, Paul stated unequivocally that *every member* of Christ's body is vital in this maturing process: "*Speaking the truth* in love, we will in all things grow up into him who is the Head, that is, Christ. From him the *whole body,* joined and held together by *every supporting ligament,* grows and builds itself up in love, as *each part* does its work (Ephesians 4:15–16).

Anyone who reads Paul's letters objectively cannot miss this critical truth. All believers—both men and women—are necessary for every local church to function as God intended. We are to "let the word of Christ dwell in [us] richly as [we] *teach and admonish one another* with all wisdom" (Colossians 3:16; see also Ephesians 5:19).

Building Up One Another

When Paul described what believers are to do for "one another" [*al-lelon*], he included, with few exceptions, *all members* of the body of Christ.[2] For example, when he wrote to the Romans, he said: "I myself am convinced my brothers [sisters], that you yourselves are full of goodness, complete in knowledge and competent to *instruct one another* (Romans 15:14).[3] In this "one another" statement, Paul used the word *noutheteo*, which means "to admonish" or to "warn," clearly a facet of the "teaching" functions mentioned throughout the New Testament.

When Paul wrote to the Thessalonians, he used the basic Greek term *parakaleo*, which means to "beseech," "exhort," "comfort," or "entreat":

☐ Therefore *encourage each other* with these words. [1 Thessalonians 4:18]

☐ Therefore *encourage one another and build each other up*, just as in fact you are doing. [1 Thessalonians 5:11]

The Spirit of Truth

The Greek term Paul used when he exhorted the Thessalonians "to encourage one another" is the basic term Jesus used three times in John's Gospel to describe the coming Holy Spirit. He would be the *parakletos*, translated "Counselor" (John 14:16, 26; 15:26). Three times Jesus also called the "Counselor" to come the "Spirit of *truth*" (John 14:16–17; 15:26; 16:13), certainly alluding to God's inspired and divine revelation that some of these men would teach orally and then inscribe in the Holy Scriptures (Acts 2:41; 2 Timothy 3:16–17). When the "Spirit of truth" comes, Jesus promised He would "teach" the apostles "all things" and would "remind" them of everything He had taught them (John 14:26).

Though Jesus stated that the apostles would have a primary, unique, and authoritative role in teaching these spiritual truths, Paul made it just as clear that every member of Christ's body—both men and women—would share in the responsibility to "teach" one another the biblical truth revealed by the Holy Spirit. Robert L. Saucy stated it well: "Consideration of the N.T. evidence thus shows that the teaching function of the church was carried on through various means involving not only *stated teachers* but also finally *all members*."[4]

ELDERS/OVERSEERS: MEN ONLY?

The Debate

Having often emphasized our unity in Christ as both men and women and that we are to minister to one another involving various kinds of "teaching" functions, Paul also taught in the Pastoral Epistles that only men should serve as elders/overseers, not women. In both his letters to Timothy and Titus, he required that this leader be a "husband of but one wife"—or more generally, a "man of one woman" (1 Timothy 3:2; Titus 1:6). He also referred to "fathers" when he required that a man selected and appointed as an elder/overseer must "manage his own family well and see that his children obey him with proper respect" (1 Timothy 3:4; see also Titus 1:6). In Paul's thinking, the church as the "family" or "household of God" was to be an extension of the intact family unit—led by spiritually mature husbands and fathers.

However, the question some Christian leaders are raising today is whether Paul was simply taking into consideration the cultural setting that existed both in the Jewish and Gentile world when he outlined these requirements. In answering this question, some have concluded that when Paul stated that "in Christ, there is . . . neither male nor female," he was stating the ideal and leaving room for movement that would eventually eliminate all role distinctions when it comes to leadership in the church.[5]

As stated earlier, most Bible interpreters would agree that Paul, at least in the New Testament context, was indeed requiring that elders/overseers be men, but some disagree as to whether this is a supracultural and thus normative requirement. After all, Paul stated that he had "become all things to all men so that by all possible means I might save some" (1 Corinthians 9:22). Is the requirement that men and not women serve as elders/overseers one of these "all things" that Paul would feel free to

change in another cultural setting? In other words, were these requirements directly related to the social situation in Ephesus and on the island
of Crete (1 Timothy 1:3; Titus 1:5)?

The Conclusion: A Supracultural Requirement

Based on our elders' own biblical, historical, and cultural research,
we've concluded that Paul's requirement in 1 Timothy and Titus is indeed supracultural and normative. In other words, this managing and
shepherding position should be held by men whenever and wherever the
church exists. Is this principle as important as the doctrines of the deity of
Jesus Christ, the Trinity, and salvation by grace through faith? Not at all!
However, if we misapply this principle, it could indeed hinder the goal
Paul so clearly stated for the church: "attaining to the whole measure of the
fullness of Christ" (Ephesians 4:13).

But how can we follow Paul's instructions to restrict the position of
elder/overseer to men without violating his other explicit teachings that
every member of Christ's body should be involved in some aspect of the
"teaching process" that leads to maturity in the church? We believe that
what has often led to either/or positions can be resolved when we rise
above the "exegetical trees" and see the "forest." In other words, as important as it is to understand the intricate details of biblical texts, we can
at times fail to see the "big picture" that emerges when we look more carefully at God's unfolding revelation through a process of time.

ASSISTANTS TO ELDERS/OVERSEERS

As we concluded in the last chapter, qualified women *can and should
assist* elders/overseers in all aspects of the ministry. "Unfortunately," as
Wayne House has observed, "attention during much of church history
has been on the limitation of women in leadership roles, but very little has
been said about the various ways in which women can serve."[6]

Paul particularly—who has been criticized severely by some as prej-
udiced against women—often showed deep appreciation to those ladies
who assisted and served with him in ministry. Even many feminists believe

Paul had a high regard for women. For example, liberal scholar Robin Scroggs defends Paul's viewpoints when he writes: "It is time, indeed past time, to say loudly and clearly that Paul is, so far from being a chauvinist, the only certain and consistent spokesman for the liberation and equality of women in the New Testament."[7]

Various Women Assistants

Several statements by Paul about specific women help verify Scroggs' conclusion. Concerning Phoebe, he wrote in Romans 16:

> I commend to you our *sister* Phoebe, a *servant* of the church in Cenchrea. I ask you to receive her in the Lord in a way worthy of the saints and to give her any help she may need from you, for she has been *a great help to many people, including me.* [vv. 1–2]

In this same closing chapter of Romans, Paul extended greetings to several other women and commended them for their diligent service:

☐ Greet *Mary,* who *worked very hard* for you. [v. 6]

☐ Greet *Tryphena* and *Tryphosa,* those women who *work hard in the Lord.* Greet my dear friend Persis, another woman who has *worked very hard* in the Lord. [v.12]

When Paul wrote to the Philippians, he again mentioned two women, *Euodia* and *Syntyche,* stating that they "contended at" his "side in the cause of the gospel." Furthermore, he noted that they had served together "with Clement and the rest of [his] fellow workers" (Philippians 4:3).

All of Paul's personal comments to various women certainly correlate with what we've concluded regarding deacons (1 Timothy 3:11). Along with qualified men, qualified women were to assist the elders/overseers in any way they were needed to help manage and shepherd the church. Though we're not told specifically how the women Paul mentioned by name helped him and so many others, we can certainly assume they carried out some very specific roles, including some "teaching" responsibilities.

Priscilla and Her Husband

Early on in Paul's final comments as he culminated the Roman letter, he extended some very special greetings to a husband and wife team that he led to Christ in Corinth: "Greet *Priscilla* and *Aquila,* my *fellow workers* in Christ Jesus. They risked their lives for me. Not only I but all the churches of the Gentiles are grateful to them" (Romans 16:3–4).

When Paul left Priscilla and Aquila in Ephesus, they heard Apollos' teaching about Jesus Christ. Though what he said about the Lord was accurate, "he knew only the baptism of John" (Acts 18:25). Consequently, both Priscilla and Aquila invited him to their home and "explained to him the way of God more adequately" (18:26). It's not accidental that in this instance Luke mentioned Priscilla's name first, no doubt indicating she initiated this opportunity with Apollos.

We must not conclude from this incident that Priscilla was the primary leader in this home. Luke seemed to make that apparent in his first reference to this couple when he introduced us to "Aquila, a native of Pontus, who had recently come from Italy with his wife Priscilla" (18:2). Prior to his conversion, he was probably a typical Jewish husband in terms of the way he viewed his patriarchal position. But when he became a believer through Paul's influence, he recognized his wife's giftedness and ability to assist in discipling others. In fact, he was evidently not concerned or threatened when Priscilla at times took the lead in making contact with people who needed spiritual help—and then may have actually taken the lead in the communication process.

WOMEN TEACHING WOMEN

There is no debate regarding Paul's viewpoint when it comes to "women teaching women." In fact, Titus was to equip the older women in the churches in Crete to teach younger women. The text in this letter speaks for itself:

"Likewise, teach the older women

   ☐ to be reverent in the way they live,

□ not to be slanderers or

□ addicted to much wine, but

□ to teach what is good.

"Then they can train the younger women:

□ to love their husbands and children,

□ to be self-controlled and pure,

□ to be busy at home,

□ to be kind, and

□ to be subject to their husbands, so that no one will malign the

word of God" (Titus 2:3–5).

Paul presented this "older woman, younger woman" model as one of the greatest teaching opportunities mature Christian women can have in the church. They can share wisdom out of their years of experience, something even mature men have no capacity to do. Furthermore, these *mature women can do what men should not do* in a personal setting—to communicate with women regarding very intimate matters. It's obvious Timothy faced this challenge in Ephesus when Paul exhorted him—particularly as a young single man—to "treat . . . older women as mothers, and younger women as sisters, with *absolute purity*" (1 Timothy 5:1–2).

Understanding a Puzzling Paragraph

We come now to Paul's comments about women's roles in the church when he wrote his first letter to Timothy—comments that have been studied extensively—particularly in recent years. Evangelical feminists have raised penetrating questions, not only regarding women in leadership roles, but also regarding their relationship with men in general.

Note first Paul's comments:

A woman should learn in *quietness* and *full submission*. I do not permit a woman *to teach* or *to have authority* over a man; she must *be silent*. For

Adam was formed first, then Eve. And Adam was not the one deceived; it was the woman who *was deceived* and became a sinner. [1 Timothy 2:11–14]

How do we correlate these statements by Paul with everything we've noted thus far when he discussed both men and women functioning in "speaking" and "teaching" roles in the body of Christ? To answer this question, we must first think logically. If Paul meant that a woman had to maintain "absolute silence" in the presence of men, Paul would be contradicting himself many times over in terms of what he taught in other letters. Even in the Corinthian church where he issued a very similar prohibition (1 Corinthians 14:33–35), he did not forbid women to utilize their "speaking" gifts (14:26).

The Scene in Eden

What then did Paul mean? What "forms" of communication used by women violate what Paul actually had in mind? To answer this question, we need to note a very important guideline in Timothy's letter that is rooted in the creation story—namely, a woman should not function in such a way as "to have authority over a man" (1 Timothy 2:12). To support this point, Paul first appealed to the order of creation—"Adam was formed first, then Eve" (2:13)—who was created to come alongside Adam to be his "helper" (Genesis 2:18). This does not mean Eve was inferior to Adam. There is no indication of inequality whatsoever in the original creation story. They were both created in the image of God, reflecting the Creator's perfection (1:27). However, even though they—together—were to "rule over" the animal creation, Adam was given from the beginning servant-leadership responsibility in this relationship because of his priority in creation.

Second, Paul stated that a woman should not have authority over a man because Eve was the one "who was deceived" by Satan—not Adam (1 Timothy 2:14). Consequently, Eve and "all her sisters" throughout history suffered the consequences. Hebrew scholar Ronald Allen seems to capture what happened after the Fall with this expanded paraphrase of Genesis 3:16:

God then spoke to the woman as a consequence of her rebellion against the beneficent rule of Yahweh, the following new realities that shall mark her life: I will bring something new into the wonder of the bringing of children into the world. I will greatly magnify your pain in giving birth. When you give birth to your children it will be in physical pain. I will also allow pain to come into your marriage relationship with your husband. You will tend to desire to usurp the role I have given to him as the compassionate leader in your home, rejecting his role and belittling his manhood. And the man on his part will tend to relate to you in loveless tyranny, dominating and stifling your integrity as an equal partner to himself.[8]

Does Paul's second reason—that Eve was first deceived and not Adam—mean that all women hereafter were more prone to deception? We believe the answer is no. What happened to Eve brought *leadership consequences* that are ongoing—but not a greater tendency toward deception than that of men. In fact, many empirical studies demonstrate that gender is not a constant issue in a tendency toward deception.[9] When I evaluate my own years of ministry, I must admit that at times I have been more prone to being deceived than my wife. I can think of instances when if I had listened to her perspective, I wouldn't have made certain errors in judgment.

The Scene in Ephesus

Against this historic backdrop, we can now look more carefully at what was happening in Ephesus. When Paul wrote to Timothy, he seemed to be addressing a very specific problem that violated the principle we just described that is rooted in the Creation story. In the Ephesian church, as well as other churches throughout the Roman world, certain women were seeking to have authority that was reserved for men—namely, to function in the same role as elders/overseers.

From a human perspective, this is understandable. Women were often treated like slaves in the Roman culture. It was a man's world. When they experienced freedom and equality in Jesus Christ, some predictably moved toward total equality in leadership roles as well. This obviously became a problem in the first-century churches.

This we believe is one reason why Paul reminded first-century Christians that women should not "teach or have authority over a man." He then proceeded to outline the requirements for this official position in the church. As Robert Saucy concludes, "On the basis of the entire pastoral concept of teaching and the immediate obviously authoritative context, most interpreters understand Paul is prohibiting women from the 'teaching' that is done in the capacity of a leader of the church."[10]

Similarly, C.L. Blomberg concludes that "the only . . . role forbidden to women in the N.T. is that of the highest 'authoritative teaching' position in the church."[11] If this interpretation is accurate—and we believe it is—there are many strategic teaching opportunities for women to assist elders/overseers in communicating biblical truth and wisdom.

NOTES

1. Gilbert Bilezikian, *Community 101* (Grand Rapids: Zondervan, 1997); see also Gilbert Bilezikian, *Beyond Sex Roles* (Grand Rapids: Baker, 1985).

2. For an extensive study of the "one another" concepts in the New Testament, see three books written by Gene A Getz: *Building Up One Another* (Colorado Springs: Chariot Victor, 1981); *Encouraging One Another* (Colorado Springs: Chariot Victor, 1981); and *Loving One Another* (Colorado Springs: Chariot Victor, 1981).

3. In many of the passages where *adelphoi* is translated "brothers," it is generic, including "sisters" in Christ. (See also Gene A. Getz, *The Measure of a Church* (Ventura, Calif.: Regal, 2001), 25–26.

4. Robert L Saucy, "Women's Prohibition to Teach Men: An Investigation into Its Meaning and Contemporary Application," *The Journal of the Evangelical Theological Society* 37 (March 1974): 79 (emphasis added).

5. Some point out that this is actually what happened in Paul's approach to slavery. Though in Christ, there is neither "slave nor free," the New Testament doesn't teach that the system should be at that time dismantled and abolished, which in that culture would have created more harm than good—particularly for slaves. Rather New Testament writers exhorted slaves to serve their masters as if they were serving Jesus Christ, and masters were to love their slaves as Christ loved them. This approach, in essence, eventually eliminated slavery in the Christian community which was God's ultimate ideal plan. Merrill L. Tenney, *New Testament Survey* (Grand Rapids: Eerdmans, 1961), 50. See also William J. Webb, *Slaves, Women & Homosexuals: Exploring the Hermeneutics of Cultural Analysis* (Downers Grove, Ill.: InterVarsity, 2001), 269.

6. H. Wayne House, "A Biblical View of Women in Ministry," *Bibliotheca Sacra* 145 (January 1988): 47.

7. Robin Scroggs, "Paul and the Eschatological Woman," *Journal of the American Academy of Religion* 40 (September 1972): 283.

8. Ronald Allen, *The Majesty of Man* (Portland, Ore: Multnomah, 1984), 145–47.

9. William J. Webb, *Slaves, Women & Homosexuals* (Downers Grove, Ill.: InterVarsity, 2001), 269.

10. Saucy, "Women's Prohibition to Teach Men," 79.

11. C L. Blomberg, "Not Beyond What Is Written: A Review of Aida Spencer's *Beyond the Curse: Women Called to Ministry*," *Criswell Theological Review* 2 (Spring 1988): 418.

THE HOUSEHOLD
MODEL (A.D. 63)

BACK TO THE SOURCE

Before proceeding, read Ephesians 5:1–6:9. What can we learn from this passage that supports male leadership in the family and the church but yet strongly supports unique male-female partnerships in ministry?

When Paul outlined the qualifications for spiritual leaders in his first letter to Timothy, he used the "biological family" as a prototype for the church—the "family of God." In 1 Timothy 3 he first addressed elders/overseers, then male deacons.

> He [the overseer or elder] must . . . manage his own family well and see that his children obey him with proper respect. (If anyone does not know how to manage his own family, how can he take care of God's church?) [vv. 4–5; see also Titus 1:6]

A deacon must be the husband of but one wife and must manage his children and his household well. [v. 12]

How is this "household model" supposed to work, both in the family and in the church? And how does a proper understanding of this model relate to a woman's role—in marriage, in the biological family, and in the family of God? Did Paul introduce a supracultural "patriarchal model" that severely limits a woman's freedom to participate in the "teaching" and "speaking" functions of the church? Rightly understood, we believe this "model" creates the opposite—unusual freedom that relates directly to what God originally designed for men and women.

When husbands and wives, and fathers and mothers become believers and begin to relate to each other as "committed brothers and sisters in Christ," this conversion experience has the potential to restore much of the freedom God designed for women—and at the same time to maintain the roles He originally created for the sexes. Though we are still impacted by sin and evil in the world, there can be unity and oneness in Christ that impacts all relationships—in our marriages, in our families, and in our local churches.

THE HOUSEHOLD MODEL DESCRIBED

When it comes to leadership roles in the church and family, some Bible-believing Christians argue that in Christ there are no longer any role restrictions based on gender. They believe that the Old Testament patriarchal model with its strong emphasis on male leadership has been replaced, not only in terms of our position in Christ, but in all human relationships. We have concluded, however, there is another model in the New Testament that retains male leadership roles in marriage, the family, and the church, yet also has the potential to restore in an amazing way what God originally intended before sin entered the world. We've identified this as the "household model."

In God's divine design, every "biological family" when converted to Christ becomes the "church in miniature." In fact, many local churches began with one extended family—such as Cornelius' household in Caesarea.[1]

Figure 5
The Household Model

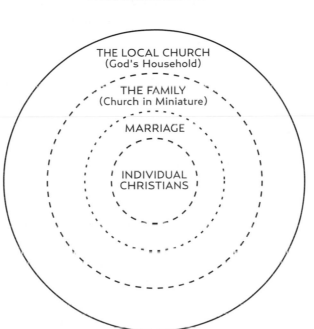

Note the circles in figure 5. Begin with the larger circle and follow the progression toward the center of the circle. The dotted lines indicate that all social units are an integral part of the church, which is represented by the larger circle.

The husband-wife relationship is, of course, the social relationship that gives birth to the family unit. Paul also used this intimate relationship—marriage—to illustrate the church's relationship to Jesus Christ. Paul wrote, "For the husband is the head of the wife as Christ is the head of the church, his body" (Ephesians 5:23). We realize that some interpret "head" as meaning "source." However, we believe this is very difficult to substantiate biblically.[2]

At the same time, all of these Christian social units—marriage, the family, and the church—are composed of individual believers (see the center of the circle in figure 5). In marriage, two individuals become one and form a new social unit. In the family, God's general plan is that what begins as two becoming one multiplies into a larger unit, where God's love is modeled and children are nurtured into a mature family unit. And, as these families mature and reflect the fullness of Christ, they become the strong building blocks of the church. In this sense, mature families automatically create mature churches.

However, the facts still remain that an individual may never marry. In fact, Paul honored singleness as an opportunity to serve Jesus Christ in a single-minded way as vital members of the church—the family of God (1 Corinthians 7:8–9, 32–35).

THE HOUSEHOLD MODEL APPLIED

As stated earlier, Paul used the believing biological household model when outlining character qualities for both elders/overseers and deacons. Being able to "manage their families well" is basic to being able to "manage the church well" (1 Timothy 3:4–5, 12). Furthermore, if married, an elder/overseer or deacon is to be loyal to one woman and one woman only—his wife (1 Timothy 3:2, 12; Titus 1:6). They are to love their wives and serve them just as Christ loved each one of us and even gave His life to pay for our sins (Ephesians 5:25).

With this "household model" in mind, we can understand more clearly how God wants leaders in the family of God to function (see figure 6). First, God has *not* given us one set of leadership principles for marriage relationships, another set for biological family relationships, and yet another for relationships in the larger family. Though each sphere of influence broadens in terms of function and responsibility, the basic leadership principles are the same. A husband is to be a *servant-leader* to his wife, a father is to be a *servant-leader* in his family, and elders/overseers are to be *servant-leaders* in the family of God.

The Husband-Wife Relationship in Marriage

However, this Christ-centered model takes us one step further in demonstrating the place of women. Though the wife is to recognize her husband's primary leadership, both are to "walk together" with one heart

Figure 6
Applying the Household Model

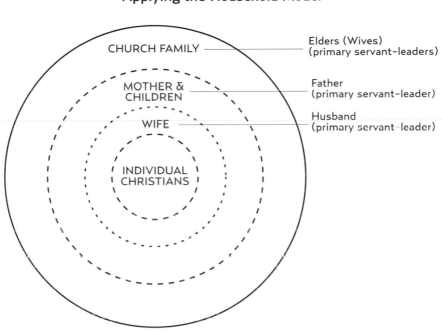

and mind, loving each other, submitting to each other, and demonstrating the oneness there is in the eternal community—Father, Son, and Holy Spirit (Ephesians 5:21).

The Father-Mother Relationship in the Family

The same principle applies to women who become mothers. Though the father is the God-ordained leader in the home, he and the mother of his children operate as a team—each bringing to this mutual leadership role oneness and unity that also reflects the eternal community. The father particularly is to reflect who God is—a loving, heavenly Father who cares and provides for His children. And the mother complements this role model with her own love and support.

With a relationship that is restored with God and one another, they lead the family together as one in Christ, reflecting the harmony and unity God originally intended: "God created man in his own image, in the image of God he created him; male and female he created them (Genesis 1:27).

Father-Mother Teams and Singles in the Church Family

Since the household—involving husbands and wives, and fathers and mothers—serves as a model for the larger family in the church, it follows that elders/overseers and their wives (if married) serve as multiple father-mother teams and servant-leaders in the church. This model also includes married couples without children.

Furthermore, this household model also provides a unique role for people who have never married. First, qualified single men can certainly serve as elders/overseers. Second, qualified single women can serve as deacons, serving alongside the elders/overseers in helping them carry out their managing and shepherding responsibilities within the church family —which certainly involves various "teaching" roles. In this model, qualified single women are serving in the same basic roles as married women with or without children.

LEADERS WHO REFLECT JESUS CHRIST

With this model, men are the primary servant-leaders in the church, the family, and the marriage—as God designed—but, as coheirs in Christ, mothers, wives, and single women as well, are serving alongside to assist, give input, teach, admonish, clarify, explain, and help make strategic decisions. This is why it is important to appoint all leaders in the church who are reflecting the fruit of the Holy Spirit (Galatians 5:22–23). Husbands and wives, mothers and fathers, elders/overseers and their wives, as well as single men and women, are to reflect Jesus Christ in their lifestyle or they cannot lead effectively as God intended, either in their families or in the church.

One note regarding "single men" who serve as elders/overseers. It's true they lack certain experiences that only come from being a husband-father. However, this is the beauty of having a multiple leadership team. In most instances, most elders/overseers will be married and will be family men. This is inherent in God's primary plan for men and women. However, single men can make unique contributions and also have the benefit of the wisdom from the other members of the leadership team.[3]

In chapter 36, I will describe how this cross-cultural household model can and should work in the church. Understood and applied properly, it allows incredible freedom to develop "cultural forms" for women to "function" in strategic leadership roles without violating God's plan for Christlike male leadership.

NOTES

1. For a very helpful analysis of "The Household in the New Testament," see George W. Peters, *Saturation Evangelism* (Grand Rapids: Zondervan, 1970), 150–159.

2. There are those who interpret "headship" for husbands in the New Testament as being a reference to "source" rather than having "authority over." Two very helpful journal articles demonstrate the serious weaknesses in this position. See Wayne A. Grudem, "Does κεφαλή ('Head') Mean 'Source' or 'Authority Over' in Greek Literature? A survey of 2,336 Examples," *Trinity Journal* 6 (Spring 1985): 38–59. Wayne A. Grudem, "The Meaning of κεφαλή ('Head'): A Response to Recent Studies," *Trinity Journal* 11 (Spring 1990): 3–72. More accessible to many would be the identical work, *Recovering Biblical Manhood and Womanhood*, eds. John Piper and Wayne A. Grudem (Westchester, Ill.: Crossway, 1991).

3. Mark Chalemin, who serves as my research assistant at Fellowship Bible Church North, has also been deeply involved in this study. I mention this to emphasize a mature single man's contributions to this process. Mark, like Timothy, has never married—at least as of this writing. Though he is not an official elder, he has met with us during these discussions and his insights, wisdom, and research efforts have been very helpful.

FINANCIAL
SUPPORT
(A.D. 63)

BACK TO THE SOURCE

*Before proceeding, read again 1 Timothy 5:17–18, this time in
the King James Version and the* New American Standard
Bible. *There are some who believe that Paul was describing two
different primary roles for elders/overseers—those who* manage
and those who teach. *Based on our study thus far and a careful
look at these verses, why does this seem to be a false dichotomy?*

Paul's first reference to supporting a leader financially appeared in
his letters to the churches in Galatia—probably written in A.D.
48–49.[1] "Anyone who receives instruction in the word," Paul wrote,
"must share all good things with his instructor" (Galatians 6:6).
Since the churches in Lystra, Iconium, and Antioch of Pisidia were
Galatian churches, and since Paul and Barnabas appointed spiritual
leaders in these churches, we can assume he was encouraging these

believers to care for their leaders financially, especially those who were teaching them the Word of God. Paul elaborated on this exhortation in his first letter to Timothy, leaving no question that churches should provide for some of these men and their families:

> The elders who direct the affairs of the church well are worthy of *double honor,* especially those whose work is preaching and teaching. For the Scripture says, "Do not muzzle the ox while it is treading out the grain," and "The worker deserves his wages." [1 Timothy 5:17–18]

MANAGING WELL

Managing and Shepherding

Before looking more specifically at what Paul meant regarding the financial support of a leader, a key part of his instructions must be interpreted correctly. Some believe that Paul was indeed dividing the elders/overseers into two categories with separate responsibilities: Those who *manage* and those who *teach.* However, from the leadership story we've seen unfolding thus far, this could not be what Paul had in mind. Nor does a proper interpretation of Paul's specific instructions to Timothy lead to this conclusion. Rather, every elder/overseer is to be a "managing" and "shepherding" leader. This is an overarching responsibility and to carry out this ministry effectively, all elders/overseers must be involved—at least to a certain degree—in the following specific functions:

☐ teaching biblical truth (Galatians 6:6; 1 Timothy 5:17; Titus 1:9)

☐ modeling Christlike behavior (1 Timothy 3:2; Titus 1:6; 1 Thessalonians 2:10–12)

☐ maintaining doctrinal purity (Acts 20:29–30; Titus 1:9)

☐ disciplining unruly believers (Galatians 6:1–2)

    ☐ overseeing financial matters (Acts 11:29–30; 2 Thessalonians 3:10–12)

    ☐ praying for those who are ill (James 5:13–15)

What Paul was saying to Timothy is that there will be those elders/overseers who will spend more time than others managing and shepherding the church and particularly in carrying out major "teaching functions," which involve encouraging, admonishing, instructing, correcting, training, preaching, explaining, etc. Furthermore, Paul was not limiting this responsibility to "teaching the Scriptures" in a formal setting but rather to all that is involved in verbal communication. As anyone knows who is in a primary leadership role in the church, maintaining efficient and effective communication is a key to unity and oneness within the body of Jesus Christ—and it is one of the most demanding aspects of ministry.

Not a Double Standard

In summary, Paul was simply exhorting Timothy to make sure that elders/overseers who were spending a lot of time carrying out all of the communication responsibilities involved in being a good manager and shepherd should be properly cared for financially. He in no way is setting up a "double standard" within the leadership team, rewarding only those who fit the modern-day approach which focuses on Bible expositors. Unfortunately, this interpretation rewards people who may be good formal Bible teachers but who are not spending sufficient time developing and utilizing communication skills in all aspects of a shepherding ministry.

A False Dichotomy

Those who divide Paul's exhortation into two categories of elders/ overseers often redefine what it means to "manage" and "shepherd" the church. They superimpose a modern-day definition of what it means to be a "good administrator"—a person who makes sure the "organizational machinery" in the church is functioning properly. On the other hand, those who are categorized as "teachers" and "expositors" often concentrate almost exclusively on instructing people in the Scriptures and leave the "administrative" duties to be cared for by those who are not involved in a direct ministry to people. Unfortunately, this can lead to a dichotomy in the leadership team—something New Testament writers never intended.

Having explained Paul's perspective, it must be said that being an effective Bible teacher in today's world is indeed a time-consuming task and certainly falls within the realm of being recognized with "double honor" —namely, financial support. However, it must also be said that a Bible teacher who spends a lot of time studying and explaining the biblical text and yet is neglectful of his role as a "shepherd" will lose contact with the "sheep"—something the Scriptures never encourage. To do so can lead to an ivory-tower mentality that can leave people with "head knowledge" and perceptions that are out of touch with their own reality. This leads to double trouble, especially if some elders/overseers have become "administrators"—which means that both "groups" are often far removed from the people they are supposed to serve.

Functions and Forms

As we've seen throughout the study, the New Testament story focuses on "functions"—not "forms." This means that it is vitally important that we clearly and correctly define elder/overseer functions. If we do not, we'll develop "forms" that perpetuate "functions" that are out of harmony with what the Bible teaches. It should not surprise us that this leads to inefficiency and even disunity when it comes to being effective managers and shepherds of the flock of God.

"DOUBLE HONOR"

The term "double" (*diplous*) in verse 17 literally means "twofold more" and the term translated "honor" (*time*) literally means "value" and "esteem of the highest degree." Together the words have both a quantitative and qualitative meaning. Paul classified "monetary support" as a means of "esteeming and honoring" faithful service and hard work.

Paul was not simply speaking of "words of appreciation"—as important as this is. Rather, he was talking about economic assistance, and in most cultures of the world "double honor" translates into "currency"—the means whereby we buy food and clothing, build homes, and care for other physical and psychological needs. Quoting the Old Testament Law that was reiterated by Jesus, Paul stated: "Do not muzzle the ox while it is treading out the grain" (v. 18; see Deuteronomy 25:4) and "the worker deserves his wages" (see Leviticus 19:13; Deuteronomy 24:15; Matthew 10:10; Luke 10:7).

Supporting spiritual leaders is rooted in the Old Testament. God commanded the Israelites to set apart one-tenth of their yearly produce and one-tenth of their flocks and cattle to support the Levites and priests (Leviticus 27:30–34; Numbers 18:21). And Jesus underscored this principle when He sent the Twelve out on a ministry tour directed at the children of Israel (Matthew 10:5). He instructed these men to "not take along any gold or silver or copper" (v. 9) since they were to be supported by those to whom they were ministering. If people in turn ministered to the apostles in a physical and material way—even if it involved only "a cup of cold water"—God Himself would reward them (v. 42).

In this letter to Timothy, Paul extended this Old Testament principle of supporting spiritual leaders into the church. When elders/overseers—like the Levites, the priests, and the apostles—devote their time and energy to ministry, they should be cared for financially. Paul also broadened the application of this principle considerably when he told the Corinthians that "the Lord has commanded that those who preach the gospel should receive their living from the gospel" (1 Corinthians 9:14). In other words, those who are involved in church planting (like the apostle Paul, Barnabas, Silas, Timothy, and Titus) should also be cared for financially. This is doubly important since these people often leave their homes, their communities and their normal source of income in order to carry out the Great Commission.

Words of Caution

Having emphasized that spiritual leaders who spend a lot of time in ministry should be financially supported by the church, Paul and other New Testament leaders also warned against abusing this privilege. An elder/overseer must not be "a lover of money" (1 Timothy 3:3) and deacons too must never be guilty of "pursuing dishonest gain" (1 Timothy 3:8; Titus 1:7). Rather, they must be "hospitable" (1 Timothy 3:2; Titus 1:8). Peter also exhorted these spiritual shepherds to never be "greedy for money, but [to be] eager to serve" (1 Peter 5:2).

Paul's Model

Paul was deeply committed to modeling this principle. Though he, of all New Testament writers, encouraged Christians to support their spiritual leaders economically, he was also the most cautious in receiving material gifts, particularly from unbelievers and even new Christians. He in no way wanted to give the impression that eternal life could be earned or that he had materialistic motives in sharing the Good News. He reminded the Thessalonian church of this very fact when he wrote: "Surely you remember, brothers, our toil and hardship; we worked night and day in order not to be a burden to anyone while we preached the gospel of God to you" (1 Thessalonians 2:9; see also Acts 20:33–35).

Though Paul was cautious about accepting material gifts, he did receive financial help from believers who were mature enough to understand his motives. Even when he was in Thessalonica—where he would not receive material gifts—he rejoiced when gifts arrived from the Philippian church (Philippians 4:16). And when he wrote to these believers from prison in Rome, one of his purposes was to thank them for the monetary gifts they had once again sent to meet his personal needs (v. 18). But even then, he wanted them to know that what they gave was ultimately a gift to the One he served—"a fragrant offering, an acceptable sacrifice, pleasing to God" (v. 18). And because Paul was serving Christ rather than himself, what they gave would be "credited" to their spiritual "[bank] account" in heaven (v. 17).

Being Honest and Accountable

What a message Paul's model sends to every Christian leader today who is receiving "double honor." It eliminates any room for manipulation, selfishness, greed, and dishonesty in any form—which includes avoiding any conflict of interest and any misappropriation of funds. Though every "worker deserves his wages," we must never serve God to "pad our own pockets."

All of us in ministry who are receiving financial support should be absolutely above reproach in how we spend our time and energy. In fact, it's important that we take the initiative—following Paul's example—to set up a system of accountability. If we do not, we may find ourselves using "our freedom" irresponsibly. Though we may never "take money from the till," we may be "stealing time" that should be invested in particular ministry efforts that are commensurate with our monetary support.

NOTE

1. Well-known scholars disagree as to when Galatians was written and to whom. For example, J. B. Lightfoot, *St. Paul's Epistle to the Galatians*, 10th ed. (London: Macmillan, 1890), 18–35, believes the letter was written after Paul's second missionary journey through northern Galatia. On the other hand, Sir William Ramsey, *An Historical Commentary on St. Paul's Epistle to the Galatians* (New York: G. P. Putnam's Sons, 1900), ii, 478, contends that "the churches of Galatia" were those of Antioch in Pisidia, Iconium, Derbe, and Lystra, which Paul established on his first missionary journey through southern Galatia. Merrill Tenney, *New Testament Survey* (Grand Rapids: Eerdmans, 1953), 266–267, points out, "The importance of the difference of interpretation is that the southern Galatian theory allows for an earlier dating of Galatians and for a better explanation of its historical setting."

PROTECTION
AND DISCIPLINE
(A.D. 63)

BACK TO THE SOURCE

Before proceeding, read Deuteronomy 19:15–19. What aspects of these Old Testament instructions are applicable to Paul's directives to Timothy?

After instructing Timothy regarding the need to make sure the material needs of certain elders/overseers in Ephesus were met, Paul went on to outline guidelines for both *protecting* and *disciplining* spiritual leaders who may be accused of wrongdoing:

> Do not entertain an accusation against an elder unless it is brought by two or three witnesses. Those who sin are to be rebuked publicly, so that the others may take warning. [1 Timothy 5:19–20]

At this point, Paul may have been thinking first and foremost about financial accountability. Perhaps some men were being falsely accused of inappropriately handling money. On the other hand, perhaps the accusations were justified, and there were those who were "pursuing dishonest gain" and taking advantage of people financially (Titus 1:7; 1 Timothy 3:3, 8). Unfortunately, this happened in the first century and it still happens in the twenty-first century. Because it does, dedicated spiritual leaders who would never be dishonest and violate ethical or moral principles in any way are sometimes put under a cloud of suspicion.

PROTECTING SPIRITUAL LEADERS

First of all, Paul was definitely attempting to protect any leader from false accusations. This was the basic intent of the Old Testament Law, which Paul was alluding to in Deuteronomy: "One witness is not enough to convict a man accused of any crime or offense he may have committed. A matter must be established by the testimony of two or three witnesses" (Deuteronomy 19:15).

This Old Testament guideline was designed to protect any person from being falsely accused—not just leaders in Israel. However, when Paul wrote to Timothy, he applied this Old Testament "general rule" in a "particular way"—to elders/overseers in the New Testament churches.

But this leads to a second observation. Paul was not saying that unless there are two or three witnesses, an accusation should be overlooked or not taken seriously. In other words, it may be "true" or "untrue." If it is "untrue," it must be corrected, especially if there are those who perceive that the accusation is accurate. This is why Moses—in the Old Testament setting—went on to say:

> If a malicious witness takes the stand to accuse a man of a crime, the two
> men involved in the dispute must stand in the presence of the LORD before
> the priests and the judges who are in office at the time. The judges must
> make a *thorough* investigation, and if the witness proves to be a liar, giving
> false testimony against his brother, then do to him as he intended to do his
> brother. You must purge the evil from among you. [Deuteronomy 19:16–19]

If an elder/overseer is falsely accused, it intensifies the need for a thorough investigation. It's a tragedy when a spiritual leader's character is assassinated by evil people. Resolving this kind of problem becomes a very time-consuming process, but it must be done carefully, thoroughly, and prayerfully—which calls for a huge amount of wisdom and discretion.

DISCIPLINING SPIRITUAL LEADERS

If a thorough investigation reveals that an accusation is untrue, the elders/overseers should do everything in their power to proclaim the accused as being innocent. However, if the accusation is true, the sin must be dealt with. This is why Paul went on to state in his instructions to Timothy that "those who sin are to be rebuked publicly, so that the others may take warning" (1 Timothy 5:20). In the Old Testament context, the "public rebuke" was intended for the ears of all Israel. However, as we've seen, Paul narrowed this concept to church elders/overseers, and so it appears he also narrowed the "public rebuke" to fellow spiritual leaders so they "may take warning" in their own lives.

Public or Private Discipline?

However, this does not mean that this kind of discipline should never be made public to the larger church community. It depends on the severity of the sin and the particular spiritual leader's response to discipline. For example, if the accusation involves immorality, it is virtually impossible to keep this kind of information within the leadership circle, especially since this kind of position involves a very public role. However, when it does become necessary to go public before the total congregation (e.g., to avoid rumors), hopefully the elder/overseer who is guilty of this kind of sin has already experienced true repentance, even if he must step aside because he is no longer "above reproach" in this area of his life. "Being forgiven" and "regaining trust" are separate issues when it comes to moral and ethical failures. Though Paul was not teaching that these failures forever eliminate a person from ministry, the total perspective Paul presented to Timothy certainly implied that those who wished to be reinstated must have demonstrated total and absolute repentance, and over a period of time have rebuilt their reputations in the Christian community.

Sadly, the need to discipline "fellow leaders" seems to be far more prevalent than having to defend those who are falsely accused. When there is "smoke," there is often "fire." Ironically, if a spiritual leader is violating God's will, particularly in a moral area, he has a built-in system for hiding his sin—namely, the moral and ethical teachings in Scripture. Who can accuse a man who vehemently preaches against these things? In reality he is using this as a smokescreen to cover up his own sins.

A Valid Witness

There are some who narrowly define what it means to be a "witness." They exclude a person who claims to be a "victim" of a leader's sin. However, "victims" are also witnesses, even in a court of law today. Their testimonies should not be disregarded because they are reporting on a sin against them personally. Granted, any such accusations must be carefully investigated—even if only one person is involved in bringing the accusation. Truth must prevail. It's at this point that Paul's instructions regarding "two or three witnesses" becomes very important—even if these two or three witnesses are also victims.

One of the most bizarre situations that I have encountered personally involved a pastor who was engaging in both seductive and promiscuous homosexual behavior. During the same period of time he served as a senior leader in a particular church, he taught the people generally and his elders particularly that Paul was teaching that the "two or three witnesses" meant there would have to be at least two, if not three, people who had observed any immoral behavior to be valid witnesses. In other words, those individuals who claimed to be "victims" of this pastor's behavior were not considered "legal" witnesses, and their testimonies were to be discounted.

Unfortunately, this interpretation not only violates biblical meaning, but it virtually eliminates any way to discover the truth in these situations. In fact, a well-known religious cult has recently come under investigation for sexual abuse of children and young people by their "elders." Sadly, they have continued to cover up this horrible sin with this self-serving interpretation. Though victims had again and again accused these "so-called" spiritual leaders, their witness has been rejected because there were no other "witnesses" to this immoral behavior.

We must remember that accusations of immorality are the most difficult to verify because they are purposely done in secret and normally "one-on-one." In most instances, there are not other witnesses to these sins—except the victims themselves. Consequently, this intensifies a need for an even more "careful investigation." Though it's possible that two or three individuals may conspire against a spiritual leader with the same "lie," it's a rare occurrence. Most people do not want to become entangled in this kind of deceptive web because they fear that they will probably be discovered.

What becomes more devastating to a church is when a spiritual leader is actually guilty and is using his position and authority to cover the sin by denying the charges and making himself appear the victim rather than the perpetrator. Unfortunately, people who are immoral will also lie and do anything they can to protect themselves.

Maintaining Objectivity

In dealing with sinful behavior in the leadership of the church, one of the most difficult challenges is to develop and maintain objectivity. Consequently, Paul next addressed this issue with Timothy:

> I charge you, in the sight of God and Christ Jesus and the elect angels, to keep these instructions *without partiality,* and to do nothing out of *favoritism. Do not be hasty in the laying on of hands, do not share in the sins of others. Keep yourself pure.* [1 Timothy 5:21–22]

When someone has worked closely with someone in ministry and has developed a trusting relationship over a lengthy period of time, it becomes very difficult to be objective in evaluating accusations of sinful behavior. I know this has been true in my own life as a pastor—to deal with individuals objectively, without "partiality" and without showing "favoritism." This is why it is so important that more than one spiritual leader be involved in sorting out all of the factors in dealing with those who are guilty of sin. It's at this point that Paul also warned Timothy not to restore a person too quickly. This seems to be the most reasonable interpretation of what Paul meant when he warned Timothy not to "be hasty in the laying on of hands." It takes time to test a person's true motives. Again, I've personally seen people who have been caught in sin respond immediately with "sorrow"—even tears. But over a period of time, it became clear that they were sorry, not because they were truly broken before God, but because they had been caught and exposed.

Avoiding Participation

Paul addressed another issue. Not only was Timothy to deal with these situations objectively and perceptively, but also he was to be careful never to share in the sins of others. In essence, Paul seemed to be saying that Timothy should never "cover up sin" by "looking the other way" and acting as if it did not exist. It's easy for all caring Christians to justify secrecy with the sincere thought that they're protecting the person. However, in doing so, they may be allowing that person to avoid the consequences that God designed to help bring the person to true repentance. Furthermore, this kind of "protection" sometimes sets the person up for continued rationalization and more failure. Obviously, exposing sin must be done sensitively, but not at the expense of violating biblical principles. If we do, we will not be helping the person to experience true repentance.

If the sin involves immorality, we must be doubly careful that we do not become a participant. Consequently, Paul warned Timothy, "Keep yourself pure" (1 Timothy 5:22). In other words, when trying to set someone free from sin, we can get trapped ourselves—particularly if this has been a weakness in our own lives.

Unfortunately, what Paul warned against happens today. I've seen elders and deacons duped and deceived by a strong spiritual leader. Not only did they "cover up" the sin, but some eventually followed their leader's example and committed the same sins. Tragically, once this happened, these men began to cover for each other and became trapped, knowing that if they blew their leader's cover, they would be blowing their own. What an insidious situation; but it demonstrates the devastating results of hiding sin, particularly in the leadership of the church.

EQUAL PROTECTION AND DISCIPLINE FOR *ALL*

The warnings and process Paul shared about both protecting and disciplining elders/overseers certainly applies to all spiritual leaders in the church regardless of their position. For example, in most churches there are pastors and teachers who are not elders/overseers. There are "deacons" and other "assistants" who help in the ministry. What Paul shared with Timothy provides instruction that can be applied in all church and parachurch ministries—regardless of the cultural dynamics. In fact, they apply to every member of the body of Christ.

SHEPHERDING
GOD'S FLOCK
(A.D. 63)

BACK TO THE SOURCE

Before proceeding, read John 9:1–10:18. Note that when Jesus identified Himself as "the Good Shepherd," He was contrasting what He had just done for the blind man with what the religious "shepherds" in Israel had just done to this man and his family.

When the apostle Peter wrote to the churches scattered throughout Asia Minor (1 Peter 1:1), he addressed the elders/ overseers as "shepherds," a much more picturesque and graphic word than "managers." Though the two words are synonyms in the biblical story, the pastoral title "shepherd" captures the role of an elder/overseer in a beautiful way.

What Peter shared seems to be as much autobiographical as exhortatory. Peering into his past and beyond these words of encouragement in his first letter, we can see a portrait of Peter himself—once a tough-minded chief executive officer of a thriving fishing business. Then he met and followed Jesus Christ, who taught him the ways of a caring and compassionate shepherd:

> To the elders among you, I appeal as a fellow elder, a witness of Christ's sufferings and one who also will share in the glory to be revealed: *Be shepherds of God's flock* that is under your care, serving as overseers—not because you must, but because you are willing, as God wants you to be; not greedy for money, but eager to serve; not lording it over those entrusted to you, but being examples to the flock. And when the Chief Shepherd appears, you will receive the crown of glory that will never fade away. [1 Peter 5:1–4]

THE GOOD SHEPHERD

Several experiences must have come to Peter's mind as he dictated this paragraph on the qualities of a shepherd. He had heard Jesus deliver a penetrating message to the Pharisees in Jerusalem—after they had thrown the "blind man" that Jesus had healed out of the synagogue. At that moment, Jesus had found him and, having opened his eyes physically, He then gently and compassionately opened the eyes of his heart (John 9:34–39). And it's not an accident that Jesus next turned to the Pharisees, contrasting His ministry to this man with their harsh and sarcastic actions:

> *I am the good shepherd.* The good shepherd lays down his life for the sheep. The hired hand is not the shepherd who owns the sheep. So when he sees the wolf coming, he abandons the sheep and runs away. Then the wolf attacks the flock and scatters it. The man runs away because he is a hired hand and cares nothing for the sheep. [John 10:11–13]

The Pharisees considered themselves "spiritual leaders"—but they were anything but "shepherds." The way they had treated the "poor beggar" as well as his family demonstrated their ravenous desire for power, prestige, and position. They acted more like "wolves." They could not have cared less about this man's body or his soul.

A Fellow Elder

Jesus' words to the Pharisees about "shepherding" were meant for Peter as well. As the Holy Spirit brought this story and Jesus' metaphorical words to his mind, he would vividly and painfully remember his role as a "hired hand" who ran away rather than being a true shepherd who would not abandon the sheep when the "wolves" attacked. He had publicly boasted that if any one of the other apostles forsook the Lord, he would not! And when Jesus predicted that Peter would deny Him three times, Peter argued that he would die with Christ before he would disown Him (Luke 22:33–34).

The end of the story is well known. Peter *did* deny the Lord and fled into the night. But when he came to his senses, he wept bitterly and then began his journey back as a humble servant. And, years later, as Peter addressed the elders/overseers in churches throughout Asia Minor, he did so from a position of great humility—calling himself a "fellow elder"—in essence, a "fellow shepherd." Though he had been called and appointed by Jesus Christ to the highest leadership position in Christendom   the leader of the apostles—he addressed these men from an equal position.

What a lesson this is for those of us who occupy primary positions in the church. Though we have a definite leadership role—as did Peter—we are indeed "fellow shepherds" with those who serve with us!

Shepherd Qualities

Eager to Serve

Peter gave elders two exhortations as shepherds: Be "eager to serve" and avoid "lording it over those entrusted to you." His exhortation to be "eager to serve" certainly grew out of another memory. It happened in the Upper Room when Jesus washed the disciples' feet. This was another embarrassing moment for Peter. He had watched the Lord get up in the middle of the Passover meal and take the place of a servant—washing their feet. Embarrassed, Peter resisted, primarily because he was well aware that this was an oversight when he and John had arranged for this event. It was unheard of for the honored guest to perform this kind of servant's task.

Again as Peter addressed the elders/overseers in his letter, he could speak out of experience, having learned a lesson from Jesus, who was definitely "eager to serve"—even though He was their Lord and teacher. "I have set you an example," Jesus said, "that you should do as I have done for you" (John 13:15). Again, what a powerful lesson for all leaders today. He that is greatest is to be servant of all! Peter was passing that lesson on to his "fellow elders"—and all of us.

Not Lording It over Others

Peter certainly had another painful recollection regarding what happened during that same Passover meal with the apostles. Just prior to the time "the Good Shepherd" was ready to lay down His life for the sheep, "a dispute arose among" the apostles "as to which of them was considered to be greatest" (Luke 22:24). Though James and John may have precipitated this argument, Peter must have been involved as well. No doubt with sorrow in His eyes, Jesus addressed them with these penetrating words:

> The kings of the Gentiles *lord it over them;* and those who exercise authority over them call themselves Benefactors. But you are not to be like that. Instead, the greatest among you should be like the youngest, and the one who rules like the one who serves. For who is greater, the one who is at the table or the one who serves? Is it not the one who is at the table? But I am among you as one who serves. [Luke 22:25–27]

Jesus had set the example of true servant-leadership. Again Peter passed on the lesson he had learned personally—not "*lording* it over those entrusted to you, but being *examples* to the flock" (1 Peter 5:3). Again, this is a powerful lesson for all of us in leadership positions in a church. True shepherds lead, but they are also servants.

A SHEPHERD TO SHEPHERDS

Peter's greatest "shepherding" lesson came early one morning on the seashore in Galilee. He had once again returned to what he did best when he was CEO of Zebedee's fishing business. But he and several other apostles even failed at that, having unsuccessfully fished all night. Once again, Jesus appeared and miraculously filled their nets.

But it was the conversation on the shore that changed Peter's life forever. Three times Jesus asked Peter if he loved Him, reminding him of that bitter experience prior to the Cross—when he denied the Lord three times. But the words that no doubt continued to ring in his ears involved Jesus' charge to him to be a "shepherd" to the other apostles. They were still "lambs" that needed to be fed (John 21:15), and though they were in actuality supposed to be "sheep," they needed special care (21:16) and encouragement (21:17). Jesus' prayer for Peter was now being fulfilled, that his faith would "not fail" and when he "turned back," to be able to "strengthen [his] brothers" (Luke 22:32) by being a "good shepherd" to "shepherds."

All spiritual shepherds need a shepherd, for whatever our position, we never cease to be sheep. Peter eventually became that kind of man. His initial task was to encourage the other apostles—and eventually the elders/overseers who would hear this letter read in their churches. Though the lessons Peter had learned about being a faithful shepherd were painful, he was now prepared for the next major event: the birth of the church on the Day of Pentecost. As Jesus' chosen leader, he began to speak the Word of God with boldness blended with humility.

Again, the lesson is clear for us today. "Shepherds" need a "shepherd." In other words, elders/overseers need a servant-leader who leads, but who serves as a "fellow elder."

OTHER SHEEP

When Jesus identified Himself as the "good shepherd," He made a statement that Peter initially missed altogether—that He had "other sheep" that were "not of this sheep pen." They too would listen to the voice of Jesus and "there shall be *one flock* and *one shepherd*" (John 10:16).

Approximately five years after Pentecost, Peter finally understood what Jesus meant. It took a vision on a housetop in Joppa and an encounter with a Gentile named Cornelius, and his family and friends, to demonstrate to Peter that Jesus died for the sins of the whole world—not just for the children of Israel. Following that experience, he declared, "I now realize how true it is that God does not show favoritism but accepts men from *every nation* who fear him and do what is right" (Acts 10:34–35).

As Peter addressed these elders/overseers who were shepherding churches "scattered throughout *various nations*"—Pontus, Galatia, Cappadocia, Asia and Bithynia—he was well aware that a large number of these men were formerly pagan Gentiles (1 Peter 4:3–4). But this was no longer an issue with Peter. Imagine a believing Jew calling converted Gentiles his "fellow elders"? Peter had long since learned that in Christ "there is neither Jew nor Greek, slave nor free, male nor female" but we are "all one in Christ Jesus" (Galatians 3:28).

Yes, Peter was called in a special way to be "an apostle to the Jews" and Paul as "an apostle to the Gentiles" (Galatians 2:8). But both understood clearly that in God's "sheep pen" there is "one flock and one shepherd" (John 10:16).

And again, the lesson is clear for all of us who serve as elders/overseers. Though we may be ministering to different segments of our society— various ethnic groups and people from different economic backgrounds, and cultures, and generations—we must never "show favoritism" (James 2:1). In God's sight, the contribution of every member of the body of Christ is important for the church to grow in love and unity.

A SHEPHERD'S HEART

What then should characterize a leader with a shepherd's heart? He is willing to give himself to the members of the body of Christ that inhabit his fold. He stands by them no matter what the cost. He *knows* his sheep. He calls them by name! The sheep know him; they know his voice.

There is no way to escape the implication of what it means to be effective elders/overseers. We must be *with* our people, not separate from them. We must know them personally—their needs, their concerns, their problems! We must be willing to leave the ninety and nine in the fold and go into the darkness of the night to find the straying lamb that has wandered away from the safety of the flock and has been caught in the thicket of disillusionment and sin (Matthew 18:12–13).

Our door must be open to the flock. We must be available—not in word only, but truly available! Our personalities must say in no uncertain way, "We love you, we care about you, and we're here beside you; you can talk with us anytime, anywhere, and about anything you wish. We won't condemn you! We will help you become the person you really want to become: a mature functioning member of His body, the church."

Obviously, these *biblical functions* have tremendous implications. We must develop *cultural forms* that enable us to be good and faithful shepherds.

THE CROWN OF GLORY

One of the most encouraging points Peter made in this paragraph relates to the fact that all shepherds have a "Chief Shepherd" who will be with them, even to the end of the age (Matthew 28:20). And some day, He will reward all faithful elders/overseers with a "crown of glory" (1 Peter 5:4). Though we cannot understand what this metaphor refers to specifically, one thing is sure. Our recognition "will not fade away," and we'll use our rewards not to glorify ourselves but to honor and worship the Lord Jesus Christ throughout eternity (see Revelation 4:9–11).

A DOCTRINE
OF CHARACTER
(A.D. 65)

BACK TO THE SOURCE

Before proceeding, reread 1 Timothy 3:1–7 and Titus 1:1–9.
What qualifications for leadership are identical in these two lists
and which ones are unique?

At some point on his post-prison journey, Paul once again met
up with Titus—perhaps in Corinth where he had previously spent
considerable time representing Paul (2 Corinthians 7:5–7, 13–16;
8:16–23; 12:18). Titus was a Gentile convert whom Paul had introduced to the Gospel early on in his ministry—perhaps in Antioch. On one occasion, he had traveled with Paul and Barnabas to
Jerusalem, perhaps as Exhibit A to demonstrate to the apostles and
elders that Gentiles can indeed be saved (Galatians 2:3).

A Ministry in Crete

After reuniting, these two men boarded a ship and traveled south to Crete. Though Paul had "sailed along the shore" of this island on his way to Rome (Acts 27:13), he had not had opportunity to preach the Gospel in this well-known and intense pagan environment. We're not told how long Paul and Titus ministered in Crete, but it could not have been a lengthy period since the time span between his first and second imprisonments in Rome was only about three years. But as happened on so many occasions, the Holy Spirit opened many hearts to the Gospel in the major cities of Crete.

Again, at some point, Paul traveled on alone, leaving Titus to "straighten out what was left unfinished and appoint elders in every town" (Titus 1:5). On the way to Nicopolis, he penned a follow-up letter, putting in writing the qualifications that Titus should look for in selecting and appointing men as elders/overseers (Titus 1:5–9).

This second list in Paul's letter to Titus *does* have some identical requirements to those listed in his first letter to Timothy. However, in these two lists, Paul also mentioned some qualifications that seem to be unique to Timothy's challenge in Ephesus and some that are definitely unique to the challenge Titus faced in Crete (see chart on next page).

The variation in these two lists raises some legitimate questions:

  ☐ How much relativity is there in measuring the maturity of men who are being asked to serve as elders/overseers in our churches today? In other words, how much cultural freedom do we have in developing criteria for selecting spiritual leaders?

  ☐ Is it appropriate to combine these two lists and use these criteria as a standard for selecting and appointing elders/overseers in our churches today?

Figure 7
Characteristics of Elders in 1 Timothy and Titus

QUALIFICATION	GREEK TERM
Above reproach (1 Timothy 3:2)	anepileptos*
Blameless (Titus 1:6)	anegketos*
Husband of but one wife (1 Timothy 3:2; Titus 1:6)	**
Manage family well (1 Timothy 3:4–5)	**
A man whose children believe (Titus 1:6)	**
Self-controlled (1 Timothy 3:2; Titus 1:8)	sophron
Hospitable (1 Timothy 3:2; Titus 1:8)	philoxenos
Not given to drunkenness (1 Timothy 3:3; Titus 1:7)	paroinos
Not violent, pugnacious, striker, quarrelsome (1 Timothy 3:3; Titus 1:7)	plektes
Not a lover of money (1 Timothy 3:3; Titus 1:7)	aischrokerdes***

* These two Greek words are basically synonyms.
** Paul used a Greek phrase to describe this concept, not a single term.
*** This Greek word is translated "not pursuing dishonest gain" in Titus.

Characteristics Unique in 1 Timothy

QUALIFICATION	GREEK TERM
Temperate, sober, alert (3:2)	nephaleos
Respectable (3:2)	kosmios
Able to teach (3:2)	didaktikos
Gentle (3:3)	epieikes
Not quarrelsome (3:3)	amachos
Not a new convert (3:6)	neophutos
Good reputation with outsiders (3:7)	marturia

Characteristics Unique in Titus

QUALIFICATION	GREEK TERM
Not overbearing (1:7)	*authades*
Not quick-tempered (1:7)	*orgilos*
Love what is good (1:8)	*philagathos**
Upright, just (1:8)	*dikaios*
Holy (1:8)	*hosios*
Disciplined (1:8)	*Egkrate*
Hold firmly to the trustworthy message (1:9)	**

* Literally, "a lover of good men"
** Paul used a Greek phrase to describe this concept, not a single term.

God-Directed Freedom

In answering these questions, we must understand the freedom the Holy Spirit gave New Testament authors to address particular issues in certain churches.

☐ When Paul wrote to the churches in Galatia, he was deeply concerned that they had reverted to a works-oriented religion.

☐ When he penned the Thessalonian letters, he corrected their false views regarding the second coming of Christ.

☐ When he wrote to the Colossians, he addressed some of the heretical teachings that had blended Jewish legalism, Greek philosophy, and Oriental mysticism with pure Christian doctrine.

☐ In his letter to the Philippians, Paul was intensely personal as he thanked these believers for their financial support and their "partnership in the gospel" (Philippians 1:4–5; 4:15–16).

☐ In his letter to the Ephesians, Paul seemed to be far less personal and more universal in his teaching, perhaps because the epistle was probably a circular letter to the churches in Asia.

☐ In Peter's first epistle, he wrote to encourage believers who were being persecuted.

☐ In his first epistle, John confronted Gnostic heresy.

☐ When Jesus Christ spoke directly to the seven churches in Asia through the apostle John, He addressed different issues in every church depending on their strengths and weaknesses (Revelation 2:1–3:22).

Viewed in this larger context where biblical authors spoke to various issues in different churches, it shouldn't surprise us that Paul addressed unique circumstances when he wrote to Timothy in Ephesus and to Titus in Crete. Though many of the challenges were the same, there were also special problems these men would have to face, and he prescribed certain requirements accordingly.

For example, in Crete, some men had already emerged and were "ruining whole households by teaching things they ought not to teach—and that for the sake of dishonest gain" (Titus 1:11). In fact, these false teachers were so blatant in their sinful actions that Paul classified them as "detestable, disobedient and unfit for doing anything good" (1:16). It is no wonder that Paul told Titus to look for spiritual leaders who were "not overbearing" (arrogant and self-willed) and "not quick-tempered," but men who loved "what is good," who were "upright, holy and disciplined" (1:7–8). And perhaps the requirement most relevant to the situation in Crete was that Paul told Titus to appoint shepherds who would "hold firmly to the trustworthy message as it has been taught, so that" in turn they could "encourage others by sound doctrine and refute those who oppose it" (1:9).

It's easy to see why Paul outlined these specific requirements in his letter to Titus but also addressed some other issues that Timothy faced in selecting and appointing spiritual leaders in Ephesus (review figure 7).

A CHARACTER PROFILE

The freedom the Holy Spirit gave Paul to tailor requirements to each cultural situation certainly gives us similar freedom. But that freedom must always be within the boundaries of God's revealed truth. We must never compromise or contradict what is taught in the whole of inspired Scripture. It's true that God's revelation unfolded over a period of time during the first century as various apostles and missionaries ministered to many different people in different cultures. But the end product is the Word of God—a body of truth that is "God-breathed and is useful for teaching, rebuking, correcting and training in righteousness, so that . . . [we all] may be thoroughly equipped for every good work" (2 Timothy 3:16–17).

Just so, when every quality outlined by Paul for selecting elders/overseers is defined properly and evaluated against the backdrop of all of the other maturity profiles in Scripture (see figure 8, which details true Christian character in eight passages [six from epistles to Timothy and Titus]), we have a "doctrine of character" that is supracultural—just as "all Scripture" reveals a doctrine of God, Jesus Christ, the Holy Spirit, man, salvation, the second coming of Christ as well as the doctrine of the church.

Consequently, even though Paul emphasized certain criteria based on specific challenges Timothy faced in Ephesus and Titus faced in Crete,[1] there is no scriptural basis for eliminating certain qualifications because they are not mentioned in both lists. In fact, since we have access to both letters—as well as the whole of Scripture—we are more accountable before God to maintain a high standard for Christian leaders. The same is true of Bible teachers today who have access to the whole Bible. Though we can certainly select areas of Scripture that will speak to particular spiritual needs at particular times, we are still accountable to teach "the whole will of God" to the whole body of Christ (Acts 20:27).

Clearly, it *is* appropriate to combine the 1 Timothy 3 and Titus 1 passages on leadership and use these criteria today as a standard for selecting and appointing elders/overseers in our churches. In fact, we have done that in our own church (Fellowship Bible Church North), developing a twenty-question measurement of spiritual maturity for leadership to evaluate elder candidates. The form for measuring this "Maturity Quotient"

Figure 8
Character Profiles

GALATIANS 5:22–23 *The Fruit of the Spirit is:*	1 TIMOTHY 4:12 *Set an example:*	1 TIMOTHY 6:11 *Pursue:*	1 TIMOTHY 2:12 *Say "No":*
Love	In speech	Righteousness	To ungodliness
Joy	In life	Godliness	Worldly passions
Peace	In love	Faith	
Patience	In faith	Love	*Live lives that are:*
Kindness	In purity	Endurance	
Goodness		Gentleness	Self-controlled
Faithfulness			Upright
Gentleness			Godly
Self-control			

TITUS 2:1–2 *Teach the older men:*	TITUS 2:3 *Teach the older women:*	TITUS 2:4–5 *Teach the younger women:*	2 PETER 1:5–7 *Make every effort to add:*
To be temperate	To be reverent	To love their husbands	To faith, goodness
To be worthy of respect	Not to be slanderers	To love their children	To goodness, knowledge
To be self-controlled	Not addicted to much wine	To be self-controlled	To knowledge, self-control
To be sound in faith	To teach what is good	To be pure	To self-control, perseverance
To be sound in love		To be busy at home	To perseverance, godliness
To be sound in endurance		To be kind	To godliness, brotherly kindness
		To be subject to their husbands	To brotherly kindness, love

is shown in appendix C and may be helpful for your church as well. (The process of evaluating our elder candidates is discussed in detail in chapter 34 under "Step 5: Evaluating the Candidates.")

GOD'S STANDARD FOR MEASURING MATURITY

It's important to note that this is not a "legalistic approach" to Christian living. If it were, Paul was definitely guilty of being a legalist. The facts are that the overall maturity profile outlined by the Holy Spirit in Scripture is God's standard for measuring spiritual maturity.

It is God's revealed will that we are responsible before God to develop these qualities in our lives—not in our own strength but with the help of the Holy Spirit (Ephesians 6:10–18). Simply becoming a Christian and accepting our new identity in Christ does not mean we'll automatically reflect the "fruit of the Spirit." If this were true, there would be no need for Christian growth—the theme and emphasis of most of the New Testament epistles. When it comes to developing character qualities, this is why there is so much emphasis on *teaching* and *training* in the Pastoral Letters (1 Timothy 2:11–13; 2 Timothy 2:1–2; 4:2–5; Titus 2:1–10).

NOTE

1. Some believe Paul was primarily influenced by Hellenistic writers when he outlined the qualifications for elders/overseers. For an excellent critique of this viewpoint, see David A. Mappes, "Moral Virtues Associated with Eldership," *Bibliotheca Sacra* 160 (April-June 2003): 201–18.

MARRIAGE AND FAMILY REQUIREMENTS (A.D. 63, 65)

BACK TO THE SOURCE

Before proceeding, revisit Paul's instructions to Timothy and Titus regarding the "husband of but one wife" and "family management" requirements (1 Timothy 3:1–2, 4–5; Titus 1:6–7). What do you believe Paul meant?

Most of the qualifications outlined by Paul for selecting and appointing spiritual leaders are relatively easy to define and apply to all cultural situations (see figure 8, previous chapter). Though we are all in process, and will be until Jesus Christ transforms us into His perfect image, most of us know whether we are morally pure, self-controlled, hospitable, not addicted to chemical substances, generous, and not materialistic, etc. Furthermore, most people who know us well can vouch for our overall reputation as a Christian—that though we are not perfect, we are growing in our relationship with Christ and others. They are aware, as we are, whether any serious flaws mar our character. They also observe that when we fail to "walk in the Spirit," we acknowledge our sins; we do so in order to restore our fellowship with God and "walk in the light as he is in the light" (1 John 1:7). Such confession and renouncing of sin, of course, develops a reputation more than any other thing we can do.

Having said this, there are two qualifications Paul listed in both Pastoral Letters that need some careful explanation. We believe they have been misunderstood throughout church history, leading to a "false standard" that eliminates some very godly men from serving as elders/overseers. Let's take a more careful look.

"HUSBAND OF BUT ONE WIFE"

The first marriage/family qualification of an overseer, that he "must be . . . the husband of but one wife (1 Timothy 3:2), has been interpreted in various ways, as noted briefly in chapter 12. Let's explore and evaluate those interpretations.

Must Be Married

Some believe that Paul was requiring that an elder/overseer be married. This would be a strange requirement indeed, as Paul in his letter to the Corinthians encouraged some to stay single—at least during the period of oppression and persecution—so as to be able to serve the Lord better (1 Corinthians 7:32–35). But it would be even more contradictory since Paul and both of his missionary companions—Timothy and Titus—were evidently single. It doesn't make sense that these unmarried church-planting missionaries would require something of local church leaders they didn't require of themselves.

Must Never Be Remarried

Some also believe that Paul was eliminating a man from this leadership position if his wife had died and he had remarried. Unfortunately, this unrealistic interpretation has led some men to "change the rules." For example, suppose a man faces this crisis in his life. He is not only an elder, but also the primary teacher in the church. His first wife dies and he remarries another godly woman. However, believing he could no longer serve as an elder, he resigns that position—but continues to function as the primary teacher. In other words, he circumvents his personal interpretation —that he cannot continue to be an elder because he has remarried—by changing his title and basically continuing to function as before.

Unfortunately, this has happened primarily because faulty interpretations can lead to unrealistic expectations that can cause us to "change the rules" in order to function within our own reality.

Must Not Be Divorced

This has probably been the most common view throughout church history— that if a man had ever been divorced, he is automatically disqualified from ever being an elder/overseer. In fact, some who interpret Paul's statement as meaning "no divorce" attempt to be consistent by adding to the requirement—that even a man who is married for the first time, but to a divorced woman, is also disqualified.

Unfortunately, this interpretation puts divorce in the category of an unpardonable sin, whereas a man could be guilty of murder and still become a spiritual leader—which characterized Paul's life (Acts 9:1, 26). In his first letter to Timothy, before listing the qualifications for an elder/overseer, Paul classified himself as "the worst of sinners"—"a blasphemer and a persecutor and a violent man" (1 Timothy 1:13–16). And yet, his position as an apostle was far more prominent as a multiple church planter than being a spiritual leader in a local church. Murder did not disqualify him from being the greatest missionary who ever lived.

Furthermore, if Paul meant "divorce and remarriage," this would allow a man who was never married but who had sexual relations with a thousand women in the Temple of Artemis in Ephesus to become an elder/overseer once he became a Christian and changed his behavior. In fact, it would allow him to occupy this position after he married because he would still be the "husband of but one wife"—even though he had become "one flesh" with countless prostitutes (1 Corinthians 6:16).

In terms of forgiveness of sins, there is no argument. The blood of Jesus Christ cleanses us from all sin (Ephesians 1:7; 1 Peter 1:18–19; 1 John 1:7). But why not the sin of divorce? Bible scholar Robert L. Saucy develops the answer to this question in a very objective and thorough fashion in an excellent journal article entitled "The Husband of One Wife." He concludes by saying: "If this interpretation is correct . . . (1) that adultery is probably not a continual state of sin, but can be forgiven even as a murder, (2) that divorce does dissolve marriage so that one married again is not considered to be the husband of two wives, then it would seem reasonable to interpret this qualification of being the husband of one wife as a present quality of a man's life."[1]

Don't misunderstand. These are not arguments to lower standards for spiritual leaders. The facts are that a divorced man may be disqualified because of a tainted reputation that has not been rebuilt or because he is not "managing his household" well. But there *are* divorced men who *are* "above reproach" in their present situation. Their past is behind them, and often the general population in their church or in the community at large knows nothing about their divorce.

Must Not Be a Polygamist

Some of the early church writers—such as Justin Martyr and Chrysostom —believed Paul was talking about polygamy. It's true that this practice in Paul's day still existed among some Jews, who may have also influenced some Gentile converts to Judaism to do the same. John Calvin concluded this was what Paul was forbidding—to have more than one wife at a time. However, most Bible interpreters today don't accept this interpretation, especially since polygamy was outlawed in the Roman Empire at the time Paul wrote his letters. It did not seem to be a serious issue. If it were, Paul would certainly have stated what he had in mind more clearly.

A One-Woman Man

We believe that Paul was simply requiring that a man be above re-proach morally, that he be a "one-woman man"—which is a legitimate translation. In essence, he was to be loyal to one woman and one woman only—his present wife.[2] This was a very necessary requirement in the New Testament world since many men were converted out of raw pagan-ism. Married men of wealth particularly, retained prostitutes at the local temples and had their own special "slave girls" in their extended family quarters. Their wives in that culture could only accept this arrangement as normal. They had very little choice. Though it was illegal to have more than one wife, it certainly was not illegal for a married man to have more than one woman in his life.

Imagine what happened in Ephesus and Crete when the Gospel pene-trated these pagan cultures. To be true followers of Jesus Christ, these men had to make a serious moral choice—to be a "one-woman man." Obviously, it took time for some of these men to become free from what had to be in-credible sexual addictions. This is probably one of the primary reasons Paul exhorted Timothy and Titus to make sure a man seeking to be an elder/ overseer had dealt with this problem in his life—and that it could be veri-fied by his reputation, both in the church and in the larger community.

A Contemporary Illustration

This problem is still true in many cultures of the world. For example, I remember meeting a young family man several years ago when I was ministering in a South American country. When he was just a young boy— entering the age of puberty—his father took him to a prostitute and of-fered her money to teach his son everything there was to know about sex. In addition, the father put this woman on a retainer so his son could visit her anytime he wished. Hard to imagine? Yes, but it's true and it's com-mon in that particular culture.

Needless to say, this young man became addicted to this kind of lifestyle. Eventually when he grew older, he decided to get married and have children. Like so many of his friends who grew up in that society, he continued to visit a prostitute regularly, even after he was married. And like so many women in that culture, his wife knew about his extramarital activities. She accepted it, though reluctantly, as normal behavior among men.

Then this man became a Christian. For the first time, he discovered the biblical standard for morality in marriage. To continue his association with a prostitute, or any other woman other than his wife, would be to continue to sin against God as well as his wife and family. Unfortunately, his addiction was so powerful that he struggled continually to measure up to this new standard.

When I met this young man, he had been victorious over his sin for several months, thanks to an accountability group. Through Bible study, prayer, and the power of the Holy Spirit, as well as being accountable for his actions, he was finally able to conquer the temptation when he left his office after work. Rather than making his regular visits to a prostitute, he returned home and spent the evenings with his wife and family. Fortunately, he had not contracted a lethal venereal disease and his wife was able to forgive him. In essence, they began a new life together, learning to love one another as Jesus Christ loved them.

If you can understand the dynamics in this story, you can also understand more clearly what happened regularly in the New Testament culture, especially among Gentiles. This, we believe, is the primary reason why Paul stated that anyone who became an elder/overseer must be "a man of one woman."[3]

MANAGING THE FAMILY WELL

Following Paul's first requirement for being "above reproach" and "blameless" in both his letters to Timothy and Titus—to be a man of one woman—Paul wrote to Titus to make sure an elder/overseer was also "a man whose children believe and are not open to the charge of being wild and disobedient" (Titus 1:6). This qualification correlates with what Paul wrote to Timothy (1 Timothy 3:4–5).

Children Who Believe

What does it mean to have "children who believe?" Is Paul first of all requiring that a prospective elder have children? If so, must they be old enough to understand the Gospel and become Christians? What if one of his children is a newborn baby? Does he have to wait until that child becomes old enough to understand the doctrine of salvation even though his older children have become believers?

First of all, we've already addressed the question as to whether a man must be married to be an elder/overseer. We believe the answer is no, and it follows naturally that an elder/overseer is not required to have children. In other words, Paul was, in essence, saying *if* a man is married, he must be loyal to one woman only—his wife. And *if* he has children who are old enough to understand the Gospel and old enough to intelligently accept or reject the Gospel, their response becomes a factor in selecting and appointing a man to be an elder/overseer. But Paul took this requirement a step further when he said that those who are of believing age and have rejected the Gospel are not to be living "wild and disobedient lives."

It's important to note that Paul was not referring to small children or even adolescents. The word he used for "children" is the same word he used in his letter to Timothy to refer to "children" who should be caring for a widowed mother—indicating these were grown children who probably were already married and had children of their own (1 Timothy 5:4).

"Wild and Disobedient"

The words "wild and disobedient" (Titus 1:6; translated "dissipation or rebellion" in the NASB) refer to older children who are living very sinful lives. The Greek word *asotia* refers to "riotous" living. Note how Peter used this word in another setting to describe a variety of very sinful behaviors: "For you have spent enough time in the past doing what *pagans* choose to do—living in *debauchery, lust, drunkenness, orgies, carousing* and *detestable idolatry*. They think it strange that you do not plunge with them into the same flood of *dissipation [asotia]*, and they heap abuse on you" (1 Peter 4:3–4).

The Greek word translated "disobedient" or "rebellious" is *anupotak-tos*. Again, note the context in which Paul used this word: "We also know that law is made not for the righteous but for *lawbreakers* and *rebels* [*anupotaktos*], the *ungodly* and *sinful,* the *unholy* and *irreligious;* for those who *kill their fathers or mothers,* for *murderers,* for *adulterers* and *perverts,* for *slave traders* and *liars* and *perjurers*—and for whatever else is contrary to the sound doctrine" (1 Timothy 1:9–10).

Obviously, Paul was talking about grown children who totally rejected the Gospel of Jesus Christ and continued to live a pagan lifestyle that actually reflected the way Eli's sons lived in the Old Testament culture—men who "were wicked" and who "had no regard for the LORD" (1 Samuel 2:12). They were both immoral and even "treated the LORD's offering with contempt" (2:17).

The Extended Family

This problem, of course, was complicated in the New Testament world in that grown children and their wives and/or husbands and families often lived in the same compound with their parents. The localized extended family was a part of this culture. It's easy to see how a grown son or daughter who continued to reject the parents' faith and flaunted his or her unbelief with this kind of sinful lifestyle would bring criticism and reproach on the parents—and particularly on one's father.

In today's Western culture particularly, our family structures and mobile society also affect the way people view our households. When children leave the home, marry, and choose to live in ungodly ways, it doesn't necessarily affect a father's reputation. Furthermore, even as godly Christian parents, we do not have a guarantee that when one or more of our children leave the home that they will not choose a very sinful lifestyle—no matter how much we as parents have modeled and taught the principles of Christian living outlined in Scripture.

Unfortunately, the world's system can at times undo everything a parent has done. But unless this hurts a man's reputation, these isolated instances should not disqualify him from being appointed as an elder/overseer. In fact, most of the men I've known over the years who love

God and have family dynamics that might hurt the cause of Christ decide on their own never to seek after or accept this kind of role. In some instances, they take this qualification so seriously they have overreacted and need to be reassured that serving in an elder/overseer role will not be a stumbling block to either believers or nonbelievers.

Again, this is not an attempt to lower the standards for spiritual leaders. Rather, we must clearly understand what Paul had in mind. To do so, we need to understand not only the meaning of words that describe character qualities but also the way in which these words were used in the historical and cultural setting. Paul was primarily concerned that every man selected and appointed to serve as an elder/overseer must have a good reputation, both in the church and in the larger community.

This becomes the overarching qualification for evaluating a man's family life: his reputation. However, when a number of children in a man's family rebel against Jesus Christ, it still raises the same question Paul raised when he wrote to Timothy: "If anyone does not know how to manage his own family, how can he take care of God's church?" (1 Timothy 3:5)

NOTES

1. Robert L Saucy, "The Husband of One Wife," *Bibliotheca Sacra* 131 (July 1974): 238.

2. For an excellent exegetical treatment of Paul's phrase "husband of but one wife," see Ed Glasscock, "The Husband of One Wife Requirement in 1 Timothy 3:2," *Bibliotheca Sacra* 140 (July 1983): 244–57.

3. This illustration was first published in Gene A. Getz, *The Measure of a Man* (Ventura, Calif.: Regal, 1974), 43–44.

SERVING WITH JOY
(A.D. 66–70)

BACK TO THE SOURCE

Before proceeding, read Philippians 1:20–26 and 2 Timothy 4:6–18. In both settings (Paul's first and second imprisonments), note his perspective on martyrdom.

By the time the biblical story on elders/overseers and other church leaders concluded in the book of Hebrews, both the apostle Paul and the apostle Peter probably had already experienced martyrdom. In fact, some believe these two great leaders who had been imprisoned in Rome were martyred on the same day. According to Jerome, it happened in the fourteenth year of Nero, June 29, A.D. 67. Peter was crucified upside down and Paul was beheaded on the Appian Way.[1]

If Paul and Peter had already paid the ultimate sacrifice, this may help us understand what the author of Hebrews meant when he wrote: "Remember your leaders, who spoke the word of God to you. Consider the outcome of their way of life and imitate their faith" (Hebrews 13:7).

We're not certain who wrote Hebrews, nor do we know exactly when it was written—but it certainly could have been written after the martyrdom of Peter and Paul. Furthermore, we're not sure why the author used a more generic title for spiritual leaders.[2]

"Remember Your Leaders"

The exhortation to "remember your leaders" is in the past tense. The author may be referring to those who first "spoke the word of God" to them while they were yet unsaved, which in turn led them to put their faith in Jesus Christ.

Those Who Had Been Martyred

As these believers "remembered" these compassionate missionaries, they were to "consider the *outcome* of their way of life" and they were to also "imitate their faith." Some believe that the Greek term *ekbasis,* translated "outcome," actually refers to the way these believers died. Could this be a reference to Paul and Peter and others who gave their lives so that the recipients of this letter could become true believers in Jesus Christ?

Why would the author appeal to these believers to "remember" these men and women—those who had been stalwart saints? It's clear the recipients of this letter were immature and wavering in their faith. They had not grown substantially in their Christian walk. Their spiritual diet still consisted of "milk, not solid food!" It was essential that they "leave the elementary teachings about Christ and go on to maturity" (Hebrews 5:11–6:1).

Later, the author reminded these same believers that in their "struggle against sin," they had "not yet resisted to the point of shedding [their] blood" (12:4)—unlike many who initially "spoke the word of God" to them. In other words, when they were tempted to revert to their old way of life, they needed to stop and think about those leaders who had literally given their lives that they might hear the Gospel. In view of these selfless examples, could they not at least live godly lives and avoid regressing into a sinful lifestyle?

The Need for Godly Models

One of the greatest ways to communicate to believers who are immature and struggling in their faith is to expose them to godly models of faith and righteousness. Thus, the writer of Hebrews exhorted these believers to "imitate" the "faith" of those who were their forefathers as well as those first-century ambassadors for Christ who died in order that they might hear the Gospel (Hebrews 11).

"OBEY YOUR LEADERS"

In the next reference to leaders, it appears that the author of this letter moved in his thoughts from those who had an "apostolic" and "church planting" ministry among them (past tense) to those who were subsequently appointed as elders/overseers in their local churches (present tense): "*Obey your leaders and submit to their authority. They keep watch over you as men who must give an account. Obey them so that their work will be a joy, not a burden, for that would be of no advantage to you*" (Hebrews 13:17).[3]

It's a difficult task to admonish believers who are deliberately living out of the will of God. Consequently, the author anticipates that many of these believers who would hear this Hebrew epistle read would react negatively. After all, many of them were very carnal and immature. He had made this clear when he stated earlier: "We have much to say about this, but it is hard to explain because you are slow to learn. In fact, though by this time you ought to be teachers, you need someone to teach you the elementary truths of God's word all over again" (5:11–12).

Though the term "authority" is not used in the Greek text, it's implied when these believers are exhorted to "obey" and "submit." Interestingly, these two words in the original are "softer" than those used more generally to encourage "obedience" and "submission," but they are still very straightforward and penetrating. More accurately, the author is exhorting Christians to live in harmony with what their leaders were teaching and to respond to the will of God.[4]

Why Obey and Submit?

The author of this letter stated three reasons Christians should obey and submit:

1. *These leaders had a sincere concern for the spiritual lives of these believers (more literally, "They keep watch for your souls").* Nothing is more important than our relationship with God. It's painful for spiritual leaders to see Christians deliberately disobeying the Lord and moving in the direction of emotional, spiritual, and physical deterioration and disaster.

2. *These leaders were representing Jesus Christ, and someday they would have to "give an account" for the way in which they carried out their shepherding responsibilities.* Paul's warning to the Corinthians elaborates on this exhortation in Hebrews. Every spiritual leader must be careful how he builds on the foundation that was laid by those who had an "apostolic" ministry by initially "speaking the Word of God" and sharing the Gospel. That "foundation" is Jesus Christ. There will come a day of accounting for all spiritual leaders, and if anyone has built on that foundation using "gold, silver, costly stones," the work will survive and that spiritual leader will be rewarded. However, if any spiritual leader builds on that foundation using "wood, hay or straw," what he has done will be "burned up." Though he will be saved, there will be no rewards (1 Corinthians 3:10–15).

3. *These believers should align their lifestyles with the truth they're being taught so their spiritual leaders will experience an immediate reward— "joy" rather than sadness and disappointment.* Again, Paul illustrated his own "emotional pain" when writing to Christians who were not growing in Christ, saying he was in "the *pains of childbirth* until Christ is formed in you[;] how I wish I could be with you now and

change my tone, because I am perplexed about you!" (Galatians 4:19–20). In other words, Paul "agonized" in helping people experience the "new birth," and when they did not move from "drinking milk" to "eating solid foods," he agonized all over again. On the other hand, he demonstrated his "joy," his enthusiasm and encouragement when Timothy returned with a great report about the believers in Thessalonica: "How can we thank God enough for you in return *for all the joy* we have in the presence of our God *because of you?*" (1 Thessalonians 3:9).

The Results of Disobedience

There is one final caution in this exhortation to "obey" and "submit" to local church leaders. If they don't, the author warned, the result will "be of no advantage" to them. In other words, there is pain, not only in being out of fellowship with God, but also in being out of harmony with those who are responsible for our spiritual welfare. When we're angry, we are unable to listen with open hearts and minds to those who teach us the truth. We want to turn a deaf ear! We even want to avoid being around other "brothers and sisters in Christ" who are obeying God. Predictably, it makes us uncomfortable, even miserable. On the other hand, living in God's perfect will brings a sense of joy and peace in our lives (Romans 12:1–2).

A NOBLE TASK

Serving as an elder/overseer is an awesome responsibility. God decidedly puts the burden to serve faithfully on those of us who are leaders. In fact, that is why this is only the second time in this leadership story that the "sheep" are exhorted to respond to the "shepherds."

In view of what we've learned, we can only conclude that the most effective way to get positive responses from those who follow us is to carry out our managing/shepherding functions diligently, first of all by modeling the life of Jesus Christ and then—against the backdrop of living out authentic Christianity—to continually "speak the truth in love." As Paul wrote to Timothy, this kind of ministry is a "noble task"—but it must be desired with a humble heart and accepted with a commitment to be a godly servant leader. The same principle, of course, applies to every leadership position in the church—including being a good husband and father and a good wife and mother.

NOTES

1. Jack Finegan, *Handbook of Biblical Chronology* (Peabody, Mass: Hendrickson Publishers, 1998), 385.

2. The author used the present participle of the Greek verb *hegeomai*—which was used to describe a variety of leadership positions in the Roman world—a prince, a governor, a military commander, as well as a leader of a religious group. It's very apparent, however, that in this letter he was referring to those who had significant authority in the church both universally and locally.

3. Since the author used the generic term for "leaders" to refer to those who had an "apostolic ministry," it would be logical to use the same nomenclature in describing spiritual leaders in the local church. This may reflect the author's unique ability as a writer—which is clear throughout this letter. Greek scholars comment on the author's elegant use of the Greek language—which may indicate that he was concerned about maintaining consistency in language forms.

4. The Greek word *peitho*, which is translated "obey" in Hebrews 13:17, is not the same as *hupakouo* which is used for children and their relationship with their parents and servants in their relationship with masters (Ephesians 6:1–5; Colossians 3:20–22). And *hupeiko* translated "submit" in Hebrews 13:17 is not the same word as *hupotasso* used for wives toward their husbands (Ephesians 5:22; Colossians 3:18; Titus 2:5; 3:1; 1 Peter 3:5); for servants toward their masters (Titus 2:9; 1 Peter 2:18); for all members of the body of Christ toward one another (Ephesians 5:21; 1 Peter 5:5); for all believers toward government authorities (Romans 13:1; 1 Peter 2:13); and for all believers toward God (Ephesians 5:24; Hebrews 12:9; James 4:7). Together the two words in Hebrews 13:17 are used not so much to indicate "subordination" as "cooperating with," "responding to," "being persuaded," and "yielding to." This does not mean members of the body of Christ should not recognize and submit to the authority of spiritual leaders as Paul indicated in 1 Thessalonians 5:12–13, but there is a softer nuance when the author of Hebrews used the words translated "obey" and "submit" in Hebrews 13:17.

SCRIPTURAL OBSERVATIONS

The following chapters look back on the biblical story that we've unfolded chronologically in part 2. We'll comment on fourteen specific observations that will help to crystallize our thinking in several important areas regarding the ministry of local church leaders: their titles, their functions, leadership selection and appointments, the concept of plurality in leadership, and the need for a primary leader. Part 3 serves not only as a systematic summary but also gives additional biblical data to help clarify more fully what we've looked at in the biblical story.

Here's a preview of the *fourteen observations* we draw from the biblical story of spiritual leadership.

OBSERVATION 1: *The Term "Elders"*

In the early years of Christianity, spiritual leaders in local churches were consistently identified as "elders" (*presbuteroi*).

OBSERVATION 2: *The Term "Overseers"*

As Paul and his fellow missionaries expanded their church-planting ministry into areas that were heavily populated with Gentiles, spiritual leaders were eventually also identified as "overseers" or "bishops" (*episkopoi*).

OBSERVATION 3: *Managing*

One of the basic terms New Testament writers used to describe the overarching function of elders/overseers was "to *manage*" (*proistemi*).

OBSERVATION 4: *Shepherding*

The second term New Testament writers used to describe the overarching function of elders/overseers was "to *shepherd* or *tend* [*poimaino*] the flock of God."

OBSERVATION 5: *A Noble Task*

When Paul outlined these overarching functions for elders/overseers, he made this opportunity available to any man who desired this "noble task" and who was qualified spiritually (1 Timothy 3:1).

OBSERVATION 6: *Specific Functions*

In order for elders/overseers to carry out the overarching responsibility of "managing" the church effectively and "shepherding" God's flock as faithful and sensitive leaders, New Testament writers described and prescribed at least six specific and essential functions.

OBSERVATION 7: *Qualifications*

The New Testament outlines very specific qualifications for serving as local church leaders, but they were not revealed in writing until Paul wrote letters to Timothy and Titus following his first imprisonment in Rome (1 Timothy 3:1–13; Titus 1:5–9).

OBSERVATION 8: *Human Responsibility*

As the biblical story unfolds, we see more emphasis on human responsibility in selecting and appointing "qualified leaders."

OBSERVATION 9: *Apostolic Representatives*

Though Timothy and Titus assisted Paul as apostolic representatives in selecting and appointing leaders in Ephesus and on the island of Crete, we're not told how other churches in the New Testament world carried out this process.

OBSERVATION 10: *A Unified Team*

As the biblical story unfolds in the New Testament, it becomes increasingly clear that each local church was to be managed and shepherded by a unified team of godly men.

OBSERVATION 11: *A Primary Leader*

The New Testament definitely teaches and illustrates that when there is a plurality of leadership, someone needs to function as the primary leader of the team.

OBSERVATION 12: *Accountability*

In the early years of the church, there was accountability for elders/overseers among themselves and also beyond their local ministry.

OBSERVATION 13: *Delegation*

The New Testament teaches that elders/overseers must maintain their priorities by delegating responsibilities to other qualified men and women who can assist them in managing and shepherding the church.

OBSERVATION 14: *Function and Form*

The biblical story on local church leadership does not describe specific "forms"—only "functions" and "directives."

TITLES AND
AN OVERARCHING
FUNCTION

OBSERVATION 1: *The Term "Elders"*

In the early years of Christianity, spiritual leaders in local churches were consistently identified as elders (presbuteroi).

Following are the chronological events in the biblical story where the term "elders" was used:

☐ *A.D. 45:* Barnabas and Paul (then called Saul) transported a gift of money from the church in Antioch which they delivered "to the elders" in Jerusalem (Acts 11:29–30).

☐ *A.D. 45–47:* James, the half brother of Christ, who had emerged as the primary leader among the Jerusalem elders, wrote a letter to Jewish believers "scattered among the nations" (James 1:1) and encouraged them to "call the *elders of the church*" for prayer for a variety of illnesses (James 5:14).

☐ *A.D. 47:* Paul and Barnabas appointed "elders" in the churches in Lystra, Iconium, and Antioch (Acts 14:23).

☐ *A.D. 49:* The "apostles and *elders*" in Jerusalem functioned as a team as they resolved the law/grace controversy (Acts 15:2, 4–6, 22–23).

☐ *A.D. 49–52:* Paul, Silas, and Timothy "traveled from town to town" and "delivered the decisions reached by the apostles and *elders* in Jerusalem for the people to obey" (Acts 16:4).

A BIBLICAL HISTORY OF ELDERS

The Elders in Israel

Jewish people had heard the title "elders" for centuries, going back to the time they were slaves in Egypt (Exodus 3:16). In those days, the "elders of Israel" were men selected to represent the various segments of the people. And once they settled into the land of Canaan, "elders" represented the various tribes and districts. These men began to wield a lot of power and control over the nation (1 Samuel 8:4).

These leaders in Israel continued to be very influential during the reigns of Kings Saul, David, and Solomon. During the exile in Babylon, they became an aristocracy. They occupied an "eldership" position because they were a part of the nobility.

By the time Jesus Christ came, every major city in the Roman Empire with a significant Jewish population had a council called the Sanhedrin, composed of twenty-three elders. Their primary responsibility was to explain and interpret the Law of Moses and to punish people for violating the law.

In Jerusalem, seventy men comprised the "Great Sanhedrin." Though this group represented a number of subgroups—priests, well-to-do families, scribes, Pharisees, Sadducees—at times they were all identified as "elders" (Luke 22:66). This elite group in Israel continued to function after the church was born. By this time, the Roman Empire had given them the authority to inflict capital punishment on those who violated Israel's religious laws—which had proliferated considerably over the centuries. It was this group of "elders" that sentenced Stephen to death (Acts 6:12, 15; 7:54–60).

Elders in the Church

Against this historical backdrop, it's easy to understand why the early church used the term "elders" to identify spiritual leaders. But what were the functional differences between the "elders in Israel" and the "elders of the churches"? Thomas M. Lindsay explained this difference well when he commented:

> When we find "elders" in charge of the community in Jerusalem, ready to receive the contributions for the relief of those who are suffering from the famine which overtook them in the reign of Claudius, *it is impossible to doubt that the name came from their Jewish surroundings.* At the same time, it must always be remembered that Christian "elders" had functions entirely different . . . and that in this case *nothing but the name was borrowed* [emphasis added].[1]

We agree with Lindsay's conclusions. Elders in the church may have had the *same title* as leaders in Israel, but they had totally *new functions.*

OBSERVATION 2: *The Term "Overseers"*

As Paul and his fellow missionaries expanded their church-planting ministry into areas that were heavily populated with Gentiles, spiritual leaders were eventually also identified as "overseers" or "bishops" (episkopoi).

Here are the chronological events in the biblical story where the term "overseers" was used:

□ *A.D. 58:* The elders in Ephesus are also called "overseers" (Acts 20:17, 28).

□ *A.D. 61:* Paul greeted the spiritual leaders in Philippi as "overseers" (Phillipians 1:1).

□ *A.D. 63:* Paul used the term "overseers" and "elders" interchangeably when he wrote his first letter to Timothy (1 Timothy 3:1–2; 5:17–20).

□ *A.D. 63:* In his first epistle, Peter also used these terms interchangeably (1 Peter 5:1–2).

□ *A.D. 65:* When Paul wrote to Titus in Crete, he once again used the term "elders" and "overseers" interchangeably (Titus 1:5–7).

ELDERS AND OVERSEERS:
INTERCHANGEABLE TITLES

The Romans often used the title *episkopos* to refer to a superintendent or leader of a colony. Consequently, Gentile converts would be well aware of this leadership terminology.

Paul, of course, was also aware of how this term was used among Gentiles. Consequently, he borrowed this word from the Roman culture, perhaps because of Luke's influence, and once again totally redefined the functions associated with this position in the pagan world. But when there was a strong mixture of both Jew and Gentile in particular communities, he identified spiritual leaders as *both* "elders" and "overseers." However, the functions were the same. These were not different positions. This demonstrates the freedom New Testament leaders felt to vary "language forms" to adapt to cultural situations and enhance their ministry.

This, of course, was not compromising biblical truth. The apostles were not guilty of syncretism—mixing Christian and pagan ideas that violated the essential doctrines of Scripture. Rather, "titles" was one of the "all things" Paul referred to when he became "all things to all men so that by all possible means" he "might save some" (1 Corinthians 9:22).

MANAGING OR SHEPHERDING:
AN OVERARCHING FUNCTION

Just as biblical writers used the titles *elders* and *overseers* interchangeably, so they also used two concepts to describe one basic function, giving overall direction to the church.

 **OBSERVATION 3:** *Managing*

*One of the basic terms New Testament writers used to describe the overarching function of elders/overseers was "to manage" (*proistemi).

Following are the situations where the function "to manage" is used chronologically in the biblical story

☐ *A.D. 51:* In Paul's first letter to the Thessalonians, he used the basic word for managing (*proistemi*) to describe the responsibility assigned to "elders" or "overseers" (1 Thessalonians 5:12).

☐ *A.D. 63:* When Paul wrote his first pastoral letter to Timothy, he used this overarching concept "to manage" two times (1 Timothy 3:4–5).

Note something very significant! When Paul referred to a man's ability to give this kind of "oversight" to his family, he used another word when he correlated this function with "overseeing" the church: "He must manage [*proistemi*] his own family well. . . . If anyone does not know how to manage [*proistemi*] his own family, how can he *take care of* [*epimeleomai*] God's church?" (1 Timothy 3:4–5).

The phrase translated to "take care of" (*epimeleomai*) is translated from the same basic word Jesus used when He told a parable to the Jewish religious leaders (many of whom were identified as "elders") to illustrate what it means to "love your neighbor as yourself" (Luke 10:25–29). Note the following paraphrase:

A Samaritan found a man robbed and beaten on the road that leads from Jerusalem to Jericho. Though two men who were considered "elders" in Israel—a "priest" and a "Levi"—saw what had happened, they both ignored this man's desperate situation and went on their way. Not so with the Samaritan. He *"took care of "* (*epimeleomai*) this bruised and beaten man. He "bandaged his wounds" and "took him to an inn." There he spent the night looking after this stranger. The next day, he paid the innkeeper to continue to do what he had already done—to *"take care of "* this wounded man (Luke 10:30–35).

What a beautiful story to illustrate what Paul meant when he outlined this particular qualification for elders/overseers. To be able to "manage" or to "take care of " the church grows out of the household model—a concept that involves being a compassionate, caring father (see also 1 Timothy 3:12; 5:17).

OBSERVATION 4: *Shepherding*

The second term New Testament writers used to describe the overarching function of elders/overseers was "to shepherd or tend [poimaino] the flock of God."

Following are the references listed chronologically where the term "shepherding" is used in the biblical story:

☐ *A.D. 56:* Paul first used the "shepherding" concept in Scripture when he defended the fact that believers are to care for the material needs of those who faithfully minister the Word of God to them (1 Corinthians 9:7).

☐ *A.D. 58:* Paul challenged the Ephesian elders to be faithful "shepherds" who would protect "the flock" from "savage wolves" (Acts 20:28–30).

□ *A.D. 63:* In his first epistle, Peter urged the elders/overseers to be faithful "shepherds" who served willingly and eagerly (1 Peter 5:1–4).

OBSERVATION 5: *A Noble Task*

When Paul outlined these overarching functions for elders/overseers, he made this opportunity available to any man who desired this "noble task" and who was qualified spiritually (1 Timothy 3:1).

For years, many have used Paul's statement about "pastors and teachers" in his letter to the Ephesians as a reference to the ministry of elders/overseers in local churches. I would like to offer another interpretation.

First, note that these were "gifts" given to "some" individuals in order to "prepare God's people for works of service":

It was he [Jesus Christ] who gave:

□ *some* to be apostles,

□ *some* to be prophets,

□ *some* to be evangelists, and

□ *some* to be *pastors* and *teachers* (Ephesians 4:11).

When we compare Jesus' "selective" distribution of gifts described in this paragraph in Ephesians with Paul's instructions to Timothy regarding selecting and appointing elders/overseers, there is no reference to either the "pastoral" or "teaching" gifts (see "The Pastoral Letters," chapter 24, regarding what Paul means in reference to the qualification "being able to teach"). In fact, in these lists of qualifications, there is no reference to a special "leadership" or "managing" (*proistemi*) gift, which is only mentioned in one Scripture verse (Romans 12:8: "If it is leadership, let him govern diligently"). Furthermore, Paul did not restrict the role of elder/overseer to "some" who were gifted supernaturally by Jesus Christ in various ways. Rather, this "noble task" was open to any man who seriously and sincerely desired to serve as a "shepherd" or "pastor" and who had the appropriate character qualities.

What, then, did Paul mean in his letter to the Ephesians? I believe he was referring to a select group of individuals that Jesus chose and definitely gifted to launch the church generally. Earlier, Paul had written that "both Jews and Gentiles" are "fellow citizens with God's people and members of God's household, *built on the foundation of the apostles and prophets,* with Christ Jesus himself as the chief cornerstone" (Ephesians 2:19–20). The grouping in Ephesians 4:11 certainly included the initial "apostles" along with others—men like Timothy and Titus ("pastors and teachers")—who were gifted to help establish churches throughout the Roman world. During this process, they equipped men who eventually became elders/overseers.

Shortly before his death, Paul summarized this conclusion in his final charge to Timothy: "And the things you [Timothy] have heard me [*an apostle and prophet*] say in the presence of many witnesses entrust to reliable men [*elders/overseers*] who will also be qualified to teach others (2 Timothy 2:2).

Though Paul did not mention elders/overseers specifically when he referred to "reliable men," it's logical to conclude that this is primarily who he had in mind, especially in view of the way this strategy unfolded throughout the biblical story.[2]

NOTES

1. David Miller, "The Uniqueness of New Testament Church Eldership," *Grace Theological Journal* 6 (Fall 1985): 315–27.

2. For a more in-depth study on how "apostles, prophets and teachers" relate to the ministry of "elders" and "overseers," see appendix D.

SPECIFIC
LEADERSHIP
FUNCTIONS

OBSERVATION 6: *Specific Functions*

*In order for elders/overseers to carry out the overarching respon-
sibility of "managing" the church effectively and "shepherding"
God's flock as faithful and sensitive leaders, New Testament
writers described and prescribed at least six specific and essential
functions.*

At least six essential functions for elders are prescribed in the
biblical story of the church. Let's look at the description and use
of each.

1. TEACHING BIBLICAL TRUTH

The specific and foundational responsibility for elders/
overseers to "teach" the Word of God takes us back to the Great

Commission. When the eleven disciples responded to Jesus' command to go to Galilee and meet Him on a certain mountain, Jesus commissioned them to do two things. First, they were to *"make disciples* of all nations" (Matthew 28:19)—initially, proclaiming the Gospel and securing conversions to Christ (converts were called "disciples" before they were called "Christians"—Acts 11:26). Second, they were to build up these disciples by *"teaching them* to obey everything" Jesus *had taught* and *commanded them* (Matthew 28:20).[1]

The Church in Jerusalem

As soon as the church was born on the Day of Pentecost, the process of teaching began. The three thousand that responded to Peter's exposition and proclamation "devoted themselves to the *apostles' teaching* [*didache*]" (Acts 2:41–42).

The Church in Antioch

When the apostles eventually heard that Gentiles had responded to the Gospel in Antioch, they sent Barnabas to assess the situation. When he arrived and discovered these "pagans" had indeed experienced God's grace—as happened to the Jews on the Day of Pentecost—Barnabas immediately began to *teach them* "to remain true to the Lord with all their hearts" (Acts 11:23).[2] And when Paul (Saul) joined him, these two men *"taught"* these disciples for a whole year (11:26).

The Churches in Galatia

When Paul and Barnabas traveled together on their first missionary journey and had "won a large number of disciples" in Antioch of Pisidia, Iconium, and Lystra, they eventually returned to these three cities, *"strengthening* the disciples and *encouraging* them to remain true to the faith" (Acts 14:21–22). Here Paul first used the basic Greek word *episterizo*, which also means "to establish." He then used the basic Greek word *parakaleo* that he used to describe Barnabas' teaching ministry in Antioch.

Passing the Baton

This leads us to the next step in the process—appointing elders/overseers in each of these churches, who would carry on the *teaching responsibility* first commanded by Jesus Christ in the Great Commission. What happened in these Galatian churches became part of the Pauline strategy. Both Timothy and Titus were to pass the baton to the elders/overseers in Ephesus and Crete who in turn were to be faithful shepherds who would "tend" or "feed" the flock of God. Note once again Paul's words to Titus regarding those he was appointing as elders/overseers: "He must hold firmly to the *trustworthy message* as *it has been taught,* so that he can encourage others by *sound doctrine*" (Titus 1:9a).

2. MODELING CHRISTLIKE BEHAVIOR

In order to communicate biblical truth in all its fullness, Paul exemplified a twofold teaching approach in his own life-on-life ministry—*modeling* Christ's likeness while *verbally instructing* believers. Again, when he wrote to the Thessalonians, he reminded them of the way he, Silas, and Timothy had utilized these two dimensions in their communication.

> *Their Model.* "You are witnesses, and so is God, of how *holy, righteous* and *blameless* we were among you who believed" (1 Thessalonians 2:10).

> *Their Teaching Ministry.* "For you know that we dealt with each of you as a father deals with his own children, encouraging, comforting and urging you to live lives worthy of God, who calls you into his kingdom and glory" (1 Thessalonians 2:11–12).

When Paul encouraged Timothy while he was in Ephesus, he emphasized the same twofold approach:

> *The Model.* "Don't let anyone look down on you because you are young, but set an example for the believers in speech, in life, in love, in faith and in purity" (1 Timothy 4:12).

His Teaching Ministry. "Until I come, devote yourself to the public reading of Scripture, to preaching and to teaching" (1 Timothy 4:13; see also Titus 2:7–8).

All elders/overseers were to follow this same two-dimensional communication style. This is one important reason why *Paul's list* of qualifications *focuses on character*, not gifts, abilities, and/or skills.

3. MAINTAINING DOCTRINAL PURITY

This specific "managing" and "shepherding" function for elders/overseers is definitely an extension of "teaching biblical truth."

Sound Doctrine

The first reference to elder involvement in resolving theological issues transpired in Jerusalem when Paul and Barnabas came from Antioch for advice and assistance. Significantly, this resolution involved the most basic doctrine in Christianity. Centuries later, Martin Luther faced the same basic issue—that we are justified by faith, not by works.

What we see in the biblical story following the Jerusalem council is that eventually the leaders in every local church became responsible for maintaining day-to-day and week-to-week doctrinal purity. This is why Paul exhorted the Ephesian elders to consistently "be on [their] guard" regarding those who would "arise and *distort the truth*" (Acts 20:30–31).

Paul recorded the most specific instructions regarding maintaining doctrinal purity in his letter to Titus. He was to appoint elders/overseers who not only taught "sound doctrine" but who could *"refute those who oppose it"* (Titus 1:9b). This was particularly important in Crete because false teachers were already having a destructive influence.

Able to Teach

When Paul outlined the qualifications for elders/overseers in his first letter to Timothy, he required that these men be "able to teach" (1 Timothy 3:2). However, it wasn't until he wrote his second and final letter that he elaborated on what kind of communication he had in mind. Timothy was to "be able to teach" (*didaktikos*) by demonstrating the "fruit of the Spirit" as he confronted people who were leaning in the wrong direction doctrinally. Consequently, Paul wrote:

> Don't have anything to do with *foolish and stupid arguments*, because you know they produce quarrels. And the Lord's servant *must not quarrel;* instead, he must be *kind* to everyone, *able to teach, not resentful.* Those who oppose him he must *gently instruct*, in the hope that God will grant them repentance leading them to a *knowledge of the truth*, and that they will come to their senses and escape from the trap of the devil, who has taken them captive to do his will. [2 Timothy 2:23–26]

Being "able to teach" is a character quality. Timothy was to confront "false doctrine" with a gentle, sensitive, and teachable spirit, avoiding arguments and quarrels. It's only in this kind of Christ-centered environment that people would listen objectively and hopefully discover what is really true. Though elders/overseers were to "speak the truth," they were always to do so "in love" (Ephesians 4:15).

Silencing the False Teachers

Having encouraged this kind of Spirit-controlled communication for spiritual leaders, Paul also drew a "line in the sand" if false teachers continued to lead people astray. He made this conspicuously clear to Titus with some very direct and deliberate instructions: *"They must be silenced"* (Titus 1:11). And, as Paul closed out his letter, he once again addressed this issue. Like Timothy, Titus was to "avoid foolish controversies" and "arguments and quarrels" (3:9). However, if a gentle, sensitive, teachable approach didn't bring a positive response, Paul outlined for Titus the next step:

"Warn a divisive person once, and then warn him a second time. After that, have nothing to do with him. You may be sure that such a man is warped and sinful; he is self-condemned" (Titus 3:10–11).

One of the specific functions, then, for elders/overseers as they "man-age" and "shepherd" the church was not only to be proactive by *teaching* and *modeling* the Word of God but also *to maintain sound doctrine*. If a lo-cal church departed from what was true, particularly at the leadership level, the "whole body" would be subject to a lethal disease that would eventu-ally lead to spiritual deterioration. Unfortunately, this happened in the New Testament world. Paul reminded Timothy that when Hymenaeus and Philetus began to teach false doctrines, what they taught "spread like gangrene" (2 Timothy 2:17–18).

4. DISCIPLINING UNRULY BELIEVERS

Just as fathers are responsible for disciplining children who are un-ruly and rebellious, so elders/overseers are responsible as "multiple fa-thers" in the "church family" to discipline believers who are determined to willfully violate the will of God. This process involves several levels of communication.

Admonishing

In Paul's letter to the Thessalonians, he introduced us to this concept, "to admonish" (*noutheteo*). Some of these believers had a false view of the second coming of Christ and were evidently using the doctrine of the Lord's immi-nent return to be lazy—not to be diligent in making a living and taking care of their families. Consequently, the elders/overseers had the awesome re-sponsibility *to admonish* and *to warn* these believers to correct their ir-responsible behavior (1 Thessalonians 5:12–13; see also 1 Corinthians 4:14).

Biblical Intervention

Closely related to Paul's instructions to the spiritual leaders in Thes-salonica is his exhortation to the Galatians. Though Paul doesn't mention elders/overseers specifically, they certainly must have been uppermost in Paul's mind when he referred to those "who are spiritual": "Brothers, if someone is caught in a sin, *you who are spiritual* should restore him gently.

But watch yourself, or you also may be tempted. Carry each other's burdens, and in this way you will fulfill the law of Christ" (Galatians 6:1–2).

Here Paul was referring to a believer who was caught in a web of sinful behavior that was common knowledge within the church. Consequently, an attempt to restore this person was a task for more than one godly Christian. This is why Paul used the plural pronoun—"*You* who *are spiritual.*" Using contemporary nomenclature, this is biblical "intervention."

Personal Offenses

During His ministry on earth, Jesus outlined a process for dealing with personal offenses.

Step 1: *"If your brother sins against you, go and show him his fault, just between the two of you. If he listens to you, you have won your brother over.*

Step 2: *But if he will not listen, take one or two others along, so that 'every matter may be established by the testimony of two or three witnesses.'*

Step 3: *If he refuses to listen to them, tell it to the church;*

Step 4: *and if he refuses to listen even to the church, treat him as you would a pagan or a tax collector."* [Matthew 18:15–17]

It's difficult to know exactly what Jesus meant since the word *ekklesia* ("church") was often used in the Roman culture to refer to an "assembly of leaders." For example, when the riot took place in Ephesus, Luke recorded that "the *assembly* [*ekklesia*] was in confusion" (Acts 19:32)—referring to an unruly crowd of people that had gathered in the theater (19:29–32). Later "the city clerk quieted the crowd"(19:35) and reminded them that their concerns "must be settled in a *legal assembly* [*ekklesia*]" (19:39)—namely, a city council.

In the same way, the Jewish Sanhedrin in local synagogues was a "legal '*ekklesia*' in Israel"—which may have been what Jesus had in mind when He told an offended individual to take his concerns to the "church." We must remember that His target audience at this time in His ministry was His fellow Jews. Nevertheless, what Jesus outlined certainly applies to the way elders/overseers should handle personal offenses that are not resolved one-on-one. After an offended party involves one or more people in the confrontation, if there is still no response, that individual can certainly appeal to the *ekklesia* (the "assembly"). In the local church, the body of elders/overseers certainly comprise that "assembly." In this sense, the elders/overseers are "the church."

This approach is in harmony with the way the biblical story describes their shepherding responsibilities. Dealing with sin is a matter to be handled by those *"who are spiritual"*—not a "general assembly" (*ekklesia*) or a "congregation of Christians"—many of whom may be "members" of the church (the larger assembly) but who are not qualified spiritually to express an opinion about another Christian's sin, let alone make a decision to discipline that believer. This kind of approach actually opens the door to Satan in that person's life. That's why Paul warned, "Watch yourself, or you also may be tempted" (Galatians 6:1b).

5. OVERSEEING FINANCIAL MATTERS

Distributing Funds for the Needy

It's not a coincidence that the first reference to elders/overseers focused on financial responsibility (Acts 11:30). Though we're not given any specific details as to how the Jerusalem elders distributed the money delivered by Barnabas and Saul (Paul), we can certainly "fill in the blanks" in terms of this Herculean task. They had to make sure these funds were allocated fairly and equitably to needy believers—not only in Jerusalem but also in other churches throughout Judea. Since this would have been an extremely time-consuming effort, these men must have appointed qualified assistants to help them.

Allocating Wages

Since the elders/overseers were the primary leaders in the church, they were also responsible for monitoring financial distributions among themselves. For example, when certain leaders were entitled to "double honor" (financial remuneration), this distribution needed to be managed in a fair and equitable way. Though we're not told how they were to carry out this function, it was certainly supposed to be done properly.

Paul consistently modeled this kind of accountability. First, he at times gave up what were his "rights" to not be a stumbling block to both unbelievers and believers (1 Corinthians 9:18; 1 Thessalonians 2:9). Second, Paul bent over backwards to avoid misunderstandings when he was raising funds. For example, when he was collecting money for needy believers in Jerusalem, he did not handle the funds personally. Rather, he exhorted the Corinthians to raise the money, store it up, and keep it until he arrived, and then to choose people whom they personally trusted to transport the gift (1 Corinthians 16:3–4). Paul wanted to be "above reproach" so no one could accuse him of raising money to benefit himself. This is why he could remind the Ephesian elders/overseers with a clear conscience and full confidence that during his ministry in Ephesus, he had "not coveted anyone's silver or gold or clothing" (Acts 20:33). In essence, he was telling them to follow his example.

6. PRAYING FOR THOSE WHO ARE ILL

As the primary leader of the elders/overseers in Jerusalem, James introduced the important function of praying for the ill in his New Testament letter early in the history of the church. Though we've listed it last, it's a very important priority function. All believers were to know that they could ask the elders/overseers for prayer regarding physical, psychological, and spiritual healing in their lives (James 5:13–16). When these spiritual leaders were not practicing this biblical injunction on a regular basis, they were bypassing an important ministry that was essential if they were going to "manage well" and "be good shepherds"

For a detailed explanation of the paragraph in James' epistle, see appendix B.

NOTES

1. For an excellent journal article on the nature of this teaching, see Roy B. Zuck, "Greek Words for Teach," *Bibliotheca Sacra* 122 (April 1965): 158.

2. Here Luke used the basic Greek word *parakaleo* to describe the communication process. This is a very specific kind of teaching—which means to exhort, to encourage. Interestingly, Jesus had called the "Spirit of truth" who would come and teach the apostles all things the *parakletos* (the "counselor" or "encourager"). See also John 14:17; 15:26; 16:13, where Jesus referred to the *parakletos* as the "Spirit of truth."

SELECTING AND
APPOINTING ELDERS

 **OBSERVATION 7:** *Qualifications*

The New Testament outlines very specific qualifications for serving as local church leaders, but they were not revealed in writing until Paul wrote letters to Timothy and Titus following his first imprisonment in Rome (1 Timothy 3:1–13; Titus 1:5–9).

Though Paul wrote the Pastoral Epistles at least thirty years after the church was born in Jerusalem, we can certainly assume that much of what he wrote to Timothy and later to Titus was in his mind long before he penned these letters. We can also assume he communicated his thoughts to his fellow missionaries during his various journeys—that elders should measure up to specific qualifications. Following is a combined list of these qualifications:

1. above reproach (a man with a good reputation),
2. husband of one wife (maintaining moral purity),

3. temperate (exemplifying balance in words and action),

4. prudent (being wise and humble),

5. respectable (serving as a good role model),

6. hospitable (demonstrating unselfishness and generosity),

7. able to teach (communicating sensitively and in a nonthreatening and nondefensive manner),

8. not given to wine (not being addicted to substances),

9. not self-willed (not being a self-centered and controlling personality),

10. not quick-tempered (void of anger that becomes sinful),

11. not pugnacious (not an abusive person),

12. uncontentious (nonargumentative and nondivisive),

13. gentle (a sensitive, loving, and kind person),

14. free from the love of money (nonmaterialistic),

15. one who manages his own household well (a good husband and father),

16. a good reputation with those outside the church (a good testimony to unbelievers),

17. love what is good (pursuing godly activities),

18. just (wise, discerning, nonprejudiced, and fair),

19. devout (holy and righteous), and

20. not a new convert (not a new Christian).[1]

THE SELECTION OF KEY LEADERS

OBSERVATION 8: *Human Responsibility*

As the biblical story unfolds, we see more emphasis on human responsibility in selecting and appointing "qualified leaders."

The Case of John Mark versus Timothy

The place of human responsibility in selecting church leaders becomes clear when Paul suggested to Barnabas that they retrace their steps and visit the churches they had started on their first journey. Barnabas agreed with Paul's idea, but he wanted to once again take John Mark and give him another chance. At this point, these two godly men had two different opinions—which demonstrate the human elements involved in this decision. Obviously, Paul believed they had made a mistake in choosing John Mark to go on the first journey, and when he eventually chose Timothy, he didn't want to make another bad choice.

It's not a coincidence Luke recorded that this young man Timothy had an excellent reputation among the church leaders in both Lystra as well as in the neighboring city of Iconium (Acts 16:2). And Paul took notice! Based on Timothy's reputation, both in the Christian community as well as in his home, Paul made his decision clear—he "wanted to take him on the journey" (16:2–3).

The Pastoral Letters

When Paul wrote to Timothy and Titus years later and outlined the qualifications for spiritual leaders, we see even more progression in terms of the human element (review chapter 12). First, Paul stated that the role of elder/overseer is "a noble task" *open to any qualified Christian man* (1 Timothy 3:1). He didn't need a "special calling"—like the original apostles or like Paul on the road to Damascus. Neither did he need to be "set apart" by some "prophetic message." Furthermore, he did not have to possess any special gift of the Spirit in order "to manage" and "shepherd" in a local church setting.

As we pointed out earlier, being "able to teach" (*didaktikos*) is not the "gift of teaching." Moreover, it would be inconsistent if Paul required the "gift of teaching" and said nothing about the "gift of pastoring" in order to be able to "shepherd God's flock"—a major responsibility for elders/overseers (Ephesians 4:12; 1 Peter 5:2). It would be even more inconsistent since Paul in this list of qualifications did not even require the "gift of *leadership*" (Romans 12:8), which is the same basic word Paul used to refer to being able to "manage [*proistemi*] his own family well" (1 Timothy 3:4–5). It would be indeed puzzling if Paul was requiring that a "father" would have to have the "gift of leadership" (*proistemi*) to be able to properly lead his family. This would certainly put "nongifted" fathers at a disadvantage.

The facts are that this "spiritual gift" was *not* a requirement. Rather, Paul was strongly implying that all Christian fathers should develop this "managing" and "shepherding" quality and skill so that they could indeed be good fathers. Then, if they functioned well in this way, they could be considered to serve as elders/overseers for the family of God.

This certainly does *not* mean the Holy Spirit was uninvolved—and is uninvolved today—in selecting elders/overseers and their assistants. In fact, the third person of the Trinity is *directly* involved when godly men and women prayerfully and carefully evaluate a potential leader's character, utilizing the Holy Spirit's inspired Word of God and at the same time, being sensitive to His personal presence and guidance in each of their lives. And the more this becomes a Spirit-directed "community effort," the more we can be sure we'll make right decisions in leadership selection. It should always be a very important divine and human process.

 OBSERVATION 9: *Apostolic Representatives*

> *Though Timothy and Titus assisted Paul as apostolic representatives in selecting and appointing leaders in Ephesus and the island of Crete, we're not told how other churches in the New Testament world have no record of having carried out this process.*

Observation 9 poses a very important question: How then were elders/overseers appointed in other churches?

OTHER APOSTOLIC REPRESENTATIVES

It's clear by implication that Paul delegated to Timothy (when he left his young partner in Ephesus) the responsibility of making sure only qualified men became elders/overseers (1 Timothy 3:1) And when the apostle left Titus in Crete, he made that assignment very specific (Titus 1:5). Beyond these references, we have no information in the biblical story as to who actually carried out this important task. However, we do have reference to a number of other men and women who served as apostolic representatives and could have participated in appointing local church leaders.

Barnabas and John Mark

When Barnabas separated from Paul, he and Mark traveled as a missionary team (Acts 15:39). We can certainly assume they continued to plant churches and appoint leaders. Furthermore, Barnabas had a powerful impact on John Mark. He eventually became an assistant to both Paul and Peter (1 Peter 5:13). During Paul's first imprisonment in Rome, Mark was by his side and possibly headed for Colossae to minister to the church in that city (Colossians 4:10). And when Paul was incarcerated a second time and wrote his final letter to Timothy, he asked Timothy to join him and to bring John Mark along to help Paul in his ministry (2 Timothy 4:11).

Aquila and Priscilla

When Paul greeted Priscilla and Aquila in his letter to the Romans, he called this couple his "fellow workers in Christ Jesus" and also mentioned that *"all the churches of the Gentiles"* were deeply thankful for their ministry (Romans 16:3–4). Since so many churches were grateful for their ministry, it's possible that "together" they helped appoint elders/overseers in these communities of faith, just as they "together" helped Apollos understand more fully the Gospel of Jesus Christ (Acts 18:24–26).

Apollos

Apollos was a brilliant Old Testament scholar. After being discipled by Aquila and Priscilla, he traveled to Corinth and helped the Jews, particularly in understanding that Jesus was indeed the promised Messiah (Acts 18:27–28). A number of years later, when Paul wrote his letter to Titus, he encouraged Titus to "do everything" he could to help Apollos with his travel plans (Titus 3:13). He certainly could have appointed elders/overseers in various churches.

Tychicus and Artemas

When Paul wrote to Titus when he was in Crete appointing elders/overseers, he mentioned that he was going to send either Artemas or Tychicus to replace him when he left to join Paul in Nicopolis (Titus 3:12). In other words, Paul had so much confidence in Tychicus that he was willing to entrust him with the very difficult task Titus had begun—to make sure that only spiritually qualified men led the churches in Crete (see also Acts 20:4; Ephesians 6:21–22; Colossians 4:7). And though this is the only reference to Artemas in the New Testament, we can certainly conclude that he had the same qualifications as Tychicus.

Andronicus and Junius and Others

When Paul concluded his letter to the Roman Christians with a series of greetings, he also mentioned two people who many commentators believe were another husband and wife team:[2] "Greet Andronicus and Junias, my relatives who have been in prison with me. *They are outstanding among the apostles,* and they were in Christ before I was" (Romans 16:7).

Here Paul used the term "apostles" the same way as he identified Silas and Timothy in his first letter to the Thessalonians (2:6). It would not be surprising, then, that this husband and wife team, just like Aquila and Priscilla, assisted Paul in selecting and appointing elders/overseers in local churches.

There are a number of other godly men mentioned by Paul who definitely could have functioned as apostolic representatives in appointing spiritual leaders in local churches: Sopater from Berea (Acts 20:4), Aristarchus and Secundus from Thessalonica (20:4), Gaius from Derbe (20:4), Trophimus from Ephesus (20:4; 21:29), and Urbanus (Romans 16:9).

THE CHURCH IN MINIATURE

In re-creating what happened regarding leadership appointments in New Testament churches, we must remember that often whole households were converted to Christ and each family unit became a "church in miniature." In other words, a local church actually began with one extended family. This may have happened in Colossae when Philemon became the first convert to Christianity—along with his whole household, including his servants. In this case, Philemon may have automatically served in a dual role—as a devoted father and, eventually, as a dedicated elder/overseer.[3]

APPOINTED LEADERS

Self-Appointed Leaders

In some instances, certain men emerged and began to function as elders/overseers, whether or not they were officially recognized. In other words, they were "self-appointed." At times, this probably worked well when these men had pure motives and were qualified. In other instances, it was a tragedy—which happened in Crete. This was a major reason Paul left Titus on the island to appoint qualified elders/overseers and to silence those who were already "ruining whole households by teaching things they ought not to teach—and that for the sake of dishonest gain" (Titus 1:11). As self-appointed leaders, they were doing more harm than good.

Leaders Appointing Leaders

When qualified elders/overseers had already been appointed in particular locations, they no doubt selected and appointed others to serve with them. In fact, they may have carried out this responsibility in other geographical areas, reaching out beyond their own local churches to assist others with this awesome task. For example, it's possible that the elders in Jerusalem selected and appointed spiritual leaders in other churches in Judea, and the elders/overseers in Ephesus may have done the same in some of the churches in Asia that came into existence because of Paul's ministry in the school of Tyrannus.

Congregations Appointing Leaders

There are some who assume that elders/overseers were somehow selected and appointed in these various New Testament churches by an official "congregational vote." We know this approach emerged at some point in church history, but it would have been virtually impossible for churches to function this way during the early years of the church since it takes strong spiritual leadership in the first place to develop a body of Christians who are mature enough to make this kind of decision. In other words, local groups of believers don't simply "organize themselves" around spiritual values without intense spiritual guidance.

Which Approach?

Which approach to appointing leaders is correct? It's clear from the biblical story that there is no specific methodology spelled out for appointing spiritual leaders, either for elders/overseers or deacons. Regarding deacons, Paul *did* say that "they must first be tested; and *then* if there is nothing against them, let them serve as deacons" (1 Timothy 3:10). However, we have no *specific instructions as to how to test these men and women.* Rather, Paul simply gave Timothy—and us—qualifications, guidelines, and principles, trusting that those of us who read his letters will develop approaches that indeed evaluate whether or not an individual is spiritually qualified to serve.

NOTES

1. This combined profile is taken from Gene A. Getz, *The Measure of a Man*, rev. ed. (Ventura, Calif.: Regal, 1995). 30. Notice that the qualifications are listed as they appear in the *New American Standard Bible*. To compare the list in Paul's letter to Timothy with the list in his letter to Titus, see figure 7, page 157–58 in this volume.

2. C. E. B. Cranfield, *Romans: A Shorter Commentary* (Grand Rapids: Eerdmans, 1985), 377; Leon Morris, *The Epistles to the Romans* (Grand Rapids: Eerdmans, 1988), 553. See William J. Webb, *Slaves, Women & Homosexuals: Exploring the Hermeneutics of Cultural Analysis* (Downers Grove, Ill.: InterVarsity, 2001), 99.

3. See also references to the "household of Stephanas" (1 Corinthians 16:15), the "household of Aristobulus" (Romans 16:10), the "household of Narcissus" (Romans 16:11), and the "household of Onesiphorus" (2 Timothy 4:19). It's feasible that all of these men naturally became the first elders/overseers in the churches that conceivably emerged from these extended households.

PLURALITY
IN LEADERSHIP

OBSERVATION 10: *A Unified Team*

As the biblical story unfolds in the New Testament, it becomes increasingly clear that each local church was to be managed and shepherded by a unified team of godly men.

Observation 10 emerges from the plural references to leaders in various local churches throughout the New Testament world. Note the following as they appear chronologically in the biblical story:

☐ The *elders* in Jerusalem (Acts 11:30).

☐ "He should call the *elders* of the church" (James 5:14).

☐ "Paul and Barnabas appointed *elders* for them in each church" (Acts 14:23).

□ The apostles and *elders* in Jerusalem (Acts 15:2, 4, 6, 22, 23).

□ "*Those* who work hard among you, who are *over you* in the Lord . . . hold them in the highest regard" (1 Thessalonians 5:12–13).

□ "Paul sent to Ephesus for the *elders* of the church" (Acts 20:17).

□ "Keep watch over *yourselves* and all the flock of which the Holy Spirit has made you *overseers*" (Acts 20:28a).

□ "Be *shepherds* of the church of God" (Acts 20:28b).

□ "All the *elders* [in Jerusalem] were present" (Acts 21:18).

□ "If anyone sets his heart on being an *overseer,* he desires a noble task" (1 Timothy 3:1).

□ "Now the *overseer* must be above reproach" (1 Timothy 3:2).

□ "The *elders* who direct the affairs of the church well are worthy of double honor" (1 Timothy 5:17).

□ "Do not entertain an accusation against an *elder* unless it is brought by two or three witnesses. *Those* who sin are to be rebuked publicly, so that the *others* may take warning" (1 Timothy 5:19–20).

□ "To the elders among you, I appeal as a fellow elder. . . . Be *shepherds* of God's flock that is under your care, serving as *overseers*" (1 Peter 5:1–2).

□ "Appoint *elders* in every town. . . . An *elder* must be blameless" (Titus 1:5–6).

□ "Since an *overseer* is entrusted with God's work, he must be blameless" (Titus 1:7).

□ "Obey your *leaders* and submit to their authority" (Hebrews 13:17).

In this unfolding set of references to local church leaders, the overall profile demonstrates that God's ideal plan was that every local church should be led by more than one elder/overseer. (Note the way Paul and Peter used the plural concept when referring to a single elder/overseer in 1 Timothy 3:1, 2; 5:19–20; Titus 1:5–7; 1 Peter 5:1.)

THE NEW TESTAMENT SETTING

To understand how plurality in leadership worked in the New Testament culture, we must avoid superimposing our contemporary, Western forms on first-century churches. In contrast to the multitude of "local churches" we have in a given population center, every mention of multiple leaders in the New Testament is made in reference to a *single church* in a *single city or town*. In the biblical story, there was only *one church* in Jerusalem, in Antioch of Syria, in Lystra, in Iconium, in Antioch of Pisidia, in Thessalonica, and in Ephesus. This is also why Paul told Titus to remain in Crete in order to "appoint *elders in every town*" (Titus 1:5). These churches were composed of all believers who lived within a particular geographical location. Though they may have met for teaching, fellowship, and worship at different locations throughout a particular city, they were still considered *one church* led by a *single body of elders*.[1]

This, of course, is a totally different structural arrangement from what we have in many cultures today. If we live in a large city—or even a small town—we often encounter different groups of believers from different denominations, who meet in buildings right across the street from each other. Furthermore, each local group has its own "board of governance"—even within "groups" that are part of the same denomination in a given city.

How, then, did the body of elders in each geographical location in the New Testament world manage the church and shepherd the people? Without being present to observe and experience this process firsthand, we can only speculate as to *how* New Testament leaders actually functioned. However, this lack of detail in the New Testament should not frustrate us. It's by divine design. God wants believers in various cultural settings to be able to create a multiple leadership plan that will function effectively regardless of whether we live in the first century of the church or the twenty-first.

THE CHURCH IN JERUSALEM:
A FUNCTIONAL PERSPECTIVE

Against this backdrop, let's look at what we *do* know from the biblical story. The "church in Jerusalem" began with three thousand baptized believers who initially met in two places—the temple courts and in their homes (Acts 2:46). The temple courts were used by the apostles especially to teach and proclaim the message of Christ to large groups of Jews as they normally gathered for religious activities. But in order to devote "themselves to the apostles' teaching and to the fellowship," believers met in homes all over Jerusalem (Acts 2:42–47). However, after Stephen's martyrdom and the "great persecution [that] broke out against the church at Jerusalem" (8:1), the temple courts became off-limits. Believers had no choice but to meet in their homes scattered throughout the city. Even then it became difficult to meet. When "Saul began to destroy the church," he went "from *house* to *house*, [and] dragged off men and women and put them in prison" (8:3).

In terms of architecture, some of these residences were relatively small and some were very large—with a variety in-between. This became very obvious to me personally when I began conducting tours to Israel. On several occasions, we visited the magnificent outdoor model of Jerusalem that represents this ancient city as it virtually existed during the time Jesus walked its streets. As I've stood on the "eastern side" of this model, viewing Herod's temple and the variety of homes clustered on the hills of Jerusalem, I've opened my Bible and read with new meaning:

> They devoted themselves to the apostles' teaching and to the fellowship, to the breaking of bread and to prayer. . . . Every day they continued to meet together in the *temple courts*. They broke bread in their *homes* and ate together with glad and sincere hearts (Acts 2:42, 46).

What was even more enlightening, however, was the opportunity to visit the underground excavations near the Temple Mount. Archeologists have discovered several large residences measuring in excess of six thousand square feet, with up to twenty rooms. Though totally covered with dirt and debris as a result of the Roman invasion in A.D. 70, when the temple was also destroyed, these excavated rooms are basically intact. One of these homes, or one like it, could have certainly belonged to Mary where many believers were meeting that day when Peter was miraculously delivered from prison (see Acts 12:11–17).

MOVING BEYOND JERUSALEM

Using private residences as meeting places became even more necessary as churches were established in cities that were populated primarily by Gentiles. Though Paul and his traveling companions often entered local synagogues in cities where they had a contingent of Jews, their message was eventually rejected. For example, in Ephesus, Paul eventually faced serious opposition and began to meet in the "lecture hall of Tyrannus" where he continued to speak daily about Jesus Christ.

In many respects, this "lecture hall" provided an environment similar to that existing earlier in the temple courts in Jerusalem. Just as the temple area provided a place for the apostles to preach and teach the message of Christ in a Judaic setting, so the lecture hall of Tyrannus provided the same opportunity for Paul to communicate the Gospel to thousands of people who came to Ephesus from all over Asia. As a result, many became believers and apparently returned to their hometowns and cities and started churches. But again, these believers had only one place to meet for worship and fellowship—in their homes. In fact, we have no record of special buildings being used for Christian worship in the Roman Empire "until the middle or end of the third century."[2]

ORGANIZATIONAL QUESTIONS

At this point, we need to address the basic question regarding the functions of elders/overseers. How did these men actually organize their shepherding ministry in these various cities and villages? Was one elder/overseer assigned to a particular "house church"? Were several elders/overseers assigned to a larger "house church"? Or was one elder/overseer asked to serve two or more smaller "house churches"? (See figure 9 for

Figure 9
Leadership Structure in Four Early Churches

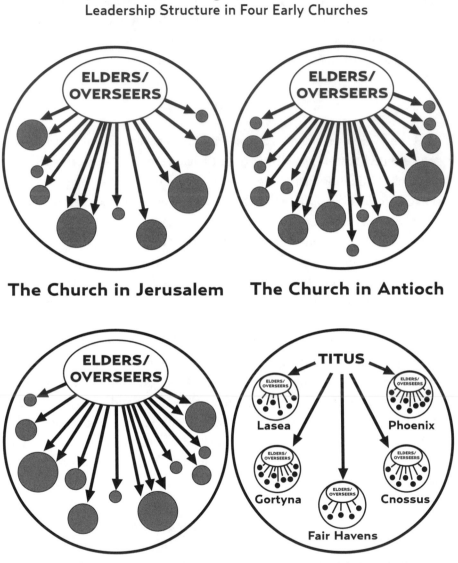

The Church in Jerusalem   The Church in Antioch

The Church in Ephesus   The Churches in Crete

the leadership structure in the churches of Jerusalem, Antioch, Ephesus, and Crete.)

These are "form issues," and the biblical story doesn't answer these questions. However, if a home was large enough to house hundreds of people, it would certainly take more than one elder/overseer to shepherd these believers effectively. Archeologists have discovered residences in some locations in the Roman Empire that could actually seat up to five hundred people in the garden room alone. This may describe a family complex owned by a well-to-do man like Cornelius in Caesarea or Philemon in Colossae.

Clearly, the Scriptures do not describe forms—only functions. The reason is just as evident. Elders/overseers are free to develop approaches that will enable them to function effectively as managers/shepherds in their own cultures. Furthermore, as the church grows numerically, so should the group of elders/overseers in order to manage effectively. But this poses a "form question" that we'll address in chapter 35: In order to function effectively, how large should a group of elders/overseers become in the average church today?

QUALIFIED LEADERS ONLY

Even though the New Testament teaches and illustrates plurality in leadership, this doesn't mean the apostles and their assistants appointed more than one elder/overseer in a given local church just to have more than one spiritual leader. Rather, they were to be appointed *only* if they were qualified to serve in this position. This is certainly why there are no references to these leaders in Antioch of Syria or in Corinth, two very pagan Gentile communities. It took years for men and their families to become mature enough to measure up to the spiritual criteria outlined by Paul for elders/overseers.

NOTES

1. Since there was only a "single local church" identified within a "single city or town" in the New Testament, there are some who believe that it's God's will that there can only be "one recognized local church" in a given city today. Unfortunately, they have missed the whole point regarding

"freedom in form." In fact, they're attempting to transport the New Testament culture into their own, wherever that might be, which certainly is an unfortunate interpretation of Scripture.

2. Graydon F. Snyder, *Ante Pacem Archeological Evidence for the Church Before Constantine* (Macon, Ga.: Mercer University Press, 1985), 166.

THE NEED FOR
A PRIMARY LEADER

 **OBSERVATION 11:** *A Primary Leader*

> *The New Testament definitely teaches and illustrates that when there is a plurality of leadership, someone needs to function as the primary leader of the team.*

It may be surprising to learn that the biblical story of local church leadership offers little data to make the specific observation that someone must function as the primary leader. However, we must remember that this story is not a self-contained historical unit. Taken out of context, it can lead to some very erroneous and impractical conclusions. In order to understand the accuracy of this observation, it's imperative that we have a *total biblical perspective.*

Jesus' Equipping Ministry

The Focus on Peter

When Jesus ascended from the Mount of Olives, He did not leave a "leaderless group" of apostles. Rather, Simon Peter was clearly their leader and spokesman, and John became his associate. While on earth, Jesus Himself had served as their primary leader. But during this time, He had taken nearly three years to prepare all of them to carry out the Great Commission. But, at the same time, He focused His efforts on equipping Peter to be their leader once He returned to the Father.

When Matthew, Mark, and John recorded their Gospels, and Luke recorded his Gospel and the book of Acts, they mentioned Peter's name dozens of times more than the other apostles (see figure 10). And when they recorded the "events" involving Peter, these episodes *far exceed* the number of events involving any other apostle. For example, Peter is mentioned specifically in fifty-seven events compared with his brother Andrew who is mentioned in only eight events (see figure 11).

Of course, many more events could have been recorded about Jesus and His association with these men (John 21:25), but we can assume that what has been recorded represents what actually happened in the larger setting. Clearly, Jesus focused on equipping Peter to be the primary leader. Furthermore, he focused next on John who was to be his associate (note again the statistics in figures 10 and 11).

An Ingenious Strategy

When Jesus eventually called Peter to leave his role in the fishing business, this rugged Galilean was already the primary leader in this enterprise. His brother, Andrew, and his friends James and John were called his "partners" (Luke 5:7, 10). From a strategic point of view, the fact that Jesus initially chose these four men first was ingenious. The social and psychological infrastructure for this new leadership team was already in place. Andrew, James, and John already looked to Peter as their leader. Furthermore, when Jesus added other men to this team, Peter already stood out as the man who would eventually lead them all.

Figure 10
Number of Times the Twelve Apostles' Names
Appear in the Gospels and the Book of Acts

APOSTLES	THE GOSPELS	THE BOOK OF ACTS	TOTAL TIMES
Peter (Simon), Cephas	117	72	189
John	35	15	50
James	16	2	18
Andrew	12	1	13
Philip	16	1	17
Bartholomew (Nathaniel)	0	1	1
Thomas	10	1	11
Matthew (Levi)	8	1	9
James, son of Alphaeus	6	1	7
Thaddaeus (Judas)	3	1	4
Simon, the Zealot	3	1	4
Judas Iscariot	20	2	22

Figure 11
Number of Events that Focus on Each Apostle
In the Gospels and the Book of Acts

APOSTLES	EVENTS* IN THE GOSPELS	EVENTS IN ACTS	TOTAL EVENTS
Peter	35	22	57
John	19	9	28
James	10	2	12
Andrew	7	1	8
Philip	6	1	7
Bartholomew (Nathaniel)	3	1	4
Thomas	6	1	7
Matthew (Levi)	3	1	4
James, son of Alphaeus	2	1	3
Thaddaeus (Judas)	1	1	2
Simon, the Zealot	1	1	2
Judas Iscariot	7	2	9

*These are not duplicated "events" in the four Gospels.

The Upper Room

When the apostles returned to Jerusalem following Christ's ascension and entered the Upper Room, "Peter stood up among the believers" (Acts 1:15) and led them in making a decision to replace Judas. Jesus had prepared him for this moment, and everyone among the one hundred twenty in that room knew that Peter was their leader. Jesus' prayers for this man had been answered. After being tried and tested by Satan—and even after he had denied the Lord three times—he was now able to strengthen and lead his "brothers" (Luke 22:31–32). Though they were his fellow shepherds, they were still sheep and also needed a shepherd (John 21:15–17). Peter was to be that man.

PETER ON PENTECOST

Though Jesus' ultimate purpose in calling these twelve men was not clear in their minds until He had ascended and sent the Holy Spirit, all of them were ready to respond to Peter's leadership. When he stood up on the Day of Pentecost and explained from the prophet Joel what was happening, not one of the apostles hesitated to follow him. Even James and John had a new perspective. They never again tried to do an "end-run" around Peter, trying to maneuver themselves into a position of power. And even James, John's eldest brother, took a backseat to his younger brother who now assisted Peter in those early days of the church. Again and again, we read that "Peter and John" took the lead and, even though these two men worked closely together, they were not coleaders. Peter was continually the primary spokesman, and John stood by his side affirming and confirming the message of Christ's death and resurrection.[1]

BECOMING SERVANT-LEADERS

Even after this high and lofty moment in Peter's life, he still had a lot of growing to do as a spiritual leader. And, as his ministry continued, he learned more and more about what Jesus had meant when He taught the first disciples about servant-leadership. This is why toward the end of his life, Peter could write to the elders/overseers in various churches and appeal to them "as a fellow elder" (1 Peter 5:1).

We see this same relationship with the other apostles. Though Peter was definitely their leader, he was also a man under authority. When Philip went to Samaria and preached the Gospel and saw many people become believers, we read the following: "When the *apostles* in Jerusalem heard that Samaria had accepted the word of God, *they sent Peter and John* to them" (Acts 8:14).

This is a very important observation. Though Peter was definitely equipped and prepared to be the leader of these men, and did so with confidence, he never forgot Jesus' words in the Upper Room at the Passover meal—that he who is greatest is to be a servant. He did not act unilaterally without seeking advice and counsel and affirmation. He was definitely a servant-leader.

More Missionary Teams

We see the same dynamic when the Holy Spirit assembled leadership teams to venture into the Gentile world. At first, it was Barnabas and Saul (later called Paul) with John Mark as their assistant. Initially, Barnabas was in the driver's seat. But once they left Cyprus, it was "Paul and his companions" who traveled on to the Galatian region (13:13). And on the next journey, it was once again Paul who led, this time with three other "companions"—Silas, Timothy, and Luke (see figure 12).

James and the Jerusalem Elders

In terms of a primary leader, we see this beginning to happen in the church in Jerusalem when James, the half brother of Christ, emerged as the key leader among the elders in Jerusalem. When Peter was released from prison and went to Mary's house, he definitely acknowledged James' leadership role (Acts 12:17). Furthermore, during the council meeting when they were resolving the law/grace controversy, Peter represented the apostles (15:7–11) and James represented the Jerusalem elders (15:13–21).

Figure 12
Paul's Team Ministry in the Book of Acts

THE TEXT	TEAM MEMBERS	MAIN GEOGRAPHICAL POINTS
13:1–13	Barnabas, Paul, and Mark	From Antioch to Paphos to Perga
13:14–14:28	Paul and Barnabas	Perga to the Galatian cities and back to Antioch
15:1–35	Paul and Barnabas	From Antioch to Jerusalem and back to Antioch
15:39–16:1	Paul and Silas	Antioch to Lystra
16:2–8	Paul, Silas, and Timothy	Lystra to Troas
16:9–40	Paul, Silas, Timothy, and Luke	Troas to Philippi
17:1–15	Paul, Silas, and Timothy	Philippi to Berea
17:16–18:4	Paul	Athens to Corinth
18:5–17	Paul, Silas, and Timothy	Corinth to Ephesus
18:18	Paul, Priscilla, and Aquila	Ephesus to Antioch
18:19–22	Paul	Antioch to Ephesus
18:23–20:1	Paul, Timothy, and Erastus	Ephesus to Philippi
20:2–4	Secundus, Gaius, Timothy, Tychicus and Trophimus	
20:5–23:30	Paul and Luke	Philippi to Jerusalem
23:31–26:32	Paul	Jerusalem to Caesarea
27:1–28:29	Paul and Luke	Caesarea to Rome
27:30–31	Paul	Two years in Rome

And years later when Paul returned to Jerusalem, he went first "to see James, and *all* the elders were present" (21:18). Call him what you will, James clearly served as the primary leader.

Timothy and Titus

Both Timothy and Titus also illustrate how important it is to have a primary leader in any given situation. In these New Testament settings, they were apostolic representatives. Though their positions were not permanent in local churches, they definitely took charge in Ephesus and in Crete to make sure that qualified leaders were appointed. Based on what we see in the total biblical story of leadership, we can only assume that they were also influential in making sure a key leader was in charge—a man who could be trusted to lead the other elders as a servant-leader.

It's God's design—from the time He chose men like Moses, Joshua, Samuel, and Nehemiah in the Old Testament, and Peter, Paul, Timothy, and Titus in the New Testament—to always have a key leader in place to lead His people. Why would we think differently when it involves elders/overseers in a local church? Those who respond to this question by explaining that a proper view of "spiritual gifts" makes it possible to function as a leadership team without a primary leader must also explain why there are no references to these "gifts" in the qualifications for elders/overseers in the Pastoral Epistles.

An Open-Ended Story

As stated earlier, the biblical story of local church leadership as recorded in the book of Acts and in the New Testament letters is "open-ended" and must not be taken out of context and made to stand alone. Jesus set the stage for the ministry of local church elders/overseers in His equipping ministry with the apostles. With Peter as their leader, they were a prototype for bodies of elders/overseers in local churches. Though we're not told who led the elders/overseers on a permanent basis after Timothy, Titus, and other apostolic representatives left and went on to other churches, we can assume it happened immediately or shortly thereafter. When the New Testament ends and the apostles and their representatives passed off the scene, we can be sure that those men who were designated as primary leaders didn't suddenly appear overnight. They were already in place, which is clear in some of the letters written by the early church fathers.

We must remember that James modeled this leadership role with the Jerusalem elders. Though James was never given a specific title in the New Testament to recognize his unique leadership role, nevertheless, others who "functioned in this role" later would be identified as *episkopoi*—overseers or bishops.

A CHANGE IN DEFINITION AND FUNCTION:
THE LETTERS OF IGNATIUS

We do not encounter a change in definition and function until we read the letters of Ignatius, who himself served as the second "bishop" of Antioch in Syria. Written at some point near the end of the first century, these letters were not considered inspired Scripture. However, they have nevertheless been established as very authentic, giving us a very accurate picture of what happened in various churches when the "biblical story" ends.

As you read these letters, it becomes obvious that Ignatius faced deep concerns about false teachers and their impact on the doctrine and unity in the churches. Imagine for a moment facing these issues without the Scriptures as we have them today. Furthermore, the apostles, including John (who may have mentored Ignatius), had passed off the scene. Those claiming to be "apostles" and "prophets" and "teachers" were everywhere, often leading people astray.

A Three-Tier System

Facing the results of what he considered a deteriorating situation, Ignatius moved the church toward a three-tier system of leadership. The primary leader of the elders/overseers in various churches in the early years of Christianity became "the bishop." Using the freedom we see in the New Testament story to use different terminology to identify spiritual leaders, Ignatius redefined the term *episkopos* to refer only to the primary leader of "the elders." In other words, the "presbytery" or "the body of elders" reported directly to a single "bishop," and the "deacons" in local churches basically reported to the "elders" and assisted them as well as "the bishop" with their ministries. As this change took place, the "bishop" in a believing community began to take on more and more authority, particularly because of Ignatius' teachings (see "Ignatius' Initial Model of Influence," figure 13).[2]

Under Ignatius' influence, this hierarchical structure impacted churches throughout the New Testament world. Onesimus became the "bishop of Ephesus" and Polycarp the "bishop of Smyrna" and Clement became the "bishop of Rome"—to name a few of the most well known. Unfortunately,

Figure 13
Ignatius' Initial Model of Influence

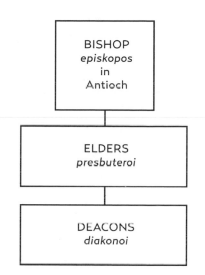

BISHOP
episkopos
in
Antioch

ELDERS
presbuteroi

DEACONS
diakonoi

this system set the stage for some of the serious leadership abuses that have haunted Christianity for centuries (see "Ignatius' Expanded Model of Influence," figure 14).

On the other hand, just because Ignatius developed an approach to leadership that was and still is out of harmony with biblical principles, it does not mean a body of elders/overseers in a particular local church do not need a primary leader. "Shepherds" need a "shepherd" who will follow the example of the Great Shepherd, Jesus Christ Himself, who came not to be served, but to serve. Practically speaking, this means a primary shepherd should be a servant-leader.

NOTES

1. As stated previously, "name order" is very important in Scripture when determining who is a primary leader in a particular situation. Matthew made this point emphatically by actually saying —"These are the names of the twelve apostles: *first* [*protos*], Simon (who is called Peter)" (Matthew 10:2). This Greek term actually means "foremost either in time, place, order, or importance" (see also Acts 1:13). Also in the book of Acts, again and again, Luke mentioned Peter's name first when he (Peter) and John ministered together in the early days of the church (Acts 3:1, 3, 11; 4:1, 3, 7, 13, 19, 23). Note also that he was again and again the primary spokesman (2:14-40; 3:4, 6, 12–26; 4:8–12; 5:3–9).

Figure 14
Ignatius' Expanded Model of Influence

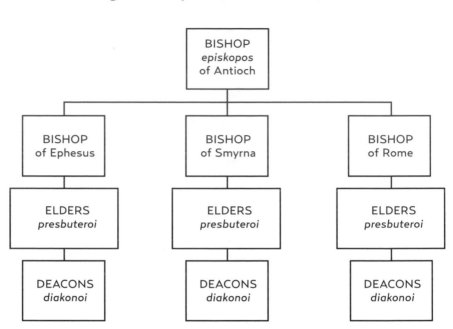

2. In "The Teaching of The Apostles" (often called the *Didache*), there is no reference to the three-tier system developed and practiced by Ignatius; however, whoever authored this document used the terms "bishops" and "deacons" rather than "elders" and "deacons." Obviously, this still reflects what we read in the New Testament story. It seems to place the date of writing late in the first century, but certainly before Ignatius wrote his letters.

We can say the same about local church leaders in the letters written by Clement of Rome. He too used the term "bishops" rather than "elders." Though he argues that believers should respect these men, he does not present the same level of authority and control as Ignatius. *The Early Church Fathers*, ed. and trans. Henry Betenson (Oxford, N.Y.: Oxford University Press, 1956), "The Teaching of The Apostles (The Didache)," 50–52; "Clemens Romanus (Clement of Rome)," 29–39.

ACCOUNTABILITY, DELEGATION, AND FORMS

OBSERVATION 12: *Accountability*

In the early years of the church, there was accountability for elders/overseers among themselves and also beyond their local ministry.

E lders/overseers were to maintain accountability among themselves. Paul made this very clear to the Ephesian elders when he exhorted: "Keep watch over yourselves. . . . Even from your own number men will arise and distort the truth in order to draw away disciples after them" (Acts 20:28, 30).

However, there was definitely accountability beyond themselves. In fact, Paul illustrated this need when he met with the Ephesian elders at Miletus and delivered the charge to be mutually accountable (see Acts 20:17–18, 28–30). It all began in Jerusalem in the early years of the church. Peter and John were influential leaders, perhaps appointing elders/overseers. But this apostolic authority extended beyond Jerusalem when the apostles agreed among themselves to send Peter and John to Samaria to follow up Philip's ministry (Acts 8:14–17). Notice, then, that these two great leaders did not act unilaterally.

ACCOUNTABILITY IN PAUL'S DAY AND BEYOND

We have more information regarding this kind of accountability when we follow Paul on his missionary journeys and read his letters. For example, when he wrote to the Corinthians, he did not hesitate to use his God-given authority as an apostle to exhort them and hold them accountable. As he closed out his second letter, he reminded them that this would be his "third visit" to see them: "I already gave you a warning when I was with you the second time. I now repeat it while absent: On my return I will not spare those who sinned earlier or any of the others, since you are demanding proof that Christ is speaking through me" (2 Corinthians 13:2–3).

This, of course, is apostolic authority. And when he authorized Timothy and Titus to appoint elders/overseers and to hold them accountable, he delegated this authority to these apostolic representatives.

Once the apostles and their direct representatives passed off the scene, we have very little biblical information as to how this kind of accountability continued to happen, particularly in the latter part of the first century. However, the moment we read the letters of Ignatius, it's clear that local bishops had already emerged and were giving leadership to the elders/overseers in given cities.

During the time Ignatius functioned as the bishop of Antioch, he eventually extended his authority to influence and teach other local church leaders how to function. At this time, his letters became very influential. As Hansen noted, "The development of hierarchical structure in the church takes another momentous change in the letters of Ignatius of Antioch. Whereas the bishops and presbyters were the same in *1 Clement*, Ignatius viewed 'the bishop presiding in the place of God and the presbyters in the place of the council of the apostles' and the deacons doing Jesus Christ's service."[1]

As second- and third-century church history unfolded, we can trace how this "hierarchy" emerged, which often led to serious theological errors and an abuse of power that continues in various ways in some denominational structures even to this day. Regardless, this distortion does not eliminate the need for elders/overseers to have "some accountability" beyond themselves.

OBSERVATION 13: *Delegation*

The New Testament teaches that elders/overseers must maintain their priorities by delegating responsibilities to other qualified men and women who can assist them in managing and shepherding the church.

In the biblical story, the first leadership appointments in local churches always involved men who could give overall spiritual direction (Acts 14:23; Titus 1:5). However, as each church grew in numbers and responsibilities increased, these spiritual leaders were to appoint qualified men and women who could assist them in carrying out their priority responsibilities.

DELEGATED AUTHORITY

In the New Testament

In the New Testament, these assistants were called "deacons," although the Scriptures focus on functions, not titles. In essence, deacons were to serve in any way they could to enable elders/overseers to concentrate on their own priority ministries.

When appointing assistants, however, the Scriptures also make it clear that men and women who are entrusted with this kind of responsibility are, in essence, to be just as qualified as elders/overseers. The reasons are obvious. To delegate responsibilities to people who are not qualified spiritually will not "lighten the load" for spiritual leaders. Rather, it will only complicate their ministry.

In the Old Testament

Delegated authority by spiritual leaders appears at key places in the Old Testament story. In Exodus, we have a very dramatic illustration of why it is important to delegate to qualified assistants. As the children of Israel camped in the wilderness after coming out of Egypt, Moses was attempting to handle all of their problems alone—a superhuman task! His father-in-law gave him some good advice. In order to keep from being overwhelmed physically and emotionally, Moses was to "select capable men" to assist him—"men who *fear God, trustworthy men who hate dishonest gain*" (Exodus 18:21).

Moses took this advice, which enabled him to make sure the needs of the people were met and at the same time to maintain his own priorities—to represent them before God and "to teach" them God's laws and decrees.

Imagine what would have happened if Moses had appointed assistants who were not qualified—dishonest and self-serving men who would have taken advantage of the people. His problems would have been multiplied many times. Just so, elders/overseers are to delegate responsibilities to highly qualified men and women who will do everything they can to enable these spiritual leaders to maintain their priorities in ministry.

OBSERVATION 14: *Function and Form*

> *The biblical story on local church leadership does not describe specific "forms"—only "functions" and "directives."*

As we've said so often throughout this study, the biblical emphasis on functions and directives over forms is by divine design. As with so many aspects of ecclesiology, the New Testament does not prescribe or even describe various "forms" for applying the "supracultural principles" that emerge from this study. This, of course, is what makes the biblical story so unique. Only the Holy Spirit could superintend this writing project that involved several key authors and spans so many years from Pentecost (A.D. 33) to the documents that were penned in the '90s.

This is what makes the message of Christianity—rightly interpreted —supracultural. It is not an ethnic religion that is so intertwined with its culture that it can only function within that culture. In other words, Christians can "function" and practice biblical Christianity anywhere in the world and at any moment in history because we have freedom to develop those unique "forms" that enable us to be truly Christian without changing the essence of the biblical message. As we'll see, this applies to the way local church leaders function in various cultures of the world.

NOTE

1. G. W. Hansen, "Authority," *Dictionary of the Later New Testament and Its Developments*, ed. Ralph P. Martin and Peter H. Davids (Downers Grove, Ill.: InterVarsity, 1997), 109 (Ign. *Magn.* 6.1). Hansen added that "the authority of the bishop was absolute: members 'must follow the bishop as Jesus Christ followed the Father' (Ign. *Smyrn.* 8.1); they 'must regard the bishop as the Lord himself' (Ign. *Eph.* 6.1); . . . 'The one who does anything without the bishop's knowledge serves the devil' (Ign. *Smyrn.* 9.1). . . . The emphasis of Ignatius on the gradation of authority —presbyters subject to the bishop and deacons to the bishop and the presbyters—and on the absolute authority of the bishop places his letters at the extreme end of the trajectory toward the development of hierarchical authority in the church." G. W. Hansen, "Authority," 109–10.

PART FOUR

SUPRACULTURAL PRINCIPLES AND PRACTICAL APPLICATIONS

These final chapters are designed to help all of us move from first-century to twenty-first-century church leadership in order to create appropriate forms that (1) harmonize with biblical principles, (2) apply lessons we've learned from history, and (3) utilize both past and present cultural insights (as depicted in figure 1).

To practice a biblical approach to leadership, this must be a dynamic, ongoing process—reviewing the biblical story, evaluating past performances as reflected in history (including our own), and understanding our cultural milieu. What God has said, of course, is foundational. Hopefully, the principles we've outlined accurately articulate God's will as revealed in Scripture.

Part 4 represents not only what we believe these principles are but our efforts in practicing some of these scriptural guidelines. As you'll see, I've chosen to focus on what we've learned from our church-planting experiences over the last number of years. Though I'm gratified and rejoice regarding what we've "done right," I believe my most helpful illustrations will be those things we could have done better. (Note: In these closing chapters, I've used the term "elders" exclusively, since we have chosen this particular title in our ministry.)

As you read the following "principles," you can begin the evaluation process in your own ministry by answering two questions:

1. As you understand the biblical story, are these principles articulated accurately?

2. Assuming these principles *are* articulated accurately, how does your own approach to leadership reflect these principles?

Here are the *fourteen leadership principles* we have uncovered from the biblical story:

PRINCIPLE 1: *First Official Appointments*

When local churches are established, the first official appointments should be spiritual leaders who are able to give overall direction to the church; however, they should not be appointed until they are qualified.

PRINCIPLE 2: *A Unified Team*

The goal of every local church should be to eventually appoint qualified leaders who serve together as a unified team.

PRINCIPLE 3: *Qualifications*

All spiritual leaders should be appointed based on the maturity profile outlined by Paul in the Pastoral Epistles.

PRINCIPLE 4: *Basic Ethics and Morality*

When looking for qualified leaders to serve the church, consider first those men and their families who've grown up in an environment where their values have been shaped by Judeo-Christian ethics and morality.

PRINCIPLE 5: *An Initial Leader*

If there are no candidates in the church who are qualified to serve as official spiritual leaders, another qualified leader needs to serve in either a temporary or permanent role until others in the church are sufficiently equipped to serve in this role.

PRINCIPLE 6: *A Primary Leader*

Every group of spiritual leaders needs a primary leader who both leads and serves, and who is accountable to his fellow spiritual leaders.

PRINCIPLE 7: *Titles*

When determining "titles" for spiritual leaders in the local church, *how they function* is far more important than *what the local body calls them.*

PRINCIPLE 8: *Multiple Fathers*

Spiritual leaders should manage and shepherd the church just as fathers are to care for their families and shepherds are to tend their sheep.

PRINCIPLE 9: *Important Priorities*

All spiritual leaders should make sure they manage and shepherd the church well by maintaining six important priorities: teaching the Word of God, modeling Christlike behavior, maintaining doctrinal purity, disciplining unruly believers, overseeing the material needs of the church, and praying for the sick.

PRINCIPLE 10: *Mutual Accountability*

Spiritual leaders in the church should hold each other accountable for their spiritual lives as well as the way they carry out their ministries.

PRINCIPLE 11: *Expanded Accountability*

To follow the model that unfolds in the New Testament story, every body of local church leaders should have some kind of accountability system that extends beyond themselves—particularly involving the primary leader.

PRINCIPLE 12: *Qualified Assistants*

In order to maintain their priorities, spiritual leaders should appoint qualified assistants who can help them meet the needs of all believers in the church.

PRINCIPLE 13: *Financial Support*

Spiritual leaders are to make sure that those who devote significant amounts of time to the ministry, particularly in teaching the Word of God, should be cared for financially.

PRINCIPLE 14: *Adequate Forms*

Spiritual leaders are responsible to make sure that adequate forms are developed to carry out the functions inherent in the above biblical principles.

PRINCIPLES FOR LEADERSHIP APPOINTMENTS (PART 1)

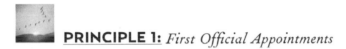

PRINCIPLE 1: *First Official Appointments*

When local churches are established, the first official appointments should be spiritual leaders who are able to give overall direction to the church; however, they should not be appointed until they are qualified.

WHEN IS IT TIME?

The length of time involved in applying Principle 1 will depend on several factors. First, Paul made it clear to Timothy in his first letter that any man appointed to the position of elder/overseer "must not be a recent convert, or he may become conceited and fall under the same judgment as the devil" (1 Timothy 3:6). If this should happen, it becomes disastrous for the individual and his family, and it can literally destroy the unity in the church.

Personally, I've seen this happen even when new Christians are platformed too quickly, particularly where they receive a lot of attention, even fame. Pride is subtle, and Satan is a master at using this sin to cause infant believers to self-destruct.

Maturity Takes Time

There is no "fast forward" way to produce maturity. Even Jesus took nearly three years to equip the apostles to fill their role. Even though they had Jewish backgrounds and basically understood the values taught in the Old Testament, it took a number of crisis experiences to deepen their commitment to Christ. It's true that they were dramatically changed after Jesus ascended and the Holy Spirit descended on the Day of Pentecost. However, it was not this unique experience per se that changed them. Rather, it was the years of preparation that enabled them to respond to the ministry of the Holy Spirit in their lives.

It takes even longer to equip men and their families for spiritual leadership when they have had pagan, secular, or non-Christian religious backgrounds. We've seen this in the churches in Antioch and Corinth. Just so, in some cultures today it will take years for men and women to develop the qualities Paul outlined in the Pastoral Letters.

A Marital Disaster

I remember one of the first appointments we made in the original Fellowship Bible Church. Though a few people had expressed concern regarding the health of this man's marriage, we proceeded to make him an elder. We knew there had been some problems in the past, but at that moment everything seemed to be in order. When we asked this couple about the situation, both the husband and the wife indicated they felt ready for this leadership role.

Unfortunately, some serious problems existed in this relationship that had never been resolved. Consequently, the man's marriage deteriorated and ended in divorce. It was a painful lesson for all of us—that nothing will jeopardize a marriage more than putting a husband and wife in this kind of shepherding role when they have serious unresolved issues in their marriage. Appointment to such a position will set the person up for an attack from Satan. This is one reason why Paul warned Timothy to "not be hasty in the laying on of hands" (1 Timothy 5:22).

Please don't misunderstand. This doesn't mean a couple has to have a perfect marriage. If so, no one would be qualified. However, it does mean there are some "relational wounds" that need more time to heal, and as a result of this experience, we soon learned that we needed a much more thorough process for selecting and appointing elders.

Older, but Not Ready

I vividly remember another personal experience that also illustrates why this principle is so important. A man who was attending seminary began to attend our church with his family. He was older than the average student since he had owned and operated his own business for a number of years. However, after he and his wife became Christians, they decided to sell their business in order to prepare for full-time ministry. Obviously, he was highly motivated to serve Jesus Christ. We sensed that it only seemed "logical" that this man, who I'll call James, would be qualified to be an elder in our church. After all, we were growing very rapidly and we needed men and their wives to "help shepherd the flock."

After serving as an elder for a period of time, James and his wife sat on the patio of our home one afternoon and shared with me the tension they were having in their relationship, primarily because the wife was not able to feel comfortable seeing him function in this role. It was then they revealed the whole story about James's background. Years earlier, he had kept two sets of books in his business—one set that was legal and the other that was illegal. With this "back room" arrangement, he was able to generate large sums of money. During these prosperous years, his wife had no idea that much of their income was generated through unlawful practices.

When James became a Christian, he confessed this sinful behavior to his wife and corrected the business problem through legal channels. During this time of significant spiritual growth, they decided to sell their beautiful home and go to seminary to prepare for full-time ministry. After arriving in Dallas, they discovered our church and became active.

However, after James began serving in an elder role and pastoring a small group of people, his wife began to experience lingering feelings of resentment, which began to impact their relationship. Though he had asked forgiveness, she could not relinquish those feelings of having been betrayed all those years. Furthermore, James confessed that even though he was serving as a spiritual leader in the church, he was not loving his wife and serving her as God intended.

Though we had moved too quickly with this appointment, the end of this story is very redemptive. I remember so well the evening they both came before the elders and shared their struggle—and why. James voluntarily and humbly submitted his resignation, and all of us as elders gathered around them as he and his wife knelt together. We laid our hands on them both and prayed for healing in their relationship.

Together this couple received counseling, enabling them to work through these issues. The most beautiful part of the story is that years later we received James back into eldership. God brought healing into this marriage, and this couple has served in a full-time ministry for years.

This story also illustrates once again why it's important to be cautious in appointing men and their wives to this shepherding role. Obviously, we should have discovered these issues *before* putting this couple in this vulnerable position. Fortunately, they faced this problem bravely and victoriously. Had they not, this premature appointment could have potentially set the stage for disillusionment, causing them to leave the ministry altogether.

James has since become a staff pastor. Looking back on these events many years ago, he reflected on his experience:

> As I think back on my resignation from being an elder, I am once again impacted by the healing process that took place. Though I was successful in business, I was not the loving, tender, godly husband the Scriptures implore all men to be. Through the pain of resignation I realized I had my priorities out of order. Biblically, I needed to put my wife before the work of the church. If I failed with her, I would

not be the husband 1 Timothy 3 described and hence, would never truly be qualified for ministry.

I also realized how important it was to have a "safe" environment in which to resign. I knew that I was loved, cared for, and that the elders had my family's best interests in mind. With this assurance, I had the freedom to resign, knowing it was the best thing for me. I can now see that if the safe environment were not in place, I could have resisted resignation. But being able to trust the leadership propelled me to take the necessary steps . . . and I'm glad today that I did.

A Grateful Pastor

PRINCIPLE 2: *A Unified Team*

The goal of every local church should be to eventually appoint qualified leaders who serve together as a unified team.

REASONS FOR A UNIFIED LEADERSHIP

When Jesus taught the apostles to love one another as He had loved them (John 13:34) and prayed that they would become one as He was one with the Father (17:20–21), our Lord laid the groundwork for the same dynamic among elders in local churches. Obviously, there are some very practical reasons for developing multiple leadership teams that reflect the same love and unity.

A More Effective Ministry

Having a number of godly shepherds in any given local church enables these men to carry out the shepherding ministry more effectively. Paul beautifully illustrated this dynamic when he, Silas, and Timothy served in Thessalonica. Because they were a team of three, they could function as parents in nurturing these new believers. Paul recorded that they "were gentle . . . , like a mother caring for her little children" and ministered to *each one* of these believers just "as a *father* deals with his own children" (1 Thessalonians 2:7, 11).

Multiple Models

A man who serves as an elder/overseer is to be (if married) a husband who is morally pure—a man who is loyal to one woman (his wife). And if he has children, he is to be a godly father who manages his family well. In this sense, he and his whole family will become a model to all believers. And when godly men and families are multiplied, there will be *multiple models* of spiritual maturity.

The Power of Love and Unity

Jesus made it clear that "oneness" among Christians sends a powerful message to unbelievers—that Jesus Christ is one with the Father and came to be the Savior of the world. This kind of unity among the apostles was to be a dynamic prototype for elders in every local church. When godly men, with the support of godly wives, manage and shepherd the church in love as a unified leadership team, it provides a dynamic example for all believers in terms of what the church is supposed to be. And when the church reflects the unity Jesus has with the Father, we will become a powerful witness in the world (John 17:23).

A Support System

No dynamic provides a greater sense of confidence for a primary leader and his family than to know that a group of godly men and their wives stand with him "with one heart and mind." On the other hand, nothing creates more insecurity, pain, and anxiety than leaders who are insensitive and unsupportive.

For years, I served with a very dedicated and qualified pastor on our staff who previously had served in another church as "senior pastor." Unfortunately, many of his elders were not godly leaders. Several men particularly thwarted my friend's sincere desires to lead the church to become a community of love and witness in the world. Sadly, this man used to come home after board meetings literally sick to his stomach. In fact, at times he would go into the restroom and regurgitate.

How tragic! I remember counseling him about this very difficult leadership position and ultimately invited him to join our staff as an associate where he was able to be a part of a group of people who were serving together in love and unity. This opportunity transformed his life and restored his motivation to carry out the Great Commission. He was and always had been a godly, sensitive, and caring pastor. Unfortunately, as Paul warned the Ephesian elders, some "wolves" had become a part of the leadership in the church, and the "primary shepherd" was their target (Acts 20:29–30). A team that supports each other will strengthen the ministry of a primary leader. Clearly an unsupportive team can undermine his ministry; conversely a unified team can energize the primary leader in fulfilling his shepherding responsibilities.

 **PRINCIPLE 3:** *Qualifications*

All spiritual leaders should be appointed based on the maturity profile outlined by Paul in the Pastoral Epistles.

EVALUATING LEADERSHIP QUALIFICATIONS

The New Testament does not give any specific methodology for applying the maturity profile found in the Scriptures. However, it's clear from the unfolding leadership story in the New Testament that selecting qualified leaders will require much careful thought, prayer, and hard work. Though the Holy Spirit at times—particularly during the early years of the church—revealed directly who should be set apart for leadership, this is the exception rather than the rule.

Misinterpreting "intuition" for the "voice of the Spirit" can lead to serious mistakes, particularly when it comes to judging character. Furthermore, most people who are being evaluated normally and naturally attempt to give positive first impressions, which definitely affects our initial conclusions. This is why God has given us a *very specific and objective standard* for evaluating spiritual maturity (found in 1 Timothy 3:1–7 and Titus 1:5–9).

A Beginning Point

When I helped launch the first Fellowship Bible Church in 1972, I began to meet with a group of men for Bible study. I suggested we use the character qualities outlined by Paul in his letters to Timothy and to Titus as a basis for our discussions. It became a dynamic and life-changing twenty-week experience for all of us. We spent one session on each character quality, defining each one biblically and then spending time sharing with each other how we could develop this quality in our lives to help us be better husbands, better fathers, and better servants of the Lord—wherever that might be. As a result of this study, we eventually selected and appointed our first elders. Shortly thereafter, I was encouraged to write a book based on these twenty qualities, entitled *The Measure of a Man*. Little did I realize this book would continue to be used as a training tool, even to this day.[1] It discusses those character qualities shown in figure 7 (chapter 19).

This twenty-week study was a life-changing experience for every man; yet we later discovered it was only a beginning point in equipping men to be spiritual leaders in the church. For those elders who are married, we must also involve wives in this process. It's also essential to give people who know them well an opportunity to evaluate their lives as a leadership couple (or as a single). Since that time, we have refined this process greatly (see chapter 34).

A Priority Principle

Taking very seriously the qualifications of maturity outlined by Paul is one of the most important leadership principles that emerges from the biblical story. It should be a priority principle. It's the key to modeling Christlike behavior for the people in the church. It is also the key to creating love and unity and one-mindedness among all of the elders as they lead the church to carry out the Great Commission. In fact, all it takes is one strong-willed and self-centered elder/overseer to destroy the unity on a church leadership team. Unfortunately, this has at times impacted unity in the whole church.

Applying this principle must never be compromised if this New Testament concept of multiple leadership is to work effectively. If we violate this principle and appoint to carry out this "noble task" men and their wives who are not qualified, it can quickly lead to disaster. On the other hand, when a group of godly men and women know who they are in Jesus Christ and are keeping in step with the Spirit and have one motive in mind—to be faithful shepherds and servants of God's people—amazing things will result.

My Most Painful Lesson

Taking these qualifications seriously not only applies when selecting men and women to serve as "lay leaders," but it is even more important when selecting an elder who is worthy of "double honor"—a person who is to give direction to the church as a primary leader (1 Timothy 5:17). In fact, one of the most serious mistakes I made was to hand over my senior pastoral position to my younger associate when I left the "home base" to start another church in a different part of Dallas. I entrusted him with a large body of elders and a multiple staff, firmly believing he would be able to carry on this dynamic and growing ministry. Unfortunately, unknown to me and others, he had serious problems in his marriage. In fact, in later conversations with him I discovered that he himself was not aware of how serious these problems were—including his internal weaknesses that certainly contributed to his marital difficulties. Though he was a brilliant seminary graduate when he took over my position, some time later we discovered that his wife never really wanted him to enter seminary or to be in the ministry.

As the pressures mounted in his new role, his problems began to surface and he began to share his issues with some other "younger elders." Tragically, they were not mature enough themselves to help him.

Ultimately he ended up with a serious moral problem—so serious he was sentenced to prison—but not before he split the church. Unfortunately, I had given up any authority to solve this problem. Though I tried, eventually I could only painfully watch and wait as this tragic story unfolded and culminated, hurting hundreds of people.

Some who were closest to this tragic event would tell you I have taken too much responsibility for this man's spiritual demise. Perhaps so, but I now know there were "signals" in his life that I totally missed. In fact, when one of my most experienced elders raised some questions about this man's ability to be in touch with his own feelings and the feelings of others, I remember assuring him that this was not a problem. I now see that I wanted so much for this man to succeed that I failed to take sufficient time to make this kind of strategic decision and to ask the tough questions of him—and myself! In this sense, I can clearly see that my judgments should have been based on a more thorough evaluation of this man's spiritual and psychological maturity.

This was indeed a painful lesson. Not only did I see this man deteriorate, but I watched the deterioration in his family as well. He has served his time in prison, and is now once again walking with God. During the process, he repented and asked forgiveness. But the damage was done. Though this man is ultimately responsible for the decisions he made that led to this personal disaster, I can now see how Satan took advantage of his weaknesses as a spiritual leader in a very significant and responsible position.

I must state that I still believe in people. Having trust in others is essential in being a successful leader. However, as I recall my misjudgments, hopefully I'm now more discerning. I'll never forget a statement made by one of my elders during this difficult time. "Gene," he said, "your greatest strength is to trust people. But your greatest weakness is to trust people you shouldn't trust." He was right! And hopefully, I've learned more about how to avoid making this mistake.

ONGOING EVALUATION

Those of us who are already serving as elders in any given church certainly must not expect more from other prospective leaders than we expect from ourselves. In fact, every time our elder team evaluates some other prospective candidates, it gives us an opportunity to once again look at our lives in the light of God's standard. This, of course, should not lead to morbid introspection but to a careful look at our Christian character. Paul set the example for all of us when he wrote to the Corinthians. Using an athletic illustration, he stated that he engaged in ongoing training so that having "preached to others," he himself would "not be disqualified for the prize" (1 Corinthians 9:27). Unfortunately, many Christian leaders today have let their guard down and fallen prey to Satan's evil attacks. This need not happen if we consistently "put on the full armor of God" (Ephesians 6:11).

NOTE

1. *The Measure of a Man*, published by Regal in 1974, was updated in 1995. The book has sold almost one million copies (including international editions) during the past three decades.

PRINCIPLES FOR LEADERSHIP APPOINTMENTS (PART 2)

PRINCIPLE 4: *Basic Ethics and Morality*

When looking for qualified leaders to serve the church, consider first those men and their families who've grown up in an environment where their values have been shaped by Judeo-Christian ethics and morality.

The question is often asked as to how Paul and Barnabas on their first missionary journey found men so quickly who were qualified to serve as elders in the churches in Lystra, Iconium, and Antioch. After all, the inhabitants of these cities were deeply influenced by the paganism that existed in the Roman world.

The answer becomes clear when we realize that both God-fearing Jews and Gentiles lived in these geographical areas, which also explains why Timothy—who grew up in Lystra—matured so quickly. His Jewish mother had taught him the Old Testament

Scriptures from infancy (2 Timothy 3:15). Once he became a Christian, all that he had learned from both his mother's example and her teaching came to quick fruition.

THE IMPORTANCE OF BIBLICAL VALUES

If this were true in the New Testament world, how much more so where Christianity has had a unique impact on the values of a particular culture. For example, in America we have churches where many attenders are basically committed to Christian values. They've grown up in Christian homes and most accept the Ten Commandments as true. Unfortunately, among these churchgoers are those who have never had a personal conversion experience. Once they understand the Gospel and receive the Lord Jesus Christ as Savior, they take giant steps forward in Christian maturity because of their understanding of Christian values. Such converts will soon become strong candidates for leadership.

I'm reminded of a couple who have served with me for a number of years at Fellowship Bible Church North. Both Mike and Sharon Cornwall grew up in religious homes. Sharon was a religion major in college and later, after they were married, Mike taught Sunday school in his church and served on the elder board. However, by their own admission, they did not know the Lord Jesus Christ as their personal Savior. Eventually, through the influence of a couple in our church who lived next door to Mike and Sharon, they became born-again Christians. Predictably, their spiritual growth happened quickly. Even when they were unbelievers, they had developed strong ethical, moral, and spiritual values because of their religious backgrounds.

I remember the time I approached Mike and Sharon to serve as an "elder couple." Compared with some of the other men and their wives who were serving with me, they were relatively new Christians. However, they had matured very rapidly because of the biblical value system that had already influenced their behaviors—in their marriage, in their family, and in the business world. Though they had a "works-oriented" approach to earning their "salvation," once they understood that they were saved by grace, not by works, they were highly motivated to build on the values that already had influenced their attitudes and actions—not to earn their salvation, but to serve out of love and appreciation for the gift of eternal life. So when I think of Mike and Sharon, I can understand the kind of people Paul and Barnabas looked for on their return trip to Lystra, Iconium, and Antioch where they appointed elders in each church.

 **PRINCIPLE 5:** *An Initial Leader*

> *If there are no candidates in the church who are qualified to serve as official spiritual leaders, another qualified leader needs to serve in either a temporary or permanent role until others in the church are sufficiently equipped to serve in this role.*

At times, particularly when starting new churches, no qualified candidates are found to be appointed as official spiritual leaders. In that case, another qualified leader should serve until potential leaders are equipped to serve.

THE INITIAL LEADER IN ACTION

This principle is clearly illustrated in the New Testament. Obviously, the apostles served as primary leaders in the church in Jerusalem until they were able to appoint elders. Barnabas and Saul (Paul) filled this role in Antioch before qualified spiritual leaders were ready. And both Timothy and Titus helped establish churches until they had permanent leaders.

In 1972, with the assistance of several men and their families, my wife and I helped start the first Fellowship Bible Church in Dallas. However, in the early days, I was considered the only "official" pastor/elder. I served in this role for at least a six-month period before we appointed other qualified men to serve with me.

In one of our most recent church plants in McKinney, Texas, we appointed one of my longtime associates at Fellowship Bible Church North to serve as the founding pastor/elder. Working closely with Bruce, our elders actually took one year to lay the foundation for this new work.

During this period of time, Bruce began to equip three other men and their wives from our church to serve as potential "elder couples." We also invited these men to attend our own board meetings as observers. In fact, as leaders at Fellowship Bible Church North, we actually served as elders for the new church for a period of time. This continued until all of us (these elder candidates as well) concluded that they were ready to assume this official role in this new church. I must add that this growing ministry has now duplicated this process further north in starting a church in Frisco, Texas. The primary leader in the new work was one of the staff pastors of the McKinney church.

There are many ways this principle can be applied in various cultural situations. The important point is that spiritual leaders should not be appointed until they are qualified. This is no doubt one of the greatest challenges missionaries face when they plant churches in pagan communities. Though it's important to help these believers form an indigenous *ekklesia,* if the work is to sustain itself, it's absolutely essential to leave the church in the hands of qualified leaders—who may need years to prepare.

PRINCIPLE 6: *A Primary Leader*

> *Every group of spiritual leaders needs a primary leader who both leads and serves, and who is accountable to his fellow spiritual leaders.*

It's clear from the total biblical story in the New Testament that God did not intend for a group of men to function without a primary leader. Neither did He plan for a church to have coleaders (see chapter 26).

WHY NOT CO-LEADERSHIP?

Though utilizing coleaders may appear to work initially, it normally leads to serious inefficiency and potential conflict, particularly as the ministry grows and the paid staff multiplies.

Flaws in Co-leadership: A Personal Experience

Frankly, in the early years in my church-planting experience, I attempted to practice a co-leadership approach for a brief period of time. The two of us were committed to making it work. However, the approach not only created efficiency problems but also confusion for the other members of our team.

In terms of our own roles, the other leader and I found ourselves tentative in leading for fear we were being inconsiderate of each other. The two of us also found ourselves attending meetings "together" when it was unnecessary—obviously not being good stewards of our time. And in some instances, it became confusing as to who should actually take the lead in these meetings. In terms of our leadership team, it also became unclear at times as to whom they should report. Wanting to be sensitive to their coleaders, both staff and nonstaff at times didn't know who to go to for advice and counsel.

Flaws in Co-Leadership: A Fellow Pastor's Experience

Recently, I received the following letter from a young man who has been attempting to serve in a co-leadership role. Though he acknowledged the benefits in this arrangement, note the weaknesses:

> There are a number of things I have appreciated about the co-leadership model that I have been part of, for the last few years . . . . [including] the "shared load" and the team approach to the pulpit. . . . However, I must admit I have grown more frustrated with the co-leadership model as time has gone by. God has designed me to be a leader, but the co-leadership structure cannot allow the full expression and exercise of my giftedness. Even in a co-leadership situation that works very well, like the one I'm in, where the two of us share a very similar philosophy of ministry, we still have different ideas and slightly different views on where the church needs to go strategically. That means that both pastors are held back from really leading the church forward. There is no primary visionary leader, and I believe our church has suffered because of that. In my mind, the

co-leadership model has been a healthy counterbalance to the idea of the domineering pastor who never truly operates as part of a team with other elders and staff. But after a few years of experiencing co-leadership, it feels like the pendulum has swung too far the other way, to where the idea of teamwork and co-leading is so overemphasized that no one can give primary leadership to the church. In my next pastorate, I'm planning on having a strong emphasis on teamwork and ministering together, but I'll be the primary leader and visionary, and hopefully I'll have the best of both worlds.

We shouldn't be surprised at the results in attempting co-leadership. First of all, it is never modeled in the New Testament. Furthermore, it violates the principles we've observed in the household model. God has designed that the husband is designated as the primary servant-leader in a marital relationship. Further, when children enter the picture, the father is to serve as the primary servant-leader in the home. Even in these intimate and unique relationships, someone must have ultimate authority to lead.

Furthermore, I've observed that in some cases, what appears to be "co-leadership" is not "co-leadership" at all. Functionally and pragmatically, one of these individuals is the primary leader. They are simply not acknowledging what is actually happening.

THE PRIMARY LEADER AS SERVANT-LEADER

Always a Servant

Clearly, the New Testament story teaches that a primary leader—to be in the will of God—must always be a *servant*-leader. There's no place in the body of Christ for authoritarianism, manipulation, and lack of accountability. Elders are not to be "yes" men who serve as "figureheads" and "rubber stamp" the dictatorial desires of their "spiritual leader."

Personally, in the early days of my church-planting ministry, I was so committed to plurality in leadership and so disappointed in what appeared at times to be one-man, ego-driven operations in the church that I often denied I was indeed the primary leader. As I stated in the introduction of this book, if you had asked me who led the church, I would always say "the elders." In essence, that was a very true statement. If you then asked me who led "the elders," I'd answer, "we lead the church together." Again, this was a true statement, but I did not answer the question adequately.

The facts are that "I led the elders" and together "we led the church." Unfortunately in those early years, I communicated a "model of leadership" I was not in actuality practicing.

My Present Role

For a number of years, I have described my role as functioning at three levels (see figure 15), which I've written into my job description.

First, I look to my fellow elders as my spiritual counselors and advisors. Ultimately, I am accountable to them. I have asked them to take final responsibility to make sure I am fulfilling my role properly. They have

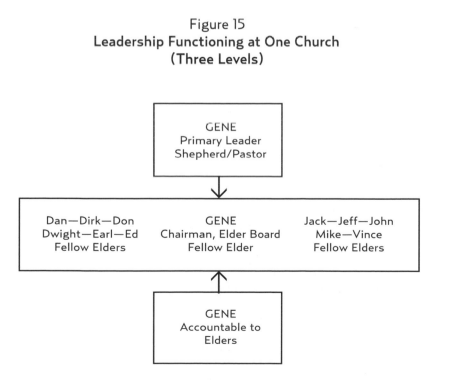

Figure 15
**Leadership Functioning at One Church
(Three Levels)**

final authority to guide me, correct me, and if need be, remove me from my position should I fail to function as a competent spiritual leader.

Second, I view my role as an elder/pastor as "one among equals" in the decision-making process. Though I bring recommendations and proposals to the elders, final decisions are made by the *total* body of elders. I consider myself as one of the decision makers when decisions are being made, even though I chair our meetings.

Third, I view my role as serving as a pastor and leader to the elders. Each of them has a right to look to me as their spiritual shepherd and leader. In this sense, I am a "pastor to the pastors" and a "leader of the leaders." I am also responsible to take the lead in consultation with the other elders to make sure all staff and nonstaff leaders measure up to biblical qualifications and fulfill their functions.

INTENSIFYING LEADERSHIP RESPONSIBILITIES

There are times when a primary leader must intensify his leadership role. This happens in times of crises or when launching significant projects. For example, in our own church we had a group of people who were strongly promoting a parachurch ministry that was operating as a supplementary educational program to our main children's and youth ministries. In fact, some families made it very clear that their primary reason for attending our church was so their children could be a part of this program. Predictably, this began to create disunity among the families of the church.

As elders, we met many times to attempt to resolve this crisis and to integrate this parachurch ministry into our total church program. At the same time, we asked several of our full-time pastors to attempt to resolve the tension. Eventually, it became such a critical issue that as senior pastor I had to intensify my leadership role to guide all of us through this difficult process. In fact, it required an unusual amount of effort on my part to help all of us as elders and the staff pastors involved to stay unified as we walked through this crisis. Ultimately, the problem *was* resolved, and when we presented the resolution, we did so as a unified team, which ultimately restored unity in the church.

Though it was very painful to lose some families because they would not accept our decision, this kind of crisis—and others like it—demonstrates why at times it becomes even more important to have a "primary leader."

But it also demonstrates the value of having a multiple leadership team. Even though I was the primary spokesman when we addressed the issue publicly, everyone knew this was not my decision, but the decision of our total team. This gave me, of course, a great sense of security and reassurance—in spite of the emotional pain I experienced in delivering our conclusions.

A MULTIPLE LEADERSHIP DISTORTION

Dysfunctional Multiple Leadership

Unfortunately, in some churches the concept of multiple leadership has taken on a strange twist. I'm aware of some situations where the elders are led by a nonstaff leader who takes charge of not only the board, but the church. The primary pastor either is not classified as an elder or simply reports to the elders. This not only violates biblical principles but puts the primary servant-leader in a very difficult position. Though he devotes full-time to the church, he really cannot lead with full support from the elders.

This happened recently to a fellow pastor we will call Bill. When he was interviewing to become the senior leader, he discovered that though he was to "lead the elders," he would not be classified as an elder. In other words, he would have no "official authority" as a board member. In actuality, he would have to come into this post and "earn" this authority on an ongoing basis.

Though this was a flashing red light, Bill accepted the position, hoping he could change this arrangement. Unfortunately, he could not make the change, which ultimately led to some very serious problems. Although the church body generally looked to him as their primary leader, the chairman of the elders used this pastor's nonelder status to do an "end run" around him by calling meetings to which he wasn't invited; there the elders discussed some complaints from older members of the church who did not like some of the changes that were taking place under this pastor's leadership.

When he discovered what was happening, Bill challenged this approach. Though he was certainly willing to be open to hear complaints, he felt it was unfair and inappropriate to call meetings where people ventilated their concerns "behind his back." Unfortunately, some of the elders convinced the other men that they should proceed with their plan.

The rest of this story is predictable. Though Bill tried desperately to resolve this issue in a mature and open way, he faced resistance from his board and ultimately decided it would be best to resign. He felt these men had violated his trust—which they had. He stepped aside with dignity, but even to this day most members of the church believe that he was wrongfully treated by the elders. Because of this dysfunctional, multiple-leadership arrangement, the church lost a number of families; indeed, they are having a difficult time surviving as a church. Obviously this has been a very painful experience for my fellow pastor and his family.

Unfortunately, that board violated a very important biblical principle. There cannot be two primary leaders in a church—a nonstaff elder and the senior pastor.

A Reverse Illustration

To demonstrate pragmatically how illogical this arrangement is, I have sometimes used a hypothetical "reverse illustration." As a full-time pastor who spends between fifty and sixty hours a week serving the church, suppose I'm invited to chair the board of a large banking corporation. (God forbid.) However, in this arrangement the CEO of this multifaceted organization must report to me and the other board members who also have full-time jobs elsewhere. We lead him. He doesn't lead us!

This would be extremely presumptuous, unrealistic, and woefully arrogant on my part—to think that I could ever lead this organization when I am not even involved in the day-to-day operations. Furthermore, in a situation like this, I would certainly lack the understanding and skills as to how to operate this kind of complicated fiscal enterprise. To top it off, I have more than a full-time job elsewhere which takes my time and energy.

Hopefully, the point is clear. It's just as illogical for a full-time businessman who works fifty hours a week elsewhere to try to lead the church with a group of other businessmen (who also have full-time vocations) and insist that the full-time pastor report to them with virtually no authority to lead them or the church. As some men have done, they insist that he devote his time to "teaching" and they'll "run the church."

This is definitely a misunderstanding of multiple leadership and of other biblical principles. I've never met a pastor who operates under these circumstances who isn't terribly discouraged—and understandably so! It's not a biblical arrangement!

Unfortunately, some primary pastors have orchestrated themselves into this position. They believe so firmly in being servant-leaders that they unknowingly have given up their authority. Admirably, they have made themselves accountable to the other elders, but in so doing they have given up their ability to lead. When this happens, it is virtually impossible to correct the problem without being accused of being self-serving and wanting "power" and "position."

PRINCIPLES FOR
LEADERSHIP
FUNCTIONS
(PART 1)

PRINCIPLE 7: *Titles*

When determining "titles" for spiritual leaders in the local church, how they function *is far more important than* what we call them.

The New Testament story on local church leadership definitely allows freedom to use various titles to identify spiritual leaders in any given local church. Both Peter and Paul exercised this freedom when they used the term "elders" (*presbuteroi*) and "overseers" (*episkopoi*) interchangeably.

CHOOSING TITLES FOR CHURCH LEADERS

Guidelines

There are, however, some biblical, historical, and cultural guidelines for making decisions regarding nomenclature. First, it is not necessary to use titles that are different from the language used in the New Testament unless these changes will serve as a more effective means to carry out the Great Commission.

Second, since the English titles "overseer" or "bishop" (translated from *episkopos*) took on a different meaning in terms of authority and position following the "biblical story," this change has often continued to be associated with this title, especially in view of the way this terminology has been used in church history. Consequently, if a church uses the term "elder," it may be easier to communicate the original functions associated with this position as they are described in the biblical story. Personally, I have found this to be the case in my own church-planting ministry. This is one reason why we use the term "elders" rather than "bishops" or "overseers."

Freedom in Nomenclature

Having said this, however, we must realize that the freedoms early church leaders used in the second century is based on a biblical principle. As we've seen, Ignatius popularized the term *"episkopos"* (most frequently translated "bishop" in the English language) to refer to the man who served as the primary leader of the "elders" in a given "city-church" community. However, even though the New Testament story allows this freedom in nomenclature, the *authority* Ignatius assigned to these men eventually violated biblical principles (see endnote 1, chapter 27). Consequently, any church or group of churches that use the title "bishops" must be sure to define and evaluate their functions biblically.

Today many churches use the same freedom to designate the primary leader of the elders as "the pastor," or in a large church, the "senior pastor." Some churches use the term "minister" or "senior minister." Other churches, of course, still use the term "bishop" to identify the primary leader. Some also use it to refer to a leader who is responsible for oversee-ing a "community of churches"—sometimes called an "archbishop." One denomination refers to this man as a "superintendent." This too is based on the freedom the New Testament allows in the use of titles. The impor-tant issue is not what they're *called* but how they *function*. Is it biblical?

Freedom of Form in Brazil

My good friend Jim Peterson, who served with the Navigators for twenty-five years in Brazil, invited me on one occasion to address the lead-ers of a number of "small groups." He made it clear that he wanted me to share biblical concepts regarding the local church. Since he served with a parachurch ministry, he felt this was a very important step in helping these Brazilian believers understand God's perspective on ecclesiology.

While ministering to these leaders, Jim explained to me the history of this unique discipling ministry. When Jim and his wife began this out-reach in Brazil, they targeted a certain segment of the society, professional people such as doctors, dentists, architects, and executives. Being a soci-ety heavily influenced by Marxist ideology at that time, these university graduates had some very negative attitudes toward the "church" as they had experienced it over the years in their particular culture. In fact, the Portuguese term for church (*igrejas*) threw up a barrier to biblical com-munication. Second, they had very negative reactions to the Portuguese term for "pastor" (*pastor*) or "priest" (*padre*). Both terms reminded them of an institutionalized religion that they had basically written out of their lives.

To overcome this communication barrier, Jim actually applied this principle of having freedom in "language forms." Rather than calling his small groups "churches" (*igrejas*), he identified them as *"turmas,"* a Por-tuguese term describing identifiable "groups." In actuality, for these peo-ple, this term represented more accurately the meaning of the Greek term *ekklesia* than the Portuguese term *igreja*. The New Testament concept, of course, refers not to an institution or to a building but to "people" who have a unique affinity—in this case, their personal relationship with God and one another.

To overcome the negative reactions to the terms *pastor* or *padre,* Jim used the Portuguese term *mestre* or "teacher" to identify the leader of each *turma.* In turn, these *mestres* formed an *equipe local,* which means a "local team" of leaders.

This change in nomenclature definitely opened the door for more effective communication, both with the people they were attempting to reach with the Gospel as well as the new believers who became a part of these *turmas.* It also illustrates Paul's philosophy of ministry—to be "all things to all men" so that "by all possible means" we might win some. Some churches, however, are so concerned about how they identify their leaders that it leads to disunity. They obviously are not aware that the Holy Spirit has given freedom to use nomenclature that will work best in any particular cultural situation. Again, the important factor is not what they're *called* but how they *function.*

PRINCIPLE 8: *Multiple Fathers*

Spiritual leaders should manage and shepherd the church just as fathers are to care for their families and shepherds are to tend their sheep.

If elders are to manage and shepherd churches as God intended, it's important to understand the breadth of function that is included in these overarching responsibilities. Fortunately, when we analyze the two models Paul used to define the overall ministry for elders, it's easy to comprehend rather quickly the parameters that God built into their "job descriptions."

TWO MODELS FOR DEFINING MINISTRIES

The Family Model

The "household model" is the most familiar, since "family life" is a universal experience. God's ideal design is that a "father" is ultimately responsible for giving Christlike overall direction to this social unit. Based on this model, Paul in essence defined the overarching role for elders.

Along with other men who qualify as effective fathers, they *together* are to become "multiple fathers" in managing the family of God. Furthermore, their wives and the mothers of their children are to serve with them in the church in basically the same way they are functioning as father/ mother teams in their homes. (See chapter 15 to see how unmarried men and women also have a significant place in this model.)

This leads to a very significant question. If the father is to "manage his family well," in what areas of his home life is he not responsible and accountable? Biblically speaking, there are no exceptions or exemptions for a father when it comes to overseeing family responsibilities. This does not mean, of course, that he is to do all the work, but ultimately he is responsible to make sure that all members of his family are loved, cared for, encouraged, and taught God's truth. In turn, he is responsible for each person to function properly (according to age levels) within this God-ordained social unit.

This leads naturally to another important question. If the household model demonstrates that a father is ultimately responsible under God for everything that happens in his family, then what functions in the church are beyond the elders' purview? In other words, in what areas are these men *not* responsible and accountable for what happens in a local church family? The answer, of course, is basically the same as the one we've asked about a father and his biological family. There are no exemptions for elders. According to the Scriptures, they are ultimately responsible under God for everything that needs to be done in the church.

Again, this does not mean they are to do all the work. As the church grows numerically and spiritually, elders need multiple, godly assistants, whom Paul called "deacons"—men and women who can help these men in any way to carry out their overarching responsibilities to effectively manage and shepherd the church.

The Shepherd Model

We can interpret the "shepherding model" in the same basic way we have interpreted the "family model." Though this leadership setting is cultural and experientially unknown to many of us, we can easily answer the following question: When it comes to caring for a flock of sheep, what responsibilities are beyond a shepherd's purview? Applied to elders as multiple shepherds, what responsibilities are beyond their area of accountability?

Again, the answer is clear. As shepherds, elders are ultimately responsible to make sure their sheep are sheltered, fed, and protected from wolves, and when injured, to be cared for. And if a wayward or naive "lamb" or "sheep" wanders off into dangerous territory and gets lost or caught in a thicket, good shepherds at least made sure that someone takes responsibility to minister to that one lost lamb.

PRINCIPLE 9: *Important Priorities*

All spiritual leaders should make sure they manage and shepherd the church well by maintaining six important priorities: teaching the Word of God, modeling Christlike behavior, maintaining doctrinal purity, disciplining unruly believers, overseeing the material needs of the church, and praying for the sick.

SIX KEY PRIORITIES

Principle 9 marks six important priorities for spiritual leaders in the church. From Teaching God's Word to praying for the sick, these duties ensure proper shepherding of the local church flock.

1. Teaching the Word of God

Once people put their faith in Jesus Christ and are "born again," the key to spiritual growth is feeding on God's truth (1 Peter 2:2). Elders are responsible for doing all they can to make sure this happens. Some will devote more time to this important function. However, all of these leaders should be involved at some level. In fact, the most strategic "teaching moments" involve "one-on-one" opportunities as people seek guidance as to how to live day by day in the will of God. This, of course, is what "fathering" is all about (Deuteronomy 6:4–9).

Recently, a businessman and his wife asked me to recommend two men who could evaluate a potential business venture. I suggested two of our elders—a retired banking executive and a younger elder who is currently operating his own employee benefit consulting company. They listened carefully to this man's vision and plans and then recommended that he not proceed because of the uncertainties and risks involved.

However, during the discussion, one of these men advised that this man and his wife also consult one of our other elders who is involved in more entrepreneurial ventures. They did—and received the same advice —affirming the results of the first consultation.

Though these three elders were not "teaching the Word of God" in a formal setting, they were functioning in a very important "teaching role" that was probably much more productive than many sermons in terms of life application. Furthermore, they had far more life wisdom than many trained pastors who have had very little, if any, business experience. This is why those of us who have been equipped theologically in educational institutions should look to elders who have this kind of business experience to give this kind of advice and counsel.

2. Modeling Christlike Behavior

Someone has said that more is learned from what is "caught" than "taught." Though an oversimplification, this is based on an important biblical truth. Though it is certainly important to communicate God's Word *didactically,* it's what people see in our lives that gives weight to our words. This is why the qualifications for elders are so important. If we are to "teach the Word of God" effectively, we must simultaneously "live the Word of God." These two realities should never be separated.

Over the years, I have found this to be one of the most significant factors in helping our people to grow and mature in Jesus Christ. Again and again I get feedback as to how much our people admire our elders and their commitment to godliness. They are aware, of course, as to how seriously we take the qualifications outlined by Paul. In fact, each time we install a new elder, we present the biblical criteria to the total congregation and explain how each elder and his wife have evaluated themselves with this biblical standard. This, of course, makes all of us as spiritual leaders more accountable to the church body. Our lives become an "open book." They certainly know we're far from perfect, but they also know that our desire is to be able to say what Paul wrote to the Thessalonians on behalf of himself, Silas, and Timothy: "You are witnesses, and so is God, of how holy, righteous and blameless we were among you who believed" (1 Thessalonians 2:10).

3. Maintaining Doctrinal Purity

It is one thing to *teach* sound doctrine. It is another to make sure members in the church are not promoting false teachings. On one occasion, we faced this challenge when a leader of one of our women's Bible study groups began to disseminate a very inaccurate view regarding the second coming of Christ. Unfortunately, this particular teacher was influenced by a man who claimed to know who the Antichrist was and when Christ would return. She was so forceful in communicating this information that a number of women became very confused. Some were even ready to sell their homes and move to safe locations so they would be protected during the Tribulation period described in detail in the book of Revelation.

As elders, we had to deal with this matter sensitively but directly. We were able to delegate the matter to one of our pastors who met with these women, exposed this erroneous view of eschatology, and asked this teacher to step aside. She did, but predictably, she left our church believing she was still right. The damage was minimal, but had we not stepped in when we did, we would have faced a much more serious problem of confusion and disunity. As elders, our responsibility was and is to maintain doctrinal purity.

4. Disciplining Unruly Believers

Perhaps the most difficult aspect of being a good shepherd is to administer discipline. On the other hand, it can be the most rewarding. Paul agonized when Christians were not growing in their Christian lives (Galatians 4:19–20). However, he rejoiced when he saw them respond to God's truth.

This kind of shepherding takes time and energy—far more than simply doing "formal teaching." It's relatively easy to "prepare" and "deliver messages" compared with those face-to-face meetings where we confront sin and potential rejection. However, being willing to carry out this kind of ministry reveals the true heart of a shepherd.

Two personal experiences come to mind. On one occasion, a very well-known Christian man in our church decided to leave his wife and family to have a relationship with a married woman. I knew this man well and was shocked. Consequently, one of my elders and I went to his place of business, walked into his office, and told him we had come to help him reverse this decision. Frankly, he was livid and asked us to leave. However, we insisted that we talk. We actually refused to leave, unless he literally escorted us out. Please understand, both of us had a very deep friendship with this man.

Finally, seeing that we were not to be deterred, he consented to talk in a private place. At one point my fellow elder—himself a businessman— placed his hand on this man's arm and with tears streaming down his cheeks, pleaded with him to reconsider his decision. After a two-hour session, he finally consented to see a Christian counselor we were recommending. Both my fellow elder and I agreed to personally meet with him and his wife during the initial session. It was then that this man made a commitment to attend at least six counseling sessions. He later told us both that he only consented to "get us off his back."

I'll never forget the day I saw this man enter the back of the church. A couple of months had gone by. After the service, he walked up to me with tears in his eyes. Putting his arms around me, he said, "Thank God you didn't let me go." His relationship had been restored with his wife, and God gave them another ten wonderful years together before she died of cancer. On one occasion during this whole process of restoration, he said: "Gene, I'll be indebted to you the rest of my life." That, of course, makes being a "shepherd" worth all the time, effort, and even the initial rejection.

This, of course, is a great story. Today, we are great friends. I wish every encounter like this turned out so well. But I also remember another elder and myself going through the same process with another man who had left his wife and family. Though we pleaded with him to reverse his decision, we never got to first base. He totally rejected our words of concern and refused to seek counsel and help. Day after day, he sat in his trailer home and played the secular song "I've Got to Be Me."

This man went on to divorce his wife and to live out of the will of God. The Lord has never promised, of course, that we'll always be successful in attempting to restore "sheep" who have wandered into the "thicket" of sin. But hopefully, in the final analysis, this man will never forget our love and concern for him and will confess his sin. Unfortunately, as far as we know, this has not happened yet.

5. Overseeing the Material Needs of the Church

Some churches believe the oversight of the financial and other material needs is the responsibility of a different group of church leaders—not the elders. They tend to classify a shepherding ministry as "spiritual" and "financial concerns" as "nonspiritual." The facts are that the "household model" does not allow for this kind of dichotomy. A "father" is ultimately responsible for the material welfare of his family—which is also a very important spiritual dimension of his responsibility.

This does not mean spiritual leaders should get bogged down with details and functions that sidetrack them from other important priorities. This is why the principle of delegation to qualified assistants is so important. But when all is said and done, the elders are ultimately accountable for the financial and material welfare of the church family.

In our own church, we are large enough to be able to delegate the leadership of the budgeting process to our business manager (who is also a staff pastor), who in turn works with other key staff leaders to prepare an initial budget. In addition, the elders have asked two fellow elders to meet with these staff leaders to give guidance during the process. Another two elders have been assigned to work with the senior pastor (myself) and the pastor who directs the budget process to evaluate salaries and incorporate these numbers into the overall budget proposal. After this process is completed, it's the four nonstaff elders involved who bring motions to the total elder board to approve the final budget.

There are, of course, a number of ways to make sure the budgeting process is efficient and adequate. However, when all is said and done, it's the elders who are ultimately responsible for the financial welfare of the church.

6. Praying for the Sick

Though listed last, prayers for the sick appears very early in the biblical story of the church. James, the primary leader in the Jerusalem church, no doubt wrote the earliest New Testament epistle, and he encouraged believers who were sick to "call upon the elders of the church to pray over [them]" (James 5:14). James made this a priority for elders (see 5:13–16).

In our own church, we have attempted to take this priority seriously. We have a group of trained leaders, identified as Stephen Ministers, who are available after each service to pray for people; however, the elders make it clear we will meet with anyone who requests prayer for healing—regardless of the nature of the illness. We often meet with people in a private setting between and after services. However, if requested, we'll visit people in the hospital or in their homes.

This study we've done together has only intensified our motivation to be accessible to people. God has honored our efforts and we've witnessed unusual answers to prayer, particularly as we've seen God bestow His grace upon those we've prayed for. (See appendix B for an extensive study of James' exhortation to elders to be available to pray for the sick. The appendix concludes with a contemporary illustration.)

PRINCIPLES FOR LEADERSHIP FUNCTIONS (PART 2)

PRINCIPLE 10: *Mutual Accountability*

Spiritual leaders in the church should hold each other account-able for their spiritual lives as well as the way they carry out their ministries.

Keep watch over yourselves!" This was Paul's exhortation to the Ephesian elders (Acts 20:28), which can be interpreted in only one way—mutual accountability. However, implementing and maintaining an accountability system is probably one of the greatest challenges all Christian leaders face. It runs counter to the way most of us think! It involves being vulnerable—which is normally threatening. We don't naturally invite others into our lives.

How to Institute Accountability

How can we apply this principle among a group of spiritual leaders? First, I'm convinced it must be initiated and modeled by the primary leader. For example, if as a senior pastor I do not take the lead in being accountable for my attitudes and actions, it will be difficult for my fellow elders and pastors to initiate and participate in this kind of accountability. Of course, the more committed we are to spiritual growth in reflecting the fruit of the Holy Spirit in our own lives, the easier it will be to be accountable. However, if we have "secret sins" that embarrass us and cause us shame, we'll naturally discover ways to circumvent this process.

Two Levels of Accountability

Among spiritual leaders in a given church, there are, it seems, two levels of accountability. For example, when elders meet together, there should be a time for sharing personal needs and concerns. In reality, the depth of this sharing will be a reflection of how mature these men really are.

A second level of accountability involves a commitment to one or two other men where there can be more openness and vulnerability regarding sensitive and personal issues. This calls for a total climate of trust—but also a commitment to being open to biblical exhortations from one another.

Questions for Level-Two Accountability

This kind of accountability also serves as a dynamic model for all men in the church. In the book *The Measure of a Man*, I've suggested a series of questions that can be used at least as a means to begin this process with another trusted friend. They are as follows:

1. How often did you meet with God this week?
2. What has God been saying to you through His Word this week?
3. What sins in your personal or business life did you experience this week that need confession?

4. Are you giving to the Lord's work regularly and proportionately as God has blessed you? What percentage did you give last month?
5. What movies did you see this past week? Do you feel good about viewing these movies? What about the Internet? Would you be able to tell your fellow Christians in your church what you have seen without being embarrassed?
6. How did you influence your marriage and family this week? How positively? How negatively? What could you do to improve?
7. Did you pray for me/us this week?
8. What challenges or struggles are weighing on your mind?
9. What lives did you influence for Christ this week?
10. Did you just lie to me?

This final question always brings a chuckle. But it's important. Even a commitment to meet for accountability and a list of questions will not be a guarantee that we will be ultimately accountable. When all is said and done, an accountability system only works when we are men of integrity.

I'm thinking of a former pastor on our staff whom I trusted implicitly. As a team, we had developed accountability partners and he met with one other pastor. Sadly, this man had a secret affair with another woman in our church for a number of months—actually while he was meeting with his accountability partner. Only in retrospect were we able to reconstruct the way he circumvented these accountability questions. "We're big boys," he said one day to his fellow pastor. "We don't need those questions. Let's just talk!" That should have been the first clue that something was wrong—but later this fellow pastor confessed that he completely missed the signal.

When all is said and done, any method for accountability can fail. However, this does not mean that as spiritual leaders we should ignore Paul's exhortation to the elders in Ephesus: "Keep watch over yourselves!" (Acts 20:28).

PRINCIPLE 11: *Expanded Accountability*

To follow the model that unfolds in the New Testament story, every body of local church leaders should have some kind of accountability system that extends beyond themselves—particularly involving the primary leader.

The principle of expanded accountability is not easy to apply, especially in nondenominational, independent churches. And in denominational groups, a bureaucratic system has sometimes emerged that leads to an institutionalized Christianity.

As I think back over my experiences in planting independent churches, *if* I could do it over, I would recommend that we set up an accountability system for the churches we've helped start, at least those in the Dallas area. Personally, I did not want that responsibility. I wanted to devote my time in serving as a local church pastor—helping to launch other churches. However, I have concluded that it would have been best if a qualified leader had been appointed to carry out this responsibility. Furthermore, when a new church was founded, there should have been mutual agreement that there was a measure of accountability on the part of the primary leader to this person. Even though a local church pastor should certainly be accountable to his elders as well as being their leader, it is the part of wisdom to have one or several people outside the organization to whom he is also accountable—at least in receiving advice regarding how to resolve tensions between himself and the elders should it be necessary. When everyone agrees on this arrangement from the beginning, it helps to solve any future problems that might develop.

An Effective Accountability Arrangement

I remember when the pastor of a large and influential denominational church was accused of trying to murder his wife. Unfortunately, whoever attempted this terrible deed left her in a vegetative state. But regardless of the fact that there was a great deal of evidence that this man appeared guilty, the problem in the church was resolved quickly. Even though I was terribly saddened by this whole event, there was one encouraging note as I watched the results of this tragedy unfold. Because of prearranged agreements within this denominational structure, the pastor stepped aside immediately—even though he denied his guilt—when the "regional bishop" came in to take over the pastoral responsibilities on a temporary basis.

Though this was a very painful experience for the church, it hardly missed a beat in terms of function and operation. Had this been the typical independent church, there probably would have been a terrible split, simply because the man accused in this case denied his involvement. In these situations, pastors have stayed to proclaim their innocence—even when it is later revealed that they were covering up their sin. The results are tragic. They often split the church, and the witness among unbelievers in the community is terribly marred.

Pastoral Incompetence

Let me share a personal illustration that demonstrates the need for accountability beyond the elders in a local church. In one of our branch churches, the pastor who was selected to lead this work was not functioning well in both his leadership skills as well as in his sermon preparation and teaching. He had a lot of enthusiasm, but he was unable to deliver in these areas. In retrospect, he was not ready to take on this strategic responsibility.

Some of the older and experienced elders in this church suggested that he resign. However, the younger elders—who were about his age—were supportive, trusting he would successfully grow into this role. At that point some of the older men who had previously been leaders in the home church approached me, asking if I would meet with this young man and suggest that it would be best that he step aside. Frankly, I concluded they were right about his skills and sincerely shared with the pastor that for the good of the church, he should indeed resign. Unfortunately, we had no agreements ahead of time regarding accountability, and when he revealed what I had suggested with his own leadership team, the elders who supported this man were understandably resentful of my recommendation. Even though I helped start the church, they felt I was interfering. Even though I was their senior pastor in the church that launched this work, once they were on their own, I had given up this kind of authority to suggest that their pastor resign. They were right!

Ultimately, this young pastor *did* resign—but not until several of the older and more experienced men quietly slipped away and came back to the home base. Eventually the younger men also concluded it was best for this pastor to step aside. In retrospect, had we developed an accountability system beyond their own elders ahead of time, we would have been able to resolve this situation much more quickly.

There's one other thing that I remember that became a significant lesson to me personally. When this man finally resigned, the church was teetering on the brink. The elders then invited an older, mature pastor to come in on a part-time basis simply to teach and to give wisdom and guidance to the elder board. Within just a few weeks, the "ship" that was about to "capsize" stabilized. The lesson I learned is that when we select men to be primary pastors in a church plant, we need to look for someone who has experience enough to lead this new work. Though most of these new works have gone well, I can point to the reason for each church's success or failure. It's the "primary leader" who has made the difference.

A Moral Issue

In a second branch church, I saw a similar pattern. However, the issue was moral. The pastor was spending hours behind closed doors with his secretary. When challenged by the elders with the impropriety of his actions, he denied that there was anything wrong. He continued this behavior, eventually splitting the elder board and then the church. Predictably, he was lying. The truth eventually came out, but not without doing serious harm to this body of believers.

Again, the older elders approached me asking if I would help resolve the issue. I was in a difficult situation. I had no authority to carry out their request—even though we launched this church from our home base. Having learned from my past experience, I chose not to get involved, knowing that it would be resented by those who were supporting the pastor. Again, if we would have had agreements ahead of time, not only I but our elders would have been able to become involved in the situation and to keep the church from at least a lengthy painful experience. Ultimately, when the truth came out, the pastor obviously resigned, but not without hurting many, many people.

THE POWER OF PRIOR AGREEMENTS

There is no perfect methodology for resolving issues like these. However, this real-life experience demonstrates the weakness in church structures when elders are not accountable to anyone beyond themselves. In situations like this, divisions and disunity are almost inevitable—unless they agree to bring in someone from the outside. However, by this time, the rift can be so deep that one side or the other will not listen.

A key is that there needs to be agreements ahead of time. Even then it's difficult, but it makes resolution easier. This is why the apostle Paul and his representatives could come into churches and resolve issues involving immaturity in the leadership. They had apostolic authority. Today we do not have that authority per se—but there is a "principle of authority" that can be established and that is recognized by all concerned.

LESSONS LEARNED

A New Church Plant

When we laid the groundwork for our most recent church plant, the pastor whom we asked to launch this church took the initiative with our elders to develop and sign a document in which we all agreed to serve as arbitrators in case their new board of elders should ever become at odds with the primary leader. In essence, in this document this pastor and the elders all agreed to abide by our recommendations for reconciliation and resolution. To this pastor's credit, he had observed the very events I've just shared, and he didn't want it to happen to him.

Hopefully, it will never become necessary to participate in this kind of meeting. However, in at least two of our branch churches, had we had this arrangement it would have helped greatly to resolve the problems.

This is a very important lesson we learned in retrospect. The challenge is to develop "forms" that enable leaders to function without becoming bureaucratic and authoritarian and interfere with the need for a local church to function freely in applying biblical principles in all aspects of the ministry—and yet be accountable.

A Personal Application

During this study, I faced the reality that I've never set up this kind of extended accountability for myself as a senior pastor. Consequently, with the approval of the elders, I approached three other senior pastors in our city and have given them the authority in writing to arbitrate, if ever necessary, any problems between myself and my fellow elders. Again, hopefully, this will never be necessary.

PRINCIPLES FOR LEADERSHIP FUNCTIONS (PART 3)

PRINCIPLE 12: *Qualified Assistants*

In order to maintain their priorities, spiritual leaders should appoint qualified assistants who can help them meet the needs of all believers in the church.

The use of qualified assistants in the early church is apparent throughout the book of Acts and the epistles. Qualified assistants are discussed specifically in Paul's first pastoral letter. While outlining the qualifications for elders, he outlined a similar list of qualifications for deacons—men and women who serve as assistants (1 Timothy 3:8–13).

Today such men and women are to help the elders to carry out all aspects of their ministry. In some churches, this role has been limited to the more material needs of the church. However, though many of the more financial and organizational aspects of the ministry may certainly be assigned to deacons, the illustrations in the New Testament demonstrate that these servants should assist elders in all aspects of their managing and shepherding functions: teaching, modeling, praying, etc.

PERMANENT AND TEMPORARY POSITIONS

These "assistant" roles may be either permanent or temporary, based on cultural needs. For example, in our own church, we have hundreds of people helping elders on a permanent basis. Some are on staff full- and part-time (paid), and others are in purely voluntary positions. We would consider all of the following leaders as assistants to our elders:

- ☐ All staff pastors who are not official elders
- ☐ Any staff person who is not classified as "a pastor," which includes administrative assistants and secretaries
- ☐ Stephen Ministers
- ☐ Small group leaders (whom we also call "pastors")
- ☐ Children and youth workers
- ☐ Property managers

In addition to permanent serving positions, on occasions our elders have also assigned people to assist in temporary roles. For example, during a serious recession in the economy, we appointed what we called an "Acts 6 Group." It so happened that this particular committee included "seven men"—though not by design. We had just entered the economic crisis during the 1980s—which, of course, affected giving in churches everywhere. This group was responsible for studying not only what was happening in the economic climate in our society but also to evaluate how this was impacting our own church and then to bring recommendations to us as elders for addressing the issue.

One of the recommendations this group made to the elders was that I as senior pastor bring a series of messages on "giving." The elders con-

curred that this would be a great idea. However, I countered with a request—that both the "Acts 6 Group" and the elders join me in a biblical study of everything the Bible teaches about how Christians should use their material possessions. In this way, they would help me do the basic groundwork in preparing this series of messages. They agreed!

HELPING PREPARE THE PRIMARY LEADER

Little did we realize the enormity of this task. We studied together every Wednesday evening for a period of six months. At the end of the process, we came up with 126 supracultural principles to guide Christians in using their material possessions. I then developed a series of messages; but all of these men had been involved with me throughout this study and felt a sense of ownership regarding the insights we had gleaned from Scripture. What a tremendous sense of support I felt when I delivered these messages! The exciting end to this story is that rather than laying off staff as some churches in the Dallas area were doing, we actually added staff to meet the needs of our growing church. God honored this "community project."

Once we had completed this task, the Acts 6 Group was no longer needed. These men had definitely served in a *temporary* "deacon's" role—which we believe is in harmony with a very important principle. Deacons in the New Testament were to assist the elders in any way possible to carry out their managing and shepherding ministries.

PRINCIPLE 13: *Financial Support*

Spiritual leaders are to make sure that those who devote significant amounts of time to the ministry—particularly in teaching the Word of God—should be cared for financially.

The whole of Scripture supports this principle. How it is carried out will vary in every culture of the world. Clearly the spiritual leaders who labor to rightly present God's Word deserve proper compensation.

(Remember Paul's injunction that elders who direct church affairs, "especially those whose work is preaching and teaching" deserve "double honor" [1 Timothy 5:17].)

DETERMINING STAFF SALARIES

In the previous section, I've already illustrated how a special "task group" helped our elders and myself study the whole of Scripture to discover what God says about how Christians should manage and use their material possessions. However, one other unexpected recommendation came out of their study. Even though we were in a financial recession, they believed that our elders should take a very careful look at our staff salary structures. Through general observations and conversations, they concluded that we were perhaps underpaying our people.

This was a rather unusual recommendation in view of the larger economic downturn. The elders accepted the proposal and once again asked the Acts 6 Group to assist. We presented this task force with extensive job descriptions for all of our staff, including additional data, such as academic preparation, years of service, etc. However, we did not present them with any specific information as to our current salaries. Rather, we simply asked them to give us recommendations based on general economic needs within our culture as well as their evaluations of the staff job descriptions and qualifications.

As a result of this process, these men recommended significant salary increases for most positions—without having known what our salary structures actually were. In this sense, it was a very objective process—and an unusual one in light of the fact that we were in the midst of a recession in our economy. As a result, God blessed the elders' decision to apply this principle. We actually increased staff salaries during this difficult economic period and made our budget. We, of course, shared with the church body what we were doing and why. Obviously, they responded in obedience to the Word of God.

AVOIDING A CONFLICT OF INTEREST

Having emphasized the biblical responsibility for believers to provide adequate care for their staff, there is also a caution for all of us who are primary pastors in large well-known churches. We live in a time in history, particularly in the Western culture, where it is possible to become very successful in ministry and to use that success to benefit ourselves financially. When this begins to happen, we need to develop a plan to avoid a conflict of interest.

I remember facing this challenge in my own ministry a number of years ago. Since I have many opportunities to speak, I became concerned about what was potentially a conflict of interest. I soon found myself in danger of devoting time and energy to ministries outside the church—for which I received compensation—and neglecting the very ministry for which I was already receiving a full-time salary.

After a lot of thought and prayer, I initiated a plan I have never regretted. I informed the elders that I wanted to set up a special mission/travel account into which I could deposit all income I generate from speaking other than my full-time salary from the church. At the same time, I requested permission to use these funds for special ministry projects—for example, to travel to mission fields of the world to minister to and with missionaries who cannot finance such trips. My fellow elders agreed to the plan, and each month this income is reported in the regular financial statements.

Again, I've never regretted this decision. For one thing, my conscience is clear from any conflict of interest. Second, I'm not tempted to accept speaking engagements based on the amount of income I can generate. Third, I've never been tempted to set up fee structures that determine whether I accept an engagement. Fourth, this additional income becomes an investment in a variety of ministries.

Frankly, I've hesitated to share this experience since some pastors are so poorly paid they have every right to generate additional income. However, without judging others—which is certainly not my intent—I believe this is something every prominent Christian leader needs to evaluate in the light of biblical principles. In short, as elders receiving "double honor," we all need accountability in order to be above reproach in terms of financial integrity.

PRINCIPLE 14: *Adequate Forms*

Spiritual leaders are responsible to make sure that adequate forms are developed to carry out the biblical functions inherent in the first thirteen biblical principles.

How should spiritual leaders carry out the biblical functions inherent in the previous principles? I've noted that various cultural forms are flexible but normative biblical function are not. The form should be developed and tailored to each local cultural setting.

I've already illustrated some of the ways this can be done. However, there are some additional "form questions" that need to be addressed:

1. How old should these spiritual leaders be?
2. What specific methodology should be used to select and appoint qualified spiritual leaders?
3. How many elders should be appointed to lead a single church?
4. How long should these leaders serve?
5. How should an elder board make decisions?
6. Is there a biblical basis for a staff-led church?
7. Shouldn't all staff pastors be elders?
8. Which is more biblical—a congregational form of church government or an elder-led church?
9. What "form" changes need to be made as the church grows numerically?
10. How does the "household model" work?

Though the New Testament doesn't give specific answers to these "form questions," in the next chapters we'll share some lessons we've learned over the years.

AGE
REQUIREMENTS

As with so many aspects of ecclesiology, the New Testament does not prescribe or even describe various forms for applying the supracultural principles that emerge from this study. This is what makes the biblical story so relevant. As I shared in the introduction, only the Holy Spirit could have superintended this kind of writing project. This "divine design" is what makes the message of Christianity—rightly interpreted—supracultural. We can "function" effectively and practice biblical truth anywhere in the world and at any moment in history because the Holy Spirit has given us freedom to develop those unique "forms" that will enable us to be truly Christian without changing the essence of the biblical message.

In this chapter and the ones to follow, we want to respond to some "form questions." There are, of course, no absolute answers. However, we can share how we've addressed these questions in our own church-planting journey.

A Word of Caution

I'm presenting the illustrations in the following chapters for one purpose: to enable other church leaders to process issues in their own churches, not to copy our "forms." If they're transferable and helpful, use them to the full. But I'm convinced that no forms should be borrowed from others without *first understanding the biblical principles that have shaped these forms.*

A Question of Age

Our first question of form is: How old should these leaders be?

The New Testament doesn't directly address the age issue, even in the list of qualifications. The same is true of deacons. Since the term "elder" (*presbuteros*) is sometimes translated "older" (1 Timothy 5:1; Titus 2:2), some conclude that the very title "elder" implies that only "an older man" should be appointed to this position. However, we cannot derive the same guideline from the meaning of the word "bishop" or "overseer" (*episkopos*), which was used interchangeably with the title "elder."

When my fellow elders and I looked at the total leadership story in the New Testament and also evaluated our own experiences in selecting elders over the years, we concluded that it's generally wise to appoint spiritual leaders who have learned from years of experience, making them wise and discerning. On the one hand, we've also concluded that "age alone" does not guarantee maturity. Neither does it mean that younger men cannot occupy strategic leadership positions.

Cultural Dynamics in the First Century

The Very Young Timothy

In answering the "age" question, it's important to consider cultural expectations. This is very obvious when we look at Timothy. He was approximately twenty years of age when Paul selected him to accompany him on his second missionary journey. In most cultures, this is considered *very* young, especially to occupy this kind of role. This was particularly true in the Greco-Roman world. In fact, Timothy was still considered "young" at approximately age thirty-three when Paul left him in Ephesus to select and appoint elders. This is why Paul instructed him: "Don't let anyone look down on you because you are young, but set an example for the believers in speech, in life, in love, in faith and in purity" (1 Timothy 4:12).

Timothy demonstrated that it is possible to be a mature leader at a very early age. In fact, Paul had sent him on some very difficult assignments probably when he was in his mid- or late twenties (Philippians 2:19 24; 1 Thessalonians 3:1–2).[1]

A Great Mentor

This maturity didn't just happen. Before he became a Christian, Timothy received the holy Scriptures from his mother "from infancy" (2 Timothy 3:15); when Timothy began his missionary experiences, Paul became a "substitute father" and a great mentor, often protecting him from involvements that could have discouraged him.

This may explain why, for example, Paul and Silas were incarcerated and brutally beaten in Philippi, and Timothy, who was with them, was not. Then, too, the fact that he was very young may have generated some leniency on the part of the Roman officials. Personally, I believe Paul purposely protected Timothy from tense situations that could have overwhelmed and intimidated him, potentially causing him to do what John Mark did—bail out when the pressure got too great. In this sense, I believe Paul had learned a lesson.

CULTURAL DYNAMICS TODAY

What should relatively young and inexperienced men do today when they graduate from a Bible college or a seminary and want to become primary leaders in a church, particularly in a culture that tends to glorify the potential of youth and often negates the wisdom of older people? I've often suggested that they look for an associate position where they can serve with and be mentored by an older leader—preferably a senior pastor.

My First Personal Mentor

This was one of the most significant things that happened to me while doing graduate work in my early twenties. A seasoned pastor had returned to school to earn an advanced degree. While there, a relatively small church invited him to be their pastor. He in turn asked me to serve as his associate. Though we were both part-time, it was a great experience for me personally. In fact, I learned some of my greatest lessons there.

On one occasion, I got myself into some fairly serious trouble by confronting a teenage girl and her boyfriend who were being overly demonstrative in the church services. Her parents were prominent members in the church and were rather upset with me—to say the least. They were more upset with the way I did it. They complained to my senior leader and he advised them to meet with me personally.

Frankly, I was scared to death. I remember so vividly that pastor taking me aside and explaining that he was going to let me go it alone. He assured me, however, that he'd be available to help bail me out if I got in over my head; but he made it clear that this would be a great learning experience. I'd gotten myself into the conflict, and he felt I needed the experience to resolve it—which I was able to do, but not without some intense anxiety. He later followed up with me and helped me learn from this experience. I covet this kind of mentoring experience for every young person going into the ministry.

In terms of appointing other younger men to be on the board of elders, I believe there are several issues to consider in making that decision. For example, are there older men who are more qualified? What is the average age of the congregation? Furthermore, how mature are the younger men?

How to Respond: Adult-to-Adult Communication

I remember one younger elder—a seminarian—who brought a proposal to one of our board meetings. It was obvious he thought his ideas were stellar! However, I also vividly remember that an older leader—a businessman—listened carefully, and then responded sensitively but very directly with at least five reasons why his ideas wouldn't work. Unfortunately, the younger man responded with inner anger. Rather than interacting in an "adult-to-adult" fashion, he reverted to an "adolescent mentality." Emotionally, he regressed to being a "son" who was reacting negatively to his "father." Unfortunately, this young man never came to grips with his immaturity and eventually failed as a spiritual leader.

By contrast, I've seen other younger men respond with openness, "teachability," and respect when their ideas are questioned by older men. They want to learn—and they do! This must have characterized Timothy when Paul chose him to be his assistant. Mature men—younger or older—relate to each other in an "adult-to-adult" fashion.

A Lesson in Humility

I remember one of our older elders who had some questions regarding a proposal. Though all of us were in agreement with the idea, he shared openly that he was hesitant to endorse the idea. He simply asked for time to think and pray about it, to get more perspective. But what I remember so vividly was his response in our next meeting. He opened the discussion by sharing that he had come to the conclusion that his reservations were not valid. He expressed total agreement with the rest of us.

At that point in my own experience as a pastor, I learned a great lesson. What this man did reflected humility. Though a very strong leader in his business and in the church, he was not embarrassed to admit he felt he had "been wrong" in his initial judgments. Obviously, at that moment, his "respect level" among all of us went even higher.

DIFFERING BACKGROUNDS

If we're honest, such stories of humility—and wisdom—have touched all of us at some point during our younger years. There are simply things we do not comprehend unless we've had life experiences that open our eyes to our own blind spots. But it is also true that some people are mature beyond their years and for various reasons. They've faced crises in their lives that most of us normally do not face. In this sense, they "age prematurely"—*if* they've been able to grow through these difficult experiences rather than allow the pain to cause them to develop shields of protection, such as rationalizations, control tactics, and other defense mechanisms.

On the other hand, age and experience per se do not guarantee maturity. I know of younger men with far more wisdom to lead than some older men. There is nothing more divisive than a fifty- or sixty-year-old man who has covered up his insecurities with control tactics. Normally this becomes obvious when he's opinionated, defensive, and unwilling to admit mistakes. However, in my own experience, I have found this to be an exception, not the rule. Most older men who are committed to Jesus Christ have learned from years of experience, indeed making them wise and discerning.

NOTE

1. William M. Ramsay, "The Age of Timothy," *Historical Commentary on the Pastoral Epistle* (Grand Rapids: Kregel, 1996), 117–21.

LEADERSHIP SELECTION

Let's consider a second form question that can help us carry out biblical functions of leadership: What specific methodology should be used to select and appoint qualified spiritual leaders?

In my own church planting experience, the methodology has been an evolving process. We've always taken the qualifications for spiritual leaders seriously. However, in the early years of our ministry, we didn't have an adequate methodology to test the degree these qualities were being fleshed out in marital, family, and ministry relationships. We simply asked people (mostly couples) to evaluate themselves, using Paul's criteria in his Pastoral Letters. In some respects this was a much better method than a "popularity contest" among members of the church at large, yet it was still not adequate. Consequently, we made some fairly serious errors in judgment, which were not fair either to the leaders whom we had appointed or to the church.

Today we have broadened and deepened our evaluation process. Admittedly, our approach is uniquely related to our particular church structures that we've developed over the years. Please keep that in mind as you read "our story."

Since the beginning of the first Fellowship Bible Church, we opted for a small-group ministry rather than the traditional adult classes. We call these groups "minichurches." Most of these "communities of faith" are led by couples that we frequently call "minichurch pastors." They're responsible to shepherd these "small flocks."

These small group leaders in turn have become the "pool" from which we select candidates for eldership. We look for those who have been successful minichurch leaders. This does not mean we expect to discover "perfect little churches." Rather, we look for faithfulness in shepherding people, even when some of "the sheep" are less than manageable. However, the overall spiritual health of the small group normally indicates good leadership.

We've established this guideline because we believe it's important for leaders to be able to lead smaller groups before taking on the responsibility to help manage and shepherd the entire church body. In fact, the believers who comprise a minichurch are the people who give a "final vote of confidence," assuring us as elders that they believe that their own "pastoral leaders" are indeed qualified to serve as an "elder couple."

A Current Process

Recently we have taken the following eight steps in making four key appointments.

Step 1: Selecting Potential Candidates

As elders, in consultation with our wives, we discussed together potential candidates—people who faithfully served as small group leaders for a significant period of time. In fact, some of our most recently appointed elders have served as minichurch leaders for ten to twenty years. We also looked for people who have developed the character qualities outlined by Paul: faithfully giving "of their time," "their talents," and "their treasures." In making these candidate selections, we had 100 percent agreement among the elders. In this kind of decision, we would not have proceeded without this unanimity.

Step 2: An Invitation to Evaluation

When we narrowed the list, we approached these couples and explained why they'd been chosen as candidates. We then asked them if they would be open to going through an evaluation process, which is described in the following steps. We also made sure that they understood that they were under no obligation to accept this role once they had taken these steps, nor were we obligated to ultimately offer them this position.

Step 3: Studying the Biblical Qualifications

We then asked these prospective candidates to meet with my associate pastor and his wife and to spend a number of weeks working through the twenty character qualities outlined by Paul for Timothy and Titus. In this case, they used my book *The Measure of a Man* as a basis for discussion and interaction. All participants, including my associate and his wife, evaluated themselves against the biblical qualities and chose one quality as a "character project" for the rest of the study.

As I'll explain later (chapter 37), as of this writing we are three years into a seven-year succession plan. We anticipate the associate pastor will replace me in 2007 and that we'll also have appointed a new group of leaders who eventually will replace most of our current elders. This explains why we asked my associate to lead the couples through this biblical study on leadership qualifications. As this plan unfolds, these are the people who will be serving with him. As one of our senior elders stated during the selection process, it's absolutely imperative that my successor be 100 percent comfortable with these new appointments.

Step 4: A Deeper Relational Experience

At the end of this evaluation process, my associate spent several days with these men and several current elders in a secluded setting (a private ranch in the Big Bend country of Texas). Here they had opportunity to get to know each other even at a deeper level—studying the Word together, praying together, sharing together—and spending time alone with God in a semi-wilderness setting. One of our long-term elders facilitated discussions about roles and responsibilities and shared his own experiences and perspectives on eldership.

Step 5: Evaluating the Candidates

Our next step was to have the following leaders each fill out an evaluation form on both "husband and wife" candidates: (1) the current elders and their wives, (2) our senior staff people, and (3) those people who are part of the minichurch this couple has pastored.

We consider these small-group evaluations very significant since they represent the people who know these candidates best, particularly regarding their marital and family relationships. For them, it's been "up close and personal."

A sample of that form is shown as appendix C. The questions regarding character are based on the qualifications Paul outlined in 1 Timothy and Titus.

Step 6: A Final Invitation

Once the elders had assessed all of these evaluations and sensed no serious reservations, we then approached the couples and formally invited them to accept the role of eldership. Please note that we consider these couples "father and mother" teams who are involved together in leading the church. (See chapter 15 again, where we discussed the "household model" as a biblical basis for this approach.)

Step 7: Presentation to the Congregation

We then presented these couples to the entire congregation, explaining why they had been chosen and the process they had gone through. We reviewed the qualifications from Paul's letters and asked anyone who may have any serious concerns to contact me (the senior pastor) by the following Wednesday.

At this point, we also invited feedback from people present who may not consider themselves a part of our church, but who may know these couples from business associations, social relationships, as neighbors, etc. The basis for this approach is that an elder is to have a "good reputation with outsiders" as well as those within the church (1 Timothy 3:7).

During this step, we made it clear to the congregation that this is not a "vote." Rather, it was an opportunity to express reservations in an open, up-front way, understanding that if there were concerns, the candidates in question desired to meet personally with any person who had these concerns in order to make appropriate changes in their lives. At the same time, we made it clear that we do not process any letters that are unsigned.

Step 8: Publicly Commissioned

Our final step was to present these couples to the total church body. At that time, all of our elders and their wives laid hands on these couples and publicly welcomed them into this official position.

VARIOUS CONCERNS

What happens if there are serious concerns that surface during this process? We address them with the individual and his or her spouse. This can be very productive. Let me share a very encouraging story. One man had consistently low marks in several areas on the evaluation form. Various people were concerned about what, at times, appeared to be contentious and argumentative behavior. On the other hand, his wife had high scores in all areas.

It became my responsibility as senior pastor along with another elder to share these concerns with this couple. It was a difficult assignment, but in the end a very rewarding experience. Reflecting on this rather difficult time in his life, here is what Ed Buford later wrote:

When Maureen said that she agreed with the evaluation that I could be contentious, argumentative and too bold in defending the views I held strongly, I knew that God wanted to get my attention—big time. I also knew down deep that the evaluation was correct. As I asked God for help, He made it clear to me that I needed to develop the fruit of the Spirit known as gentleness.

He also gave me a plan. I was to get my family to hold me accountable. One evening I called my family together and asked each one to forgive me for not being gentle and asked for their help. I explained to them that every time they saw me using my verbal skills to steamroll over them, raise my voice, show anger, or be contentious in any way, they were to put an X on the family calendar in the kitchen. To my dismay, the next day I got five Xs. I considered changing the rules! But I was committed and my family helped me learn to be gentle.

What started out as a crushing blow to my Mr. Charge Ahead ego has turned into a wonderful blessing in my life. I now know that viewpoints spoken in gentleness with energy are much more acceptable and effective with the listener. I certainly have not arrived at my goal but I am on my way.[1]

All of us who know Ed well saw immediate changes in his life. Eventually, he became an elder. He has a heart for God, a heart for the ministry, and a heart for people. He really always did. He simply needed to change his style of communication. He didn't mean to appear contentious, authoritarian, or argumentative, and controlling. But when he learned that other mature leaders thought he was contentious and controlling, he made some permanent and lasting changes. I've heard him share this experience on several occasions with the interns in our church as well as other people. In every situation, Ed has "teared up"—not with a sense of sorrow, but gratitude. He has also publicly thanked me for continuing to believe in him during this "change process." This, of course, is a very rewarding result, even though I found it difficult to initially share those concerns.

Forgetting What Is Behind

In no way does this mean that any of the leaders of Fellowship Bible Church North consider themselves to be "perfect." At times, we all fail to "measure up" but when we do fail, our commitment is to seek forgiveness, if necessary, and make changes. Like the apostle Paul, we want to be able to say:

> Not that I have already obtained all this, or have already been made perfect, but I press on to take hold of that for which Christ Jesus took hold of me. Brothers, I do not consider myself yet to have taken hold of it. But one thing I do: Forgetting what is behind and straining toward what is ahead, I press on toward the goal to win the prize for which God has called me heavenward in Christ Jesus. [Philippians 3:12–14]

The process I've just described has evolved over a period of time. Needless to say, each time we go through this experience, it becomes an opportunity for all of us—men and women—to once again take a look at our lives, using biblical criteria that reflect the life and character of the Lord Jesus Christ. Furthermore, it gives us one more opportunity to refine the process.

Note

1. Gene A. Getz, *The Measure of a Man*, rev. ed. (Ventura, Calif.: Regal, 1995), 174.

BOARD SIZE
AND LENGTH
OF SERVICE

Two additional form questions regarding biblical leadership deal with some very practical issues: How large should the elder board be and how long should the leaders serve?

Once again, the biblical story doesn't answer these questions. As we've noted, the "church forms" in the New Testament world were related to the functions of a "single church" in a "single city" (see 211–15). This cultural dynamic definitely impacted the number of elders in a given city. Some speculate that in Jerusalem the number of believing elders equaled the number of Jewish elders in the Sanhedrin (i. e., seventy).

A NUMBERS LESSON

To be perfectly honest, I believe I made a serious mistake in the first church I helped plant. Since we had created a small group ministry that needed a number of pastors, I falsely concluded that only official elders and their wives could carry out this kind of ministry.

After all, the Scriptures are clear these leaders should "shepherd God's flock." Consequently, as we launched new groups in a very rapidly growing church, we in turn appointed elders to care for these minichurches.

What happened is predictable. We ended up with an elder board that was too large to function effectively. Furthermore, we were not as selective as we should have been as to whom we appointed as elders. To meet a need, we moved too quickly. In retrospect, we became more pragmatic than biblical. In the final analysis, some of these individuals did not measure up adequately to the character qualities outlined in Scripture.

As I recall, the board eventually grew to approximately forty-five men. With this many elders, we faced another problem. Approximately one-quarter to one-third of these men would be absent for meetings because of business traveling schedules, family priorities, or emergencies. In the next meeting, this group of men would be present and another group gone. And so it went—meeting after meeting! We lost continuity and we bogged down having to review the reasons for decisions. The process became incredibly inefficient, and we found it very difficult to keep communication lines open.

Such situations can become a seedbed for disunity. To avoid this problem, I often spent many hours on the telephone communicating with the men who were absent from a particular meeting in order to bring them up to speed for the next meeting. This helped significantly in solving the communication challenge; unfortunately this kept me from meeting other biblical priorities as a senior pastor.

In our present church structure, we have attempted to keep our board size to approximately seven or eight men. However, since we are now in a succession plan (see chapter 37), we now have twelve elders. This may continue to increase over the next several years until the transition is complete. At that time, the board should once again become smaller as many of our long-term elders turn the reins of leadership over to those who have been appointed in the last several years. We're trusting this will go as planned. Only time will tell.

In terms of shepherding the small groups, we have developed a large group of "pastors" who are not elders, but who are certainly qualified spiritually to be shepherds. The basic difference between these minichurch leaders and our elders is that the elders have decision-making authority to manage and shepherd the church at large. The minichurch leaders are responsible for managing and shepherding a "small flock" within the "larger flock"—but always operating as assistants to the elders.

A CLOSED SYSTEM

If we limit the board size in order to be efficient, doesn't this become a "closed system"? That is indeed a real danger. In fact, as the church grows, this plan closes the door to many godly men and women who are or will become qualified to serve in this role. In fact, I know of one church that began with a small group of elders. As the church grew, the board size remained the same and these men more and more became "reclusive" decision makers. Since they did not have an effective plan to continue to be shepherds, they often made these decisions out of touch with people's needs. Their work became primarily "administrative."

What happened next is predictable! There were godly men and women in the congregation who had no way to relate to what appeared to be the "power people" in the church. When they tried to communicate their concerns, they felt their voices were not being heard. Sadly, the church eventually split. Fortunately, these men "got the message" but not until it was too late to avoid the division.

I know this situation well, since I was invited to come in from the outside to evaluate what happened. In actuality, these men were godly and measured up to the qualifications outlined in Scripture. They had simply put in place a "form" that wasn't evolving with the growth of the church. Though I was a consultant in this situation, I learned a very valuable lesson myself. We must have "forms" that allow elders to be in touch with people regardless of the size of the church.

A ROTATING SYSTEM

One way to resolve this problem is to have a rotating system. However, what normally occurs is that new leaders often come on the board but have very little continuity in terms of philosophy, experience, and the reasons decisions have been made in the past. Ask any senior pastor about this plan! It may take a year to bring these new elders and their wives up to speed. And then, the process begins all over again with new appointments. This is one reason why some churches have opted for a "staff-led church." The leadership team doesn't bog down because of lack of continuity.

ANOTHER OPTION:
SMALL-GROUP LEADERS

To avoid this problem in our own church, we have discovered that our small groups led by a large number of "lay pastors" provide a very gratifying shepherding ministry for a great host of mature people. But there is another factor. Most of our elders serve as "care pastors" to these minichurch shepherds in an attempt to stay in touch with their needs—and the needs of the people under their care. For example, should there be some serious needs in these small groups, the elders usually hear about it within a very short period of time. We want these "pastoral assistants" to know that they have access to the elders at any time. We are not only their leaders, but their servants.

This, of course, is our goal. We elders don't always operate as efficiently as we would like. But we have discovered that this approach keeps the number of elders on the board at a workable size, maintaining continuity and at the same time not creating a totally "closed system" that becomes ingrown. Even so, it's very important for elders to continue to be shepherds. If we do not, we are failing to carry out the functions outlined in Scripture. We're headed toward an "administrative role" that is never prescribed in the biblical story. And if this happens, we'll lose the confidence and trust of the people.

There's another "must" with this approach. When we make significant decisions for the whole body, we want minichurch leaders to be the first to know what is happening *before* it happens. Furthermore, since they serve as our "eyes" and "ears," they can give us valuable input regarding the pulse beat in the church at large, which helps us make wise decisions. We have learned that adequate communication is the key to building trust and maintaining unity.

LENGTH OF SERVICE

Concerning the length of service, some believe that once a man becomes an elder, he is always to be an elder. They assume this because the Scriptures lack any guidelines for length of service. Without specific directions, they conclude that it is the will of God that these men are "elders for life." Unfortunately, this is once again superimposing "form" on Scripture. It is also arguing from silence.

The facts are, the biblical story is open-ended. There are many details that are missing—and by divine design. God wants every local church to develop "forms" that enable elders to do the very best possible job "managing" and "shepherding" the church within a particular culture.

In this sense, a rotating system certainly falls within the realm of "freedom in form." But, as stated earlier, among the major weaknesses in this approach are loss of continuity and an inefficiency. Some churches attempt to resolve this problem by allowing elders to serve several terms. On the other hand, if elders are indeed appointed to serve indefinitely—as they are in our church—there is the challenge of what to do with elders who do not or cannot function as they should. What if they become disqualified?

In actuality, we have discovered that when we take the qualifications seriously (as we do) and when elders themselves are accountable to each other (as they are), men will naturally step aside when it's appropriate. If they feel they have become disqualified, they should be able to resign with dignity (see James' story in chapter 28, "Older, but Not Ready"). If they feel there are too many other demands on their time, they can also step aside with full prayer support from the other elders. Over the years, we've had this happen, but it happened not because they were asked to step aside for one reason or another, but because they initiated the decision.

However, there are situations where an elder may become divisive and because of his pride and selfish ambitions, refuse to step aside. To deal with this potential problem, it is wise for every elder (including present elders) to sign an agreement that if the other elders believe he should resign, he will abide by their decision. Fortunately, we have not faced this problem, and pray it will never be necessary.

Remember that one of the most noble decisions an elder can make is to resign his position so he can devote more time to his family. Who can fault this man? Only those who are less than spiritual will criticize this kind of decision. When this happens, there is nothing but admiration from those "who are spiritual."

MORE FORM
QUESTIONS

In chapters 33–35, we have looked at four form questions—questions of methodology and procedures that help local churches to function effectively as they declare and practice biblical truth. They are: (1) How old should leaders be? (2) What specific methods should be used to select and appoint qualified spiritual leaders? (3) How many elders should there be in a single church? (4) How long should these leaders serve?

Here are six more form questions.

QUESTION 5:

HOW SHOULD AN ELDER BOARD MAKE DECISIONS?

Seeking Full Consensus

Early in my church-planting experience, I was enamored with the concept of "consensus." If we're all being led by the Holy Spirit, shouldn't we all come to agreement on all issues? This sounds very spiritual, and it works quite well when the group is small and the decisions are not critical. But I soon sensed several problems with this method.

First, a "consensus" approach at times puts intense pressure on an elder who may have reservations about a particular decision. To avoid standing in the way, some men simply outwardly agree but internally disagree. This often leads to inner tensions and even resentment that will eventually surface.

Second, when a group is committed to this approach, but an elder or two continues to raise objections to important decisions, our tendency as "primary leaders" is to put subtle pressure on these men to conform. Though our intentions are to move the ministry forward, those who are under pressure sense our frustration and once again often agree because they do not want to be a "wrench in the machinery." Unfortunately, this also creates "outward" conformity but, again, no "inward" convictions. This too will lead to resentment and feelings of being manipulated. Furthermore, the person objecting may be presenting a perspective the Lord wants the group to hear and consider.

It dawned on me one day that striving for a consensus is simply a "lopsided voting" system. I used to say, "Does anyone object?" If there was silence, we assumed total agreement. However, I discovered that not everyone spoke up for fear of being a dissenter and hindering progress.

Seeking Full Support

Since then, we have been committed to taking a vote when making decisions on certain issues. We simply follow parliamentary procedure which over the years has proven to be very effective. For example, once a motion is on the table, if someone still feels out of harmony with a proposal, he has an opportunity to voice his concerns in open discussion. However, if he still is not convinced and the majority of elders still feel comfortable with the motion, he can then cast a "negative vote" but then "agree" to support the majority. In essence, this is an effective way to arrive at "consensus."

On the other hand, if several elders continue to be concerned about a particular proposal, it's always wise to table the matter to give ample time for reflection and prayer and then to revisit the issue. Having said this, I'm convinced that very godly men do not always agree on all issues. This shouldn't surprise us. Though I have my personal opinions about Paul and Barnabas and their intense disagreement that led to a separation, I have never questioned their godly character. Both of these men were "prophets and teachers" and received direct messages from the Holy Spirit. Yet they came to conclusions about John Mark that were 180 degrees apart.

QUESTION 6:
IS A STAFF-LED CHURCH BIBLICAL?

Strengths and Weaknesses of a Staff-Led Church

There is nothing in Scripture that states it is wrong to lead a church with a paid staff. However, as with any organizational system, there are both strengths and weaknesses. Normally, the people who occupy these paid positions are younger leaders who do not have the insights that come with age and experience. I have also found that godly men who have been successful in the business world bring wisdom to the decision-making process that none of us as staff pastors have, simply because we haven't functioned long-term as leaders in that environment. This does not mean that "businessmen" automatically bring positive input to eldership. In fact, they may attempt to operate with a "business model" that at times contradicts biblical principles of leadership. However, there is no substitute for an experienced businessman who is spiritually mature, who has a biblical perspective on leadership and who has integrated these scriptural concepts into his own leadership style.

A Case Study of Interaction Between Elders and Staff

In terms of our evolving forms, there was a point in time that the elders invited our administrative staff to attend elder meetings regularly as input people. However, I'll never forget the meeting when several elders raised a very significant question: Are we an "elder-led church" or a "staff-led church?" I appreciated that openness. The point they were making was that the staff had inadvertently become such a strong influence in these meetings that as elders they didn't feel they were indeed the leaders of the church. In essence, the staff had begun to function as if they were elders. Consequently, the elders asked the administrative staff to discontinue attending regular elder meetings.

It didn't take long for all of us to see the problem. Though some felt a bit disenfranchised, they eventually saw the wisdom of this decision. One of our pastors was disappointed because he sincerely wanted to learn everything he could from the elders and their interaction on issues. However, he understood the reasoning behind this decision.

To facilitate interaction between elders and staff, we schedule significant times for fellowship with one another, often including our wives. And when we schedule staff retreats, we invite any elder who can break away from his business obligations to join us.

QUESTION 7:
SHOULDN'T ELDER MEMBERSHIP
INCLUDE STAFF PASTORS AS WELL?

Making staff pastors part of the elder board may work in a small church where the paid staff is limited. However, as the church grows and as the number of paid pastors increases, if all were official elders they would soon outnumber the nonstaff elders. For example, Fellowship Bible Church North now has close to twenty full-time staff pastors. If all of these men became official elders, board functions would quickly become inefficient because of sheer size. Further, this would create an unhealthy power block, particularly when it comes to making decisions where the staff would naturally have a vested interest.

Though every staff pastor should be "qualified" to be an elder, nowhere in Scripture does it say he must have "elder authority."

QUESTION 8:

WHICH IS MORE BIBLICAL—A CONGREGATIONAL FORM
OF CHURCH GOVERNMENT OR AN ELDER-LED CHURCH?

The question of whether church government should be led by the congregation or its elders is definitely one of "form," as the Scriptures do not answer this question definitively and absolutely. However, as we look at the biblical story carefully, we can gain some insights that enable us to evaluate various approaches to church governance.

Congregational Versus Representative Government in the Early Church

Some leaders and congregations are rather adamant in proposing that a congregational form of government is the only biblical system. They cite examples in the book of Acts, such as when Luke recorded that "the Twelve gathered *all the disciples together*" and told them to "choose seven men" to care for the Grecian widows. We also read that the "whole group" chose these men and the apostles affirmed these men (Acts 6:2–6).

It may appear that this was a "congregational" decision on the part of the Jerusalem church. We must remember, however, that at this point in time there could easily have been fifty thousand to one hundred thousand believers in Jerusalem who couldn't even gather in one place. Second, a closer look at the passage reveals that the apostles probably met with just those Grecian Jews who had widows who were affected—not the Hebrew believers who were residents of Jerusalem and Judea. Chances are that this may have been a very small representative group as well. Clearly, this is not a model for "congregationalism." If we draw this conclusion, we are simply superimposing on Scripture a "form" that isn't there.

Some also point to the decisions made during the council meetings on law versus grace (Acts 15). When Judas and Silas were chosen to accompany Paul and Barnabas as they delivered the letter composed by the "apostles and elders," we read that the "whole church" was involved in selecting these two men (v. 22). However, we must remember that Luke frequently used these inclusive terms ("all," "whole") to refer to a very select group or a representative group. For example, when he recorded that "*all* except the apostles were scattered through Judea and Samaria," following Stephen's death, he may have been referring to the six remaining Grecian Jews who were appointed to serve tables (see chapter 5, "The Larger Scene").[1]

Similarly, when he referenced the "whole church" that was involved in the decision to select Judas and Silas, Luke may have been referring to a relatively small group of dedicated believers who had voluntarily joined the apostles and elders in these discussions about "law and grace," perhaps meeting in Mary's home as they had done earlier when Peter was released from prison (Acts 12:12). This was not a "congregational meeting" as we often define it today.

A Personal Perspective Favoring Elder-Led Decisions

Having experienced both "congregational" and "elder-rule" systems, I must admit my own bias. The weaknesses I have seen in congregationalism almost always concern church members who are involved in making decisions who are not mature believers. Church membership is often based on a profession of faith and expressing that faith through baptism. However, this does not mean that these believers are mature enough in Christ to make critical decisions for the church.

In a family setting, we would not allow a three-year-old to vote on whether we're going to build a new home or whether Dad should change jobs. And we certainly wouldn't allow a young child to vote on the family budget. And what father would allow a child to be a part of making a decision regarding disciplining a brother or sister? Just so, there are "infants in Christ" who have "joined the church" and are not mature enough to make important decisions for the church. These dynamics represent some of the major weaknesses in a congregational form of government.

That's not to say there are no dangers in elder-led decision making. Within the elder-led church, if qualifications for eldership are not taken seriously and an effective system is lacking for selecting and appointing spiritual leaders, we can have a group of immature Christian men making decisions for the church. There is nothing more devastating than having carnal believers as elders.

Another problem relates to elder accountability beyond themselves. Even having final authority rest in the local congregation does not keep churches from splitting. A divided elder board usually also divides the church. The safest plan is to have accountability "outward" rather than "inward" as described under Principle 11 in chapter 31.

Personally, I've been involved in an elder-led system since beginning my church-planting experiences. Frankly, the most serious problems I've seen relate to having men and their wives in leadership who lack the character qualities outlined by the apostle Paul in the Pastoral Epistles. On the other hand, when these qualifications are carefully considered and applied, I've discovered there is no more effective decision-making system. When these men and their wives have one goal in mind—to serve others and not themselves—it's a great blessing for the whole church.

It must be said that biblical freedom also allows leaders to combine these two approaches in various ways. The important factor is that we must go back to the leadership principles of Scripture and measure our particular forms against these principles. If we do, we'll be able to develop approaches that will work best in our particular cultural situations.

QUESTION 9:
WHAT "FORM" CHANGES NEED TO BE MADE AS A CHURCH GROWS NUMERICALLY?

When a church is small with a few elders and one staff pastor, it's relatively easy to function. But as a church grows and more than one pastor is added to the staff, it becomes very important that lines of authority be established. I know of churches where several staff pastors each report to the elders as a group. This, of course, creates serious challenges in terms of accountability. It's very unrealistic to believe that nonstaff leaders can as a group properly supervise individual pastors—especially since they are not involved with the day-to-day operations. It sets the stage for serious misunderstandings, "power plays," and inadequate accountability.

This becomes even more important when determining job performance and salaries. It's at this point that a primary leader is absolutely essential. The staff leaders must be accountable to this leader who in turn reports to and makes recommendations to the "elder body." And as the paid staff continues to grow, it becomes more and more essential that an adequate system of accountability continues to develop throughout the organization without becoming institutionalized and bureaucratic.

In our own church, where we now have almost twenty staff pastors, only two of us are elders—myself and the associate pastor. As a total elder body, we concentrate on giving overall direction to the church but delegate the day-to-day operations to the staff. However, as senior pastor, it's my responsibility (with my associate) to adequately represent the staff and have them interface regularly with the elders in order to present their ministry needs. It's also my responsibility (along with my associate) to adequately represent the elders to the staff.

QUESTION 10:
HOW DOES THE HOUSEHOLD MODEL WORK?

Welcoming the Input of Elders' Wives

As stated in chapter 15, our elders' wives function alongside their mates just as in the home. They often attend church-based training sessions, participate in discussions, work through the same projects as the elders and make significant contributions. On some occasions, we have also invited these women to attend special elder meetings to give us input on particular issues. This does not mean they have "elder" status anymore than they have "husband" or "father" status.

In terms of women participating in the life of the church, the "household model" opens up unusual opportunities. For example, one of the most beautiful experiences for our congregation is when a small group (minichurch) pastor has helped baptize a father, the father in turn has baptized the mother, and the mother—standing beside her husband—has baptized the children. On another occasion, the husband baptized his wife, and in turn the wife baptized the husband. Another time, a young woman who serves faithfully in our church led a young man to Christ and baptized him in one of our main services. We believe this is in perfect harmony with the "household model."

Some ecclesiastical groups may consider this a violation of Scripture. They point to "ordination" as the biblical criteria for baptizing, serving communion, or even taking the offering. However, the New Testament never defines "ordination" as many do today. This practice evolved beyond the biblical story. In other words, it has its roots in "tradition," not Scripture.

This does not mean official "ordination" is inappropriate. In fact, in our culture it is essential to enable those of us who are paid by the church to receive government-approved tax benefits. In some states, this kind of ordination is also necessary to perform weddings. But to use "ordination" to restrict members of the body from functioning as just described is to superimpose a very "restrictive form" on the New Testament.

Communion in the Church

In terms of communion, we encourage believing fathers and mothers to remember the Lord with their believing children—making it a part of a meal just as they did in New Testament days. We must remember that in most instances, the early church could only meet in homes. They had no official "church buildings" for the first two centuries. Furthermore, the "Lord's Supper" became an extension of the Jewish Passover meal. This is what was happening in Jerusalem when these new believers "broke bread in their homes and ate together with glad and sincere hearts" (Acts 2:46).

Regarding communion practices, we should remember that most churches did not begin to practice "the token meal" until much later in church history. Many believers today do not realize that we are already practicing "freedom in form" when it comes to the early church model.

We also encourage our minichurches to have communion together when they meet in homes. This enables believers to have this experience in conjunction with a fellowship meal. Though official minichurch leaders often conduct this service, they also share the responsibility with other members of the group. This, we believe, is true biblical freedom in form.

It always surprises me when some people actually believe the Bible teaches you cannot have a communion service unless there is an official elder or deacon present. They, of course, do not understand that these "traditions" have grown out of church history—not the Scriptures. And there are those who believe a communion service must be in a church building— which is even more surprising since believers could not meet in special buildings for a couple centuries. They *had* to meet in homes.

A FINAL WORD

This takes us back to where we began in this study. Scriptural principles reflect biblical functions and directives that give us freedom to develop forms that will enable us to practice biblical Christianity in every culture and at any moment in history. To be able to differentiate between "function" and "form" is to be able to distinguish between what should never change and what *should* change in order to carry out the Great Commission of our Lord Jesus Christ.

NOTE

1. In his article, "The Acts of the Apostles: 1:1–5," Richard N. Longenecker gave us a helpful comment regarding how Luke used the Greek word *pantes* in both his Gospel and in the book of Acts: "Throughout his two volumes Luke uses the word 'all' as a general expression that the context in each case must define. So we cannot assume he meant his Gospel to be any more exhaustive than Acts. In a number of places in the NT 'many' (*polloi*) and 'all' (*pantes*) are used interchangeably (e.g., Matt. 20:28; Mark 10:45 [cf. 1 Tim. 2:6]; Matt. 12:15, Mark 3:10; Rom. 5:12–21), with the context alone determining in each case the precise nuance." *The Expositor's Bible Commentary*, vol. 9, ed. Frank E. Gaebelein (Grand Rapids: Zondervan, 1981), 253.

A SUCCESSION
PLAN

As I've watched the multiplication of megachurches that have developed a large staff and have built multimillion dollar facilities, one of my concerns is what will happen when the founding pastor retires or moves on to another ministry. Without question, the success of these churches relates directly to their dynamic leaders. This is not a criticism but an observation based on reality. God uses the personality and gifts of primary leaders to accomplish very significant goals. I would be less than honest if I did not admit that my own style of leadership has significantly impacted Fellowship Bible Church North where I currently pastor.

This concern has definitely influenced my own thinking and strategy as a pastor. I'm sharing our succession plan at this point because Bob Buford and Brad Smith—who graciously wrote the foreword to this book—have encouraged me to tell our story. Hopefully, it will be helpful.

In essence, this chapter is about leaders preparing leaders— the next primary leader of the church and future elder leaders as well. If you have a large church or a church with one or more leaders near retirement age, here is one model to consider.

BEGINNINGS

When I began my church-planting ministry, I was committed to multiplying churches from the home base rather than simply building a larger and larger centralized church body. This is not to say that this latter approach is not appropriate. I soon discovered that even though you attempt to plant churches, if you're doing things right in a heavily populated area, it will not keep the mother church from continuing to grow. This is certainly true at Fellowship Bible Church North. We *are* a megachurch— and so are several churches we've planted in the Dallas area.

As our own pastoral staff at Fellowship Bible Church North continued to expand, I began to share the teaching and preaching ministry with several of these men, particularly surrendering the pulpit when I was traveling or on vacation. I decided not to bring in guest speakers "to fill the pulpit" (except for very rare occasions), but rather to give some of the other pastors an opportunity to speak. Jeff Jones, one of several men who shared this responsibility periodically, began to get some rather difficult questions to answer, such as: "Do you know something that we don't know?" It was obvious that many in the congregation were responding in a particular way to Jeff's teaching and leadership in other areas. Furthermore, most of our people knew I had passed age sixty-five and wondered if perchance we were preparing Jeff to be my successor.

A NEW MILLENNIUM

This positive feedback and the ensuing questions put Jeff in a very awkward position. As we talked together about this matter, I knew we had to "get out front" of what was happening. This kind of speculation can lead to false conclusions and rumors. Consequently, I scheduled meetings with each elder privately and asked a pointed question: "Of all the people on staff, who do you think should possibly take over my role in seven years?" This question, of course, was based on the assumption that I could continue to function effectively until I was seventy-five. Without knowing what the other elders were thinking, each man without equivocation mentioned Jeff Jones. Interestingly, we were headed into the year 2000—a very important point in history. It also turned out to be a very important moment in the history of our church.

I decided to approach the other staff pastors who had also been speaking in my absence. Again, these men responded the same way. They all affirmed Jeff's ability to teach the Scriptures and to lead others effectively. Not one person felt he was being passed over, which is a tribute to their own maturity and a confirmation to the elders that Jeff was indeed a very viable candidate.

A HUSBAND-WIFE TEAM

With the blessing of the elders, I approached Jeff and his wife, Christy, and told them what we had been doing behind the scenes. They were honored, of course, that there was such unanimity in the responses to my question. After prayerful consideration with his wife, Jeff accepted this invitation—realizing that seven years is indeed a long period of time. However, I will never forget his initial response to the invitation. "It will," he said, "take me seven years to get ready." I could sense these were not mere words or an obsequious platitude. He meant every word of it!

As elders, we next developed a plan to communicate our decision to the entire church body. Since we are not a congregational church, it was not necessary to call for a church-wide vote. However, the response of the people was spontaneous and unanimous. We could sense that everyone who was committed to our fellowship was encouraged with our decision. It actually gave our people a sense of security relative to their future commitment to the church.

BECOMING ASSOCIATE PASTOR

At this point, we promoted Jeff to serve as the associate pastor. In this role, he does about one-third of the teaching, and my stated goal is to help him build his team for the future. At this point in time, he has effectively led our total leadership team through an alignment process. Though we were not seriously "compartmentalizing" in our many different ministries, it was beginning to happen—which is predictable when an organization gets to a certain size. Churches are not exempt. They become institutionalized just like any large enterprise.

It's a great experience to sense that all of our ministry leaders are headed in the same direction and committed to the same core values. Jeff has led this charge and though it caused all of our staff to look carefully at their ministries and how these ministries relate to our corporate values, we've never been more united around these core values. We're praying regularly that Satan will not disrupt what is happening. We must be on guard—making "every effort to keep the unity of the Spirit through the bond of peace" (Ephesians 4:3).

In His Own Words

How does such a succession plan affect the future leader? I asked Jeff to comment on the process, including its impact on the church. Here are his words:

"When Gene first approached me with the idea of becoming his successor, I was both excited and scared half to death. I was excited because there is no one I would rather have as a mentor in my life. Yet I was, of course, scared because stepping into Gene's shoes is intimidating. He is the founder of our church, a well-known teacher, author and leader, and is the person whom God used to restore my own passion for the local church. . . .

"A significant key to a successful extended transition is that both leaders have to leave their egos behind and learn to lead and serve together. This is generally more of a challenge for the outgoing pastor than for the incoming one. A succession process means that one person is slowly letting go and the other is slowly taking on more. Most of us have a harder time letting go than we do accepting more. Gene has balanced this unusually well.

"Gene has been incredibly freedom-giving, allowing me space to lead and grow. Under his supervision, I help lead the staff and work with him and the elders to set the direction of the ministries. This has allowed me to assume executive level leadership, yet still with his wisdom and experience. In this sense, we lead the church together. I am very careful not to move forward unless we are both fully onboard. This may lengthen the decision-making process, but decisions reached this way are generally far better than they would have been otherwise. It is imperative in succession for both parties, as much as possible, to have maximum ownership of key directional choices.

"This takes a significant amount of communication. I remember times over the last couple of years when Gene would ask my input and I might have a different perspective. At times I have said, 'Gene, which hat do you want me to wear? Do you want me to wear the associate pastor hat, and then I'll tell you what I think and we'll move forward with whatever you want to do? Or I can put on my future senior pastor hat, and it will be a more involved discussion.' He has always said, 'Jeff, put on your future senior pastor hat. That is the only way this will work. If you act like you are okay but you really aren't, this could derail the succession plan.'

"A significant advantage of an extended succession process is that the sheep have time to know my voice in addition to Gene's. As I lead and teach, people get to know my heart. They are learning to follow not just Gene, but me as well. Starting out, I was working on borrowed credibility from Gene, since people knew how much he believed in me. Over time, my own leadership credibility is emerging as people become accustomed to and excited about my leadership. That natural process is essential, though it would be threatening to a senior pastor who is insecure.

Leadership Styles

"Another key to a succession process is demonstrating continuity while at the same time allowing for differences. Gene and I are different people, and therefore our leadership styles and speaking styles are different. When the elders met to ask me to be Gene's successor, [they explained] . . . 'We want Jeff Jones to be the future pastor of this church, and we don't expect or want you to try to be like Gene. You lead the way God has called you to lead.'

"This gives me incredible freedom. Yet it also gives security to the church. Though we are different stylistically, our ministry philosophy is the same. Our values are very similar. The more we can emphasize that, the better. People love it when we talk about each other positively. They enjoy seeing us on the platform together and enjoying life together. They need to know that while we are different, we love each other and are committed to the same basic principles that form our church.

"The three years have gone remarkably well, but transition is still transition—meaning, it is not always easy. As succession becomes more and more a reality in people's minds, those who have been around a long time begin to grieve Gene's impending absence. Others are excited for the transition to happen as soon as possible. Some have anxiety about the unknowns of the future under my leadership; others have great anticipation. Some leaders in addition to Gene also have had to let go, while other younger leaders are learning to assume leadership. With all of these different feelings, we have to recognize how natural they are and keep communicating as much as possible to help people process these feelings well.

A Prayerful Process

"We are excited about the process and equally prayerful. We believe it is the best path for our church in leading us forward in unity. We are prayerful, because we also know that any organization in transition is at a vulnerable place. . . . Satan would like nothing better than to build a wedge between Gene and me, or divide the church into factions."

Jeff concluded his comments with a personal reflection:

"As for me, I am thankful for a church with the foresight to have a succession plan. I praise God for an opportunity to be mentored into the role of senior pastor by a leader like Gene. And I am also grateful for a mentor who is empowering, doing all he can to help me be successful and the church be vibrant long after his leadership tenure comes to an end. That kind of servant-leadership is rare."

Elder Succession

As stated in the previous chapter, once we launched this succession plan, all of the other elders concluded that they needed a similar plan. Consequently, they've agreed together that none of them would continue in an elder role beyond age seventy-five. Since several of these men have served with me since the beginning of my church planting ministry, they're approximately my age.

We then launched a plan to bring new elders on the board—men Jeff particularly felt comfortable to have serve with him in the future. Once we all agreed on who these men and their wives should be, we then assigned Jeff the responsibility to disciple and prepare these couples for eldership (see chapter 34). We began with two couples and as of this writing have added two more. Over the next couple of years, we'll no doubt add more new elders until the succession plan is complete and the men who have served for a number of years begin to step aside and turn the ministry over to this new body of elders led by my associate.

"If It's the Lord's Will"

From the very beginning of this process, we've realized that each step is in the Lord's hands. I've often quoted James:

> Now listen, you who say, "Today or tomorrow we will go to this or that city, spend a year there, carry on business and make money." Why, you do not even know what will happen tomorrow. What is your life? You are a mist that appears for a little while and then vanishes. Instead, you ought to say, "If it is the Lord's will, we will live and do this or that." [James 4:13–15]

Not one of us knows what a day will bring forth. We can and must say, "'If it is the Lord's will' we will complete this succession plan." Jeff has accepted this challenge with "open hands," ready to let go. The process can only be finalized at the end of the seven-year journey—or sooner if something unforeseen happens to me personally that makes it impossible to continue to function in my role. Though the first three years have gone remarkably well, as of this writing we still have four years to go! The greatest concern for both of us is that the church we love will never miss a beat in its ongoing ministry, that it will be healthier four years from now and healthier still when the succession plan is completed and ongoing.

FINAL WORDS

Let me say a final word to men who may be at my stage of life—or even younger—and are pastoring large churches. The future of your ministry in many respects is in your hands. Don't wait until it's too late to begin this process. The ongoing fruit that you've given your life to produce depends on your plans for succession.

Over the years, I have believed in what for me is a very important spiritual and psychological guideline: *"When I need the church more than the church needs me, I have stayed too long."* In other words, when my ego needs are more important than the needs of the people in the church, I have stepped over the line and I'm reflecting carnality rather than spirituality.

On occasions, I have asked my elders to help me keep this guideline in mind! We all know stories in the corporate world where CEOs have allowed their egos to drive their longevity and they "hang on" too long—to the detriment of the organization. Unfortunately, senior pastors are not exempt from experiencing the same ego trip and can hinder God's kingdom work. When this happens, the "applause of people" has become far more important than the "applause of God." I sincerely trust that this will never happen in my life. That is my ongoing prayer—to continue to seek and be grateful for the applause of God.

USE OF THE WORD "CHURCH" (*EKKLESIA*) IN THE BOOK OF ACTS AND THE EPISTLES

As you study this chart, you may wish to check out each reference in the biblical context. You'll discover it's an inspiring investigation, taking you more deeply into *why* the "church" is such a foundational and pervasive concept in the New Testament. But before you do, scan the following profile and answer these questions:

1. How many times did New Testament authors use the word "church" to refer to the *universal* church? Do you agree with these categories? If not, why not?
2. How many times did the New Testament authors refer to a *group of local churches* and how many times did these authors refer to a *single local church?* Do you agree with these categories? If not, why not?
3. What other significant observations can you make about this profile?
4. In what ways do your observations affirm or challenge your previous conclusions about the church?

Verse[1]	The Universal CHURCH	A Group of Local Churches	A Specific Local Church
Acts 5:11			Church
Acts 8:1			Church
Acts 9:31		Churches	
Acts 11:22			Church
Acts 11:26			Church
Acts 12:1			Church
Acts 12:5			Church
Acts 13:1			Church
Acts 14:23			Church
Acts 14:27			Church
Acts 15:3			Church
Acts 15:4			Church
Acts 15:22			Church
Acts 15:41		Churches	
Acts 16:5		Churches	
Acts 18:22			Church
Acts 20:17			Church
Acts 20:28			Church
James 5:14			Church
Galatians 1:2		Churches	
Galatians 1:13	CHURCH		
Galatians 1:22		Churches	
1 Thessalonians 1:1			Church
1 Thessalonians 2:14		Churches	
2 Thessalonians 1:1			Church
2 Thessalonians 1:4		Churches	
1 Corinthians 1:2			Church
1 Corinthians 4:17			Church
1 Corinthians 7:17		Churches	
1 Corinthians 10:32	CHURCH		
1 Corinthians 11:16		Churches	
1 Corinthians 11:18			Church

Verse	The Universal CHURCH	A Group of Local Churches	A Specific Local Church
1 Corinthians 11:22	CHURCH		
1 Corinthians 12:28	CHURCH		
1 Corinthians 14:4			Church
1 Corinthians 14:5			Church
1 Corinthians 14:12			Church
1 Corinthians 14:19			Church
1 Corinthians 14:23			Church
1 Corinthians 14:28			Church
1 Corinthians 14:33		Congregations	
1 Corinthians 14:34		Churches	
1 Corinthians 14:35			Church
1 Corinthians 15:9	CHURCH		
1 Corinthians 16:1		Churches	
1 Corinthians 16:19		Churches	
2 Corinthians 1:1			Church
2 Corinthians 8:1		Churches	
2 Corinthians 8:18		Churches	
2 Corinthians 8:23		Churches	
2 Corinthians 8:24		Churches	
2 Corinthians 11:8		Churches	
2 Corinthians 11:28		Churches	
2 Corinthians 12:13		Churches	
Romans 16:1			Church
Romans 16:4		Churches	
Romans 16:5			Church
Romans 16:16		Churches	
Romans 16:23			Church
Ephesians 1:22	CHURCH		
Ephesians 3:10	CHURCH		
Ephesians 3:21	CHURCH		
Ephesians 5:23	CHURCH		
Ephesians 5:24	CHURCH		

Verse	The Universal CHURCH	A Group of Local Churches	A Specific Local Church
Ephesians 5:25	CHURCH		
Ephesians 5:27	CHURCH		
Ephesians 5:29	CHURCH		
Ephesians 5:32	CHURCH		
Colossians 1:18	CHURCH		
Colossians 1:24	CHURCH		
Colossians 4:15			Church
Colossians 4:16			Church
Philippians 3:6	CHURCH		
Philippians 4:15			Church
Philemon 2			Church
1 Timothy 3:5			Church
1 Timothy 3:15	CHURCH		
1 Timothy 5:16			Church
Hebrews 2:12	CONGREGATION		
Hebrews 12:23	CHURCH		
3 John 6			Church
3 John 9			Church
3 John 10			Church
Revelation 1:4		Churches	
Revelation 1:11		Churches	
Revelation 1:20		Churches	
Revelation 2:1			Church
Revelation 2:7		Churches	
Revelation 2:8			Church
Revelation 2:11		Churches	
Revelation 2:12			Church
Revelation 2:17		Churches	
Revelation 2:18			Church
Revelation 2:23		Churches	
Revelation 2:29		Churches	
Revelation 3:1			Church

Verse	The Universal CHURCH	A Group of Local Churches	A Specific Local Church
Revelation 3:6		Churches	
Revelation 3:7			Church
Revelation 3:13		Churches	
Revelation 3:14			Church
Revelation 3:22		Churches	
Revelation 22:16		Churches	

SOURCE: Gene A. Getz, *The Measure of a Church* rev. ed. (Ventura, Calif.: Regal, 1995), 245–48. Used by permission.

NOTE

1. After the book of Acts, the New Testament letters are listed in the order they were probably written.

A BIBLICAL
PERSPECTIVE
ON HEALING

The first function for elders that is described in detail in the biblical story is their responsibility to be available to pray for the sick. James, the half brother of Christ and the lead elder in the church in Jerusalem, made this very clear (James' epistle was probably the first letter written that is included in the New Testament canon). His instructions in James 5:13–16 are:

> Is any one of you in trouble? He should pray. Is anyone happy?
> Let him sing songs of praise. Is any one of you sick? He should
> call the elders of the church to pray over him and anoint him with
> oil in the name of the Lord. And the prayer offered in faith will
> make the sick person well; the Lord will raise him up. If he has
> sinned, he will be forgiven. Therefore confess your sins to each
> other and pray for each other so that you may be healed. The
> prayer of a righteous man is powerful and effective.

To understand what James meant, we first must understand

the healing ministry of Jesus as recorded in the Gospels and of the apostles particularly, as well as several other individuals who are mentioned in the book of Acts.

JESUS' HEALING MINISTRY

When Jesus began His ministry, He often healed people—a miraculous demonstration of God's power that verified His deity, specifically that He was "the Word [who] became flesh" (John 1:1, 14). John's primary purpose in writing his Gospel was to demonstrate this truth. As he concluded this marvelous treatise on who Jesus really is, he summarized this purpose: "Jesus did many other *miraculous signs* in the presence of his disciples, which are not recorded in this book. But *these are written that you may believe that Jesus is the Christ, the Son of God,* and that by believing you may have life in his name (John 20:30–31, italics added).

Four of the miracles John chose to record in this Gospel in order to prove Christ's deity involved His healing ministry:

☐ He healed the sickness of a royal official's son (4:46–53)

☐ He enabled the invalid in Jerusalem to get up and walk after he had been incapacitated for thirty-eight years (5:1–13)

☐ He gave a man sight who had been born blind (9:1–41)

☐ He actually restored Lazarus' life after he had died four days earlier (11:38–44)

THE APOSTLES' HEALING MINISTRY

Jesus gave the same power to the eleven apostles, especially Peter, and later to Paul who described himself as "the least of the apostles and do not even deserve to be called an apostle, because I persecuted the church of God. But by the grace of God I am what I am" (1 Corinthians 15:9–10).

It's very interesting and significant that though there are several general references to miracles performed by the apostles (for example, Acts 2:43; 5:12), Luke only recorded and described in detail three specific healings by Peter and three specific healings by Paul:

The Apostle Peter	The Apostle Paul
The *crippled man* at the temple gate (Acts 3:1–10).	The *crippled man* in Lystra who had been lame from birth (Acts 14:8–10).
Aeneas, a paralytic who had been bed-ridden for eight years (Acts 9:32–35).	*Eutychus*, raised from the dead at Troas (Acts 20:7–12).
Dorcas, raised from the dead (Acts 9:36–43).	*Publius*, healed—the chief official on the island of Malta (Acts 28:7–8).

Though Peter and Paul certainly performed more healings than those recorded (see Acts 5:15–16; 28:9–10), Luke without a doubt graphically recorded these six specific healings (three for Peter and three for Paul) to demonstrate their apostolic calling. When Paul wrote to the Corinthians, he spoke of this special calling and the way miracles verified this calling: "The things that mark an apostle—signs, wonders and miracles—were done among you with great perseverance" (2 Corinthians 12:12).

Peter, of course, was called in a special way to be "an apostle to the Jews," whereas Paul was called to be "an apostle to the Gentiles" (Galatians 2:8). It is not an accident that Luke recorded almost three identical healing events for each of these men, obviously to verify their apostleship.

THE HEALING MINISTRY OF OTHERS

Though several other men including Philip the evangelist (8:5–7), are mentioned in the books of Acts—men who could miraculously heal people—this ability seems to have been given only to a select few by the Holy Spirit. Paul also spoke of those who had the "gifts of healing" in his letter to the Corinthians (1 Corinthians 12:9), but we have no specific illustrations regarding how these gifts were exercised.

This leads to a second observation. Healing gifts were not only given to verify apostleship but also to verify the message of the Gospel. The author of Hebrews addresses this purpose when he wrote: "This salvation, which was first announced by the Lord, was confirmed to us by those who heard him [eyewitnesses]. God also *testified to it by signs, wonders and various miracles, and gifts of the Holy Spirit* distributed according to his will" (2:3–4, italics added).

James' Instructions to Elders (James 5:13–20)

When James instructed believers to "call the elders of the church" to pray over them when they are ill, he broadened the healing ministry to include the primary spiritual leaders in every local church (elders or overseers) and included "anyone who desired to have prayer for healing." The question we must explore is what kind of "illness" and "healing" did James have in mind?

To answer this question, it's important to see that the healings described in the Gospels by Jesus and by a select few in the book of Acts were performed for specific purposes. Though the welfare of the individuals certainly is important, as we've seen, the stated purpose was:

☐ To demonstrate Christ's deity

☐ To affirm apostolic calling

☐ To verify the message of the Gospel

By contrast, James' focus was primarily on *the welfare of believers*. It is not to affirm the elders' calling and position or to verify the Gospel, but to minister to every member of the body of Christ who desires prayer for healing.

To further explore the answer to this question (what kind of "illness" and "healing" did James have in mind), we need to make one other important observation. Nowhere in Scripture are we guaranteed that we will always be healed physically of every sickness and disease. If this were true, we could stop the aging process and never die. Even the apostle Paul, who performed various healing miracles, including raising Eutychus from the dead—did not experience healing himself. When he wrote to the Corinthians, he talked about a "thorn" in his flesh. We're not told what this "thorn" was, but we can assume that it was probably some type of physical ailment. Some believe it was blindness or even some kind of disfigurement from having been beaten and stoned. Regardless, Paul stated: "Three times I pleaded with the Lord to take it away from me. But he said to me, 'My grace is sufficient for you, for my power is made perfect in weakness'" (2 Corinthians 12:8–9).

What then did James have in mind? Paul's statement about himself in 2 Corinthians helps us with the answer to this question—particularly when we look carefully at the words James used to describe "sickness."

A CLOSE LOOK AT JAMES' INSTRUCTIONS

James used three Greek words to describe "sickness" that have their roots in the soul or heart. Though each word adds uniqueness in defining this "sickness," in essence they are synonymous in meaning. Note the following:

☐ 5:13 "Is any one of you in *trouble?*" (This Greek word coming from *kakopatheo* means to be afflicted or to be enduring hardship.)

☐ 5:14 "Is anyone of you *sick?*" (This Greek word comes from *astheneo* and means to be feeble, weak, exhausted.)

☐ 5:15 "Make the *sick* person well" (This Greek word comes from *kamno* and means to be faint, weary, weak, worn out, exhausted.)

The Physical and Psychological Effects of Stress

In this passage, James is addressing the issues he referred to throughout his letter. In chapter 1, he referred to "trials of many kinds" (1:2, 12) and in chapter 5, just before the paragraph under discussion, he referred to having "patience in the face of suffering" and used the Old Testament prophets as an example (5:10). It follows naturally that he then outlined what happens to people who are being persecuted and facing these "hard-ships." We experience the psychosomatic results—weariness, exhaustion, and physical weakness. It's in this context James exhorted these believers to "call the elders of the church to pray over him and anoint him with oil in the name of the Lord" (5:14).

Healing for the Soul and Body

There is an Old Testament proverb that correlates with the issues that James dealt with in this passage: "Pleasant words are a honeycomb, sweet to the soul and healing to the bones" (Proverb 16:24). In essence, we are basically two-dimensional creatures—both soul/spirit and body. To put it another way, we are both psychological/spiritual beings and physical beings. These are interrelated dimensions, so much so that we can experience "psychosomatic" conditions (from the Greek words *psuche*, meaning "soul," and *soma* meaning "body."), that is, conditions affecting both the "soul" and "body." Solomon reminds us in the proverb that pleasant words affect both our psychological and physiological being in a positive way.

On the other hand, Solomon also reminds us that "an anxious heart weighs a man down, but a kind word cheers him up" (Proverb 12:25). In this New Testament setting, James was certainly addressing the stress that resulted from persecution, unkindness, rejection, etc., and he encouraged these people to call for the elders to pray for them.

In our world today, we may not experience the kinds of persecution James addressed in his letter. But we do face many circumstances that are often beyond our control that have the same impact on our minds and bodies: tensions in our work, job loss, marital tensions, family difficulties involving our children, illnesses, etc. And some of the greatest causes of anxiety, of course, are physical problems caused by accidents, birth defects, bodily dete-rioration, and the whole aging process. All of these stressors affect our mind and body, and when we face these difficulties, we need help bearing these burdens. During such times, we should feel free to call for the elders of the church to pray for us. God's promise through James is that these prayers of faith will cause these weary, discouraged, and exhausted persons to become "well." The Greek word here is *sozo* and means to be "whole again."

Paul's Experience

Paul's testimony in his letter to the Corinthians is very helpful in understanding James' statements about healing. Though people may not be healed from certain physical maladies—their particular "thorn in the flesh" such as a serious heart condition, diabetes, Alzheimer's, or the effects of other deteriorating or injured body parts—God promises that His "grace is sufficient" for us. His "power is made perfect in weakness," enabling us to even "delight in weaknesses, in insults, in hardships, in persecutions, in difficulties" (2 Corinthians 12:8–10). With Paul we can say: "Now we know that if the earthly tent we live in is destroyed, we have a building from God, an eternal house in heaven, not built by human hands (2 Corinthians 5:1).

This does not mean that God will not use this process to bring physical healing—particularly if the problem is rooted in stress and emotional pain. Healing of the soul often brings healing to the body. But, further, God may also choose to heal a person supernaturally and even instantaneously from some physical ailment that seems to be primarily biological in nature. In fact, I heard recently from a valid source of several unusual physical healings among Muslim families. In these instances, God chose to validate the Gospel message regarding Jesus Christ just as He did during the first century. In some instances, whole families have put their faith in Jesus Christ.

However, these healings seem to be rare—even though God can still choose to work the same kinds of healings as those that are described in the Gospels and the book of Acts. We must never limit God, but we must not "put words in God's mouth" that He has not uttered—that we can *always* be healed from bodily ailments if we have enough faith. If we do, we can create false hope, and guilt feelings for failing to have enough faith. This kind of false biblical interpretation can even lead to disillusionment and doubt regarding the Christian faith. And from the viewpoint of spiritual leaders, it can also lead to false claims that are at times sincere but at other times insincere and deceptive. We want so much to believe in miraculous healings that we try to merge what we believe are "biblical realities" with personal experiences. When we do this, we can deceive ourselves as well as others, regardless of our sincerity.

Spiritual Effects of Sin

James went on to extend the cause of the kind of "sickness" he mentioned in his letter. Christians experience psychosomatic illness, not simply because of persecution and trials, but from allowing sin to come into their lives. In fact, James addressed this issue throughout his letter when he referred to an inappropriate use of the tongue (1:26; 3:1–12). He also referred to the results of showing favoritism to the wealthy and insulting poor people (2:1–12). He actually got very specific when he talked about the fights and the quarrels that existed among some of these believers (4:1–3). In fact, in 4:11 he wrote, "Brothers [sisters], do not slander one another."

"Sinful behavior" not only affects people who are victims of our sinful actions, but it affects those who are living in sin. As Christians, we cannot continue to live deliberately out of the will of God without "reaping what we sow." Therefore, James included this as a cause for being emotionally and physically weak. It's rooted in our spiritual condition. Consequently, he wrote, "Therefore confess your sins to each other and pray for each other so that you many be healed" (5:16).

It should be noted, however, that confessing our sins to one another is not necessary for God's forgiveness (1 John 1:9). However, this kind of confession is very helpful in terms of experiencing emotional and physical healing. This kind of openness to a group of godly believers enables others to pray for this kind of healing. This process actually helps us to forgive ourselves—which is also very important in terms of healing. Through this process of prayer, we experience love and support from spiritually mature people in the church who really care.

JAMES' INSTRUCTIONS AND
THE TWENTY-FIRST CENTURY CHURCH

Since our study, the elders want to take James' instructions more seriously than ever before. Our new and fresh study of this passage has motivated us to encourage all of our people to seek prayer for healing— regardless of the nature of that sickness.

Fortunately, this prayer process is not limited to calling only for the elders of our church. The important principle is that all believers can seek prayer from godly people. This is why James wrote that "the prayer of a righteous man is powerful and effective"—and then used Elijah as an example (James 5:16b–18).

At Fellowship Bible Church North, we have many people in leadership who are godly people. This is certainly true of our minichurch leaders who pastor and shepherd small groups. This is also true of our Stephen Ministers, who are committed to being available to people who are going through and/or are recovering from serious crises in their lives. But this principle applies as well to all brothers and sisters in Christ who are living in the will of God.

All true believers have access to God through this "new and living" way described so beautifully in Hebrews 10:19–22. Regarding "anointing with oil," we believe this was actually practiced in the New Testament days as a healing balm. However, we believe this practice is very appropriate today as a symbol of our concern and of God's healing touch and can be used by any group of spiritual leaders in the church who are living in the will of God.

A TWENTY-FIRST CENTURY STORY

I had the privilege of interviewing Kyle Duncan and his lovely wife, Suzanne, on my daily radio program called *Renewal*. They have a remarkable story. Because of a genetic weakness, the child they conceived inherited a serious condition that was terminal. Little Joseph would either die in the womb or shortly after birth. The sonograms revealed a child with multiple disorders and deformities. The doctor suggested that he be allowed to put this little infant (four months along) to sleep, which would cause a natural abortion.

Due to their faith, they chose to carry the child as long as he was alive, knowing the prognosis for a normal birth was beyond any medical correction. They realized that God could heal this little boy, but they also knew that it would be a virtual re-creation of many parts of the body—the brain, the heart, etc. Trusting God's providential care, they accepted the reality of deformity and death, but still were open to a complete miracle. They simply prayed that God's will would be done.

When Joseph was born, the doctors and nurses had a difficult time even knowing whether or not he was dead or alive. Kyle had grabbed a small bottle of oil from the kitchen when he left home to join Suzanne who had already given birth; his purpose was simply to anoint his infant son and dedicate him to the Lord Jesus Christ.

When Kyle arrived at the hospital, he dabbed some of the oil upon his own finger. Holding his child in his arms, not knowing if there was even life in his tiny deformed body, Kyle placed his oil-coated finger on Joseph and made the sign of the cross on his little forehead. To the surprise of the doctors and nurses and others in the room, at that very moment Joseph opened his eyes.

Was he healed of all his diseases? No. But God gave this little child three days of life that from a medical point of view should never have happened. Those special days were a gift from God to every family member who was able to hold this child and experience God's grace at this moment in Kyle and Suzanne's lives—and in the lives of their two young daughters.

I share this story to demonstrate that God responds to faith and prayer in ways that are different from our expectations. Though this child was not re-created on earth but went to be with Jesus, God in His mercy honored Kyle's obedience to the process in James' letter. In this case, this father served as shepherd and elder in his household—certainly an action based on biblical truth. Furthermore, the healing that day involved spiritual and emotional healing for the whole family.

DETERMINING A CANDIDATE'S "MATURITY QUOTIENT"

At Fellowship Bible Church North, we use the following form, based on criteria for elders found in 1 Timothy 3:1–7 and Titus 1:6–9 (NASB), to evaluate candidates for spiritual leadership in the church.

Above Reproach

1. How do you evaluate his/her reputation as a Christian both among fellow believers as well as among non-Christians?

   Dissatisfied   1   2   3   4   5   6   7   Satisfied

The Husband of One Wife

2. How do you evaluate his/her relationship with his/her spouse?

   Dissatisfied   1   2   3   4   5   6   7   Satisfied

Temperate

3. How do you evaluate the degree to which he/she is maintaining balance in his/her Christian experience?

Dissatisfied   1   2   3   4   5   6   7   Satisfied

Prudent

4. How do you evaluate his/her ability to be wise and discerning?

Dissatisfied   1   2   3   4   5   6   7   Satisfied

Respectable

5. How satisfied are you with the way his/her life reflects the life of Jesus Christ?

Dissatisfied   1   2   3   4   5   6   7   Satisfied

Hospitable

6. How do you evaluate his/her level of generosity?

Dissatisfied   1   2   3   4   5   6   7   Satisfied

Able to Teach

7. How do you evaluate his/her ability to communicate with others who may disagree with him/her?

Dissatisfied   1   2   3   4   5   6   7   Satisfied

Not Addicted to Wine

8. To what degree are you satisfied with his/her ability to control various kinds of obsessions and compulsions?

Dissatisfied   1   2   3   4   5   6   7   Satisfied

Not Self-Willed

9. How satisfied are you with his/her ability to relate to other people without being self-centered and controlling?

Dissatisfied   1   2   3   4   5   6   7   Satisfied

Not Quick-Tempered

10. How satisfied are you with the way he/she handles anger?

    Dissatisfied   1   2   3   4   5   6   7   Satisfied

Not Pugnacious

11. How satisfied are you with his/her ability to control any form of verbal or physical abuse?

    Dissatisfied   1   2   3   4   5   6   7   Satisfied

Gentle

12. How objective and fair-minded is he/she in his/her relationships with others?

    Dissatisfied   1   2   3   4   5   6   7   Satisfied

Uncontentious

13. How satisfied are you with his/her ability to avoid arguments?

    Dissatisfied   1   2   3   4   5   6   7   Satisfied

Free from the Love of Money

14. How satisfied are you with his/her ability to be nonmaterialistic?

    Dissatisfied   1   2   3   4   5   6   7   Satisfied

One Who Manages His/Her Own Household Well

15. If they are a father or mother, how satisfied are you with his/her ability to function in this role according to God's plan?

    Dissatisfied   1   2   3   4   5   6   7   Satisfied

Loving What Is Good

16. To what degree are you satisfied with his/her efforts at "overcoming evil with good"?

    Dissatisfied   1   2   3   4   5   6   7   Satisfied

Just ["upright"]

17. How satisfied are you with his/her ability to be just and fair in his/her relationship with others?

Dissatisfied   1   2   3   4   5   6   7   Satisfied

Devout ["holy"]

18. To what degree are you satisfied with the way his/her life reflects God's holiness?

Dissatisfied   1   2   3   4   5   6   7   Satisfied

Disciplined

19. How satisfied are you with his/her ability to live a disciplined Christian life?

Dissatisfied   1   2   3   4   5   6   7   Satisfied

Overall Spiritual Maturity

20. How do you evaluate his/her overall maturity as a Christian?

Dissatisfied   1   2   3   4   5   6   7   Satisfied

Signed: _____

APOSTLES, PROPHETS, AND TEACHERS

As I've studied the New Testament over the years, I've concluded for some time that God has outlined for us two important leadership phases. The first phase involves those leaders particularly who were identified as the "greater gifts" to the whole body of Christ and who were responsible to equip elders/overseers and deacons who could serve as permanent leaders in local churches. This fresh study of the New Testament as well as a careful look at the writings of the early church fathers has affirmed my previous conclusions.

It's also my personal opinion and experience that we need not be confused regarding these two phases. As we've seen in the biblical story, any qualified man can be appointed to be an elder/overseer in a local church and every qualified man or woman can be appointed to serve as a deacon. Though these leaders are to manage/shepherd and serve others, no spiritual gifts or special divine calling are mentioned in the list of qualifications in the pastoral letters.

On the other hand, those who were called to launch the church at large were selected and appointed by deity Himself and were endued by the Holy Spirit with certain spiritual gifts and abilities that enabled them to carry out the Great Commission. These leaders in phase one initially became Christ's witnesses, beginning in Jerusalem, "and in all Judea and Samaria, and to the ends of the earth" (Acts 1:8); however, as they established local churches throughout the Roman Empire, they appointed permanent local church leaders who were spiritually qualified to shepherd or manage and serve various communities of faith.

The "Greater Gifts"

Paul referred to those leaders involved in phase one in two key passages—first in his letter to the Corinthians and then in his letter to the Ephesians.

The Corinthian Correspondence

When Paul wrote his first letter to the Corinthian believers, the church evidently had not entered phase two. There are no references to elders/overseers. The believers' source of nurture came primarily from those Paul identified as *apostles*, *prophets*, and *teachers*. Even then, they were so immature and carnal that Paul had to exhort them to pay attention to these gifted individuals. Consequently, he wrote:

> And in the *church* God has appointed first of all *apostles*, second *prophets*, third *teachers* . . . but eagerly desire the *greater gifts*. [1 Corinthians 12:28, 31; all emphasis added]

The Corinthians were part of a divided church. Some were still devoting their allegiance to the apostle Paul. Some, however, were rejecting Paul as an apostolic leader and following the apostle Peter. Still others had rejected both Paul and Peter and were devoted to a teacher named Apollos. Then there were those who would not follow any of these gifted men and prided themselves on following only Jesus Christ (see 1 Corinthians 1:12).

To help these Christians overcome their divisiveness, Paul clearly identified these three foundational gifts as the most important gifts and urged the believers as a church to give attention to those who *had* and actually *were* these gifts.[1]

The Ephesian Correspondence

Those Paul identified in the Corinthian letter as the "greater gifts" in the church also appear in his letter to the Ephesians, but with more elaboration:

It was he [Jesus Christ] who gave

> *some* to be *apostles,*
>
> *some* to be *prophets,*
>
> *some* to be *evangelists,*
>
> and *some* to be *pastors* and *teachers,*
>
>> to prepare God's people for works of service, so that
>>
>> the body of Christ may be built up (Ephesians 4:11–12).[2]

At this point, let's take an in-depth look at who these "greater gifts" were and how they functioned in the New Testament setting.

THE APOSTLES

In the Gospels

When Jesus began His ministry, those who followed and listened to His teachings were called "disciples." Early on, Jesus had issued a special call to four fisherman—Peter, Andrew, James, and John—and a tax collector named Matthew or Levi (Matt. 4:18–22; 9:9). Everywhere Jesus went, they followed, and as the group of disciples expanded, Jesus eventually chose these five men and seven more (often called "The Twelve") and designated them as "apostles" (Matt. 10:1–4; Mark 3:13–19; Luke 6:12–16).

The name *apostle* (*apostolos*) literally means "one sent"—as a messenger and ambassador. However, even though the twelve men Jesus chose that day on a mountainside in Galilee were called "apostles," the Gospel writers continued to use the term *disciples* to describe their activities. In fact, this basic term is used more than 80 percent of the time in the four Gospels to refer exclusively to one or more of the twelve apostles, which indicates how prominent these twelve men are in the biblical story. Though Jesus ministered to the multitudes as well as to a smaller group which He identified as disciples, His primary focus was on preparing these twelve men to continue the work once He returned to the Father.

In the Book of Acts and the Epistles

As Luke continued to unfold the New Testament story in the book of Acts, he quickly focused on "the apostles" Jesus "had chosen"(Acts 1:2), which now numbered eleven. Following the Resurrection, they were still filled with questions regarding the future, the final question being, "Are you [now] going to restore the kingdom to Israel?" (1:6). Jesus' answer was vague, but one thing was clear. Though it was not time for them to know the "times or dates the Father has set by his own authority," they would "receive power when the Holy Spirit" came on them when they returned to Jerusalem and they would be His witnesses not only in the Holy City, but "in all Judea and Samaria, and to the ends of the earth" (1:7–8).

The apostles obeyed Jesus' final words and returned to Jerusalem. They entered an upper room and prayed with a number of other disciples (1:12–14). While waiting, and as the primary leader of the apostles, Peter's first task was to replace Judas with another eyewitness of Christ's ministry from the time John was baptized until Jesus ascended. Specifically, Peter stated that Judas' replacement "must become a witness with 'them' of his resurrection" (1:21–22). Two were qualified, but Matthias was chosen by lot and "was added to the eleven apostles" (1:26).

When the Holy Spirit descended on the Day of Pentecost, these twelve men were singled out with "what seemed to be tongues of fire that separated and came to rest on each of them" (2:3). Furthermore, they were supernaturally enabled to speak various languages and dialects so that "God-fearing Jews from every nation under heaven" could hear and understand the apostles' message regarding the crucified and resurrected Messiah. Amazed, those who witnessed this phenomena asked: "Are not all these men who are speaking Galileans?" (2:5–7). And from this point forward, the Holy Spirit continued to verify the apostleship of these twelve men in a supernatural way through "wonders and miraculous signs" (2:43; cf. 4:33; 5:12).

Paul, "an Apostle to the Gentiles"

Though the New Testament clearly focused on the original twelve apostles during the early years of the church, God expanded this number to include Paul, who met the resurrected and ascended Christ face-to-face on the road to Damascus. He was definitely numbered with "the Twelve" as having a unique apostolic ministry. Paul's claim that he was "an apostle, sent not from men nor by men, but by Jesus Christ and God the Father" was also verified by the other apostles—particularly by Peter and John. They recognized Peter "as an apostle to the Jews" and Paul as "an apostle to the Gentiles" (Galatians 1:1; 2:7–9).

Apostolic Representatives

There came a point in time that the term "apostle" was also used in a broader sense. For example,

☐ On the first missionary journey, Luke identified both Paul and Barnabas as *apostles* (Acts 14:14).

☐ When Paul wrote to the Thessalonians, he identified not only himself as an *apostle,* but also his fellow missionaries, Silas and Timothy (1 Thessalonians 2:6).

☐ When Paul wrote 2 Corinthians, he referred to a group of brothers as "*representatives* [*apostoloi*] of the churches" (8:23).

☐ When Paul wrote to the Romans, he stated that his relatives Andronicus and Junias (probably a husband and wife team) were "outstanding among the *apostles*" (16:7).

There are several other references in the New Testament letters where the term *apostles* may have been used, particularly by Paul, to refer to missionaries generally who were not among the men chosen by Christ who were eyewitnesses of His resurrection. However, the distinction is clear. As the late theologian George Peters wrote: "The unique position of the apostles in the beginning ministries of the church is recognized throughout the New Testament—only they are known as the *apostles of Jesus Christ,* while others are known simply as *apostles* or as *apostles of the church.*"[3]

At this point, it seems that the "apostles" Paul referred to in 1 Corinthians 12:28 and Ephesians 4:11 were those who were eyewitnesses of Christ's ministry, death, and resurrection. He identified them as "super apostles" (literally "highest apostles") because of their calling as well as their ability to perform "signs, wonders and miracles" (2 Corinthians 12:11–12). More specifically, Paul called these demonstrations a "mark" of an apostle—which also set Paul himself off as an eyewitness of the resurrected Christ and one the Holy Spirit verified as one of the original apostles (12:12). Because of God's grace in choosing him to be an "apostle to the Gentiles"—even though he at the time was persecuting the church—he sincerely identified himself as "one abnormally born," "the least of the apostles" and one who did "not even deserve to be called an apostle" (1 Corinthians 15:8–9).

THE PROPHETS

Though the term *apostle* is basically a New Testament concept, the term *prophet* is not. The Old Testament refers again and again to those who declared and announced God's will to the people of Israel. As Merrill F. Unger states, "The true prophet was God's spokesman to man, communicating what he had received from God."[4]

When we look carefully at the Old Testament documents, it's clear that the prophets declared and announced *doctrinal truth* about God and His will as well as *predictive truth* regarding God's will in the future. When true prophets spoke, they were divinely inspired by God Himself (2 Peter 1:20–21). In terms of predictive prophecy, some Bible students estimate that as much as 25 percent of the Bible is predictive in nature.

In the Book of Acts

Throughout Luke's historical treatise, twenty-five out of thirty-four statements about "prophets" or "prophecy" (74 percent) refer to Old Testament prophets who predicted the first coming of the Messiah.[5] And though there are not as many references to prophets who were gifts to the church, yet seven of these thirty-four statements (21 percent) refer to New Testament prophets. Since they are the focus of our attention, here is the complete list:

1. Joel's prophecy regarding New Testament prophets: "In the last days, God says, I will pour out my Spirit on all people. Your sons and daughters will prophesy . . ." (Acts 2:17).
2. Prophets from Jerusalem: "During this time some prophets came down from Jerusalem to Antioch" (Acts 11:27).
3. Agabus: "One of them, named Agabus, stood up and through the Spirit predicted that a severe famine would spread over the entire Roman world" (Acts 11:28; cf. 21:10–11).
4. Barnabas, Simeon, Lucius, Manaen, and Saul: "In the church at Antioch there were prophets and teachers" (Acts 13:1).
5. Judas and Silas from Jerusalem: "Judas and Silas, who themselves were prophets, said much to encourage and strengthen the brothers" (Acts 15:32).
6. Twelve men in Ephesus: "When Paul placed his hands on them, the Holy Spirit came on them, and they spoke in tongues and prophesied" (Acts 19:6).
7. Philip's four unmarried daughters: "He had four unmarried daughters who prophesied" (Acts 21:9).

In the Epistles

In the New Testament letters, there are approximately forty-two references to "prophets" or "prophesying."

1 Corinthians. Fifteen references appear in Paul's first letter to the very immature and carnal Corinthian church (1 Corinthians 3:1–4). Since these believers were misusing the gifts of the Spirit, Paul gave some very specific instructions regarding the prophetic gift; namely, to give priority attention to this gift since it was designed by God to edify and build up believers (1 Corinthians 14:1–4). As we've already noted, when "Judas and Silas, who themselves were *prophets*" in the church in Jerusalem came to Antioch, they "said much to *encourage* and *strengthen*" their fellow believers. Clearly, this was one of the major purposes for this "greater gift."

Ephesians. In this letter, no doubt a circular letter that focused more on the universal church than a single local church, we see how clearly the prophetic gift is aligned with the apostolic gift in God's overall plan for the body of Christ:

> ☐ You are members of God's household . . . built on the foundation of the *apostles* and *prophets.* [Ephesians 2:19–20]

> ☐ The mystery of Christ [the church], which . . . has now been revealed by the Spirit to God's holy *apostles* and *prophets.* [Ephesians 3:4–5]

> ☐ It was he who gave some to be *apostles,* some to be *prophets.* [Ephesians 4:11]

1 Thessalonians. When Paul penned his first letter to the church in Thessalonica, he gave some specific instructions regarding how to evaluate those who supposedly had the gift of prophecy but did not. He wrote: "Do not put out the Spirit's fire; do not treat *prophecies* with contempt. Test everything. Hold on to the good" (1 Thessalonians 5:19–21).

Clearly, Paul was cautioning these believers to discern between "false prophets" and "true prophets." On the one hand, they were not to restrict the Spirit's voice through gifted believers; on the other hand, they were to evaluate everything that was being said and to only listen to prophetic messages that were from God.

Revelation. Finally, there are ten references to prophets or prophesying in the book of Revelation. Most of these refer to those who will receive and exercise this gift after Jesus Christ has removed the church from this world.[6]

THE EVANGELISTS

Though Paul includes "evangelists" in the lists of "greater gifts" in his letter to the Ephesians (4:11), there are only three references to the title (*euangelistes*) in the New Testament:

1. Philip: "Leaving the next day, we reached Caesarea and stayed at the house of Philip the evangelist, one of the Seven" [Acts 21:8]
2. The Greater Gifts: "It was he who gave some to be apostles, some to be prophets, some to be *evangelists*, and some to be pastors and teachers" [Ephesians 4:11]
3. Timothy: "Do the work of an *evangelist*." [2 Timothy 4:5].[7]

From *Euangelizo*

Though there are only three references to "evangelists" (*euangelistes*), when we look at the functions of these individuals described with the basic word *euangelizo*, there are at least forty references in the book of Acts and the New Testament letters, and almost all refer to key men, such as the apostles, Philip the evangelist, Paul, Barnabas, Silas and Timothy, *proclaiming* or *preaching* the Gospel to unbelievers.[8]

From *Kerruso*

In analyzing the ministry of "evangelists," we must not only look at the process described by *euangelizo* but at other words that describe evangelism. For example, the basic word *kerruso* is used approximately thirty times in Acts and the epistles and is often translated to "preach, to be a herald and to proclaim."[9] Again, almost all these references are to the same key leaders (Philip, Peter, Paul, Silas and Timothy) who were presenting the Gospel to unbelievers.

From *Katangello*

The New Testament writers also used the word *katangello* to describe the ministry of evangelism. This basic term, which means "to tell, declare plainly, openly, loudly," is used approximately eighteen times in Acts and the epistles and is also used primarily to describe the ministry of the apostles in communicating the Gospel to unbelievers.

From *Diamarturomai*

In terms of presenting the Gospel, another Greek word used to describe this process is *diamarturomai*. It means "to attest, or to solemnly testify and to earnestly bear witness to the truth of the Gospel message." The preaching of Peter, John and Paul is associated with this word in the book of Acts.[10]

At this juncture, it's clear from the biblical text that the gift of evangelism was in the most part combined with the gift of an apostle, which may be one reason Paul omitted referring to "evangelists" in the list of "greater gifts" in his letter to the Corinthians (1 Corinthians 12:28). On the other hand, there were gifted individuals who were *not* apostles in a primary sense who were gifted evangelists. Though Philip is the only individual mentioned specifically, it may be that Stephen and the other five Grecian Jews mentioned in Acts 6 also had this gift. It appears that at least several of these men were the ones that first presented the Gospel in Antioch.[11]

PASTORS-TEACHERS

When the term *pastor* or *shepherd* is associated with the term *teacher* (as it is in Ephesians 4:12) and described as a special gift from God, it seems to indicate a single gift. Furthermore, this is the only time the Greek word *poimen* (pastor or shepherd) is identified as a gift of the Spirit.[12] Though elders/overseers are to be shepherds, this function is never defined as a supernatural gift but rather as a responsibility for any man who serves in this role. On the other hand, the term *teacher* (*didaskalos*) is used more frequently and, as we've seen in 1 Corinthians 12:28 and Ephesians 4:11, is defined as a supernatural gift. Interestingly, there is only one reference to gifted teachers in the book of Acts (13:1), and on two occasions, Paul stated that he "was appointed a herald and an apostle and a teacher" (2 Timothy 1:11; see also 1 Timothy 2:7). Like the gift of "evangelist," the teacher's function (*didasko*) is described more often than the title.

In the Gospels

To understand this unique gift of pastor-teacher, we must go back to that unusual scene in the Upper Room shortly before Jesus went to the cross. The Savior had told the eleven remaining apostles He would be leaving them. To encourage and comfort them, He quickly reassured them He would send "another Counselor . . . the Spirit of truth" to "teach [them] all things" and to "remind [them] of everything" he had taught them (John 14:16 17, 26). Furthermore, Jesus said, "But when he, the *Spirit of truth*, comes, he will *guide you into all truth* . . . and he will tell you what is *yet to come*" (John 16:13). Armed with this "unfolding truth" from God Himself, the apostles would be able to communicate this truth to others.

In the Book of Acts

This Upper Room discourse (recorded in John 13–16) set the stage for what happened on the Day of Pentecost. When the Counselor came as Jesus promised, the "Spirit of truth" began to carry out what Jesus said would happen. As He revealed truth, He also supernaturally enabled the apostles to begin teaching this truth to both unbelieving and believing Jews. Responding to this truth about the Messiah, "three thousand believed" and then "devoted themselves to the apostles' *teaching* [*didache*]" (Acts 2:42).

From this point forward in the book of Acts, the term *teaching* is used almost exclusively to describe the apostles' evangelistic ministry, particularly among the Jews. In fact, this "teaching process" is at times associated with three other words we've already looked at (*euangelizo, kerusso,* and *diamarturomai*) that describe presenting the Gospel to unbelievers. For example, in the early days of Christianity, we read that the apostles (the Twelve) "never stopped *teaching* and *proclaiming* [*euangelizo*] the good news that Jesus is the Christ" (Acts 5:42). And years later when Paul was in prison in Rome, he was still engaged in this process of evangelistic teaching among unbelieving Jews. We read: "Boldly and without hindrance he *preached* [*kerusso*] the kingdom of God and *taught* about the Lord Jesus Christ" (Acts 28:31).

In the Epistles

Though the basic term for *teaching* (*didasko*) is used almost exclusively by the apostles in the book of Acts with a strong focus on an evangelistic ministry, when it is used in the New Testament letters, it refers more frequently, though not exclusively, to edifying believers. Furthermore, the *"didache"* that was presented by "gifted teachers" like Paul enabled *all* members of Christ's body to communicate biblical truth to one another enabling them to mature in Jesus Christ. For example, Paul wrote to the Colossians: "Let the word of Christ dwell in you richly as you *teach* and *admonish* one another with all wisdom" (Colossians 3:16; see also 1:28; 2:6–7).

And when it came to equipping people for special service and ministry—including eldership—Paul wrote to Timothy: "And the things you have heard me say in the presence of many witnesses *entrust to reliable men who will also be qualified to teach others*" (2 Timothy 2:2).[13]

THE APOSTLES' TEACHING

The process of "teachers teaching" has pervaded every culture of the world since the dawn of creation. However, communication within the Christian community is unique since it is based on God's revealed truth.

This supernatural process was at first introduced by the Creator at Mount Sinai when God revealed His will to Israel. God then continued to reveal Himself and His will through the numerous Old Testament prophets. And when Jesus sent the "Spirit of Truth" on the Day of Pentecost, He began to reveal the body of truth initially delivered orally and called the "apostles' teaching [*Didache*]" (Acts 2:42).

This process continued throughout the first century, according to the biblical record. In the initial days of the church, the religious leaders were alarmed and threatened. On one occasion, the apostles were brought before the Sanhedrin. The high priest addressed them angrily: "We gave you strict orders not to teach [*didasko*] in this name," he said. "Yet you have filled Jerusalem with your teaching [*didache*] and are determined to make us guilty of this man's blood" (Acts 5:28).

Paul particularly used another Greek term, *didaskalia*, to describe a body of biblical truth. Combining these two ideas, he told Titus that an elder/overseer "must hold firmly to the trustworthy message as it has been *taught* [*didache*], so that he can encourage others by *sound doctrine* [*didaskalia*] and refute those who oppose it" (Titus 1:9; see also Ephesians 4:14; 1 Timothy 1:10; 2 Timothy 3:10, 16).

What began on the Day of Pentecost with the "apostles' teaching" continued for a number of decades and eventually resulted in a body of literature we call the New Testament. In essence, these documents are the *didache* and the *didaskalia*—a complete fulfillment of what Jesus promised these men in the Upper Room. As primary apostles, Matthew gave us one of the Gospels, Peter wrote two letters, and John composed his Gospel, three epistles and the book of Revelation. Paul, of course, was the most prolific apostle, penning thirteen letters.

However, there were at least four other men gifted by the Holy Spirit to record the holy Scriptures. James, the half brother of Christ, wrote one of the letters in the New Testament and so did Christ's half brother Jude. John Mark wrote one of the Gospels and an unnamed author wrote Hebrews. I believe all of these writers were pastor-teachers, bringing into being the New Testament, which is the foundation for preparing all of us "for works of service" so that we will "become mature, attaining to the whole measure of the fullness of Christ" (Ephesians 4:12–13). It is this body of truth that can keep us from being "tossed back and forth by the waves, and blown here and there by every wind of *teaching*" (v. 14); that is, from accepting a corpus of "teaching" that is out of harmony with the revealed will of God.

If this assumption is correct, the gift of *pastor-teacher* was a supernatural, revelatory gift—just as the gift of prophecy was. In fact, all of the original apostles seemingly had both the gift of prophecy and pastor-teacher. There were others, however, who were not apostles in the primary sense but who also had both the prophetic and teaching gifts (see Acts 13:1).

Often it's difficult to distinguish functionally one of the "greater gifts" from the others. For example, Agabus was definitely a prophet, being able to predict the future with detailed accuracy (Acts 11:27–28; 21:10–11). But did he have more than one of the "greater gifts"? We're not told. However, we know that Paul had *all* of the "greater gifts" (Acts 13:1; 1 Timothy 2:7; 2 Timothy 1:11).

We also know that Philip was not an original apostle, but he was definitely an evangelist who was empowered by the Holy Spirit to work incredible miracles (Acts 8:5–7; 21:8). By contrast, Peter, like Paul, was also multigifted. This is why it is very important not to over-categorize the "greater gifts." Apparently some individuals had one of the gifts. Some had two, while others had three. But the apostles particularly had all four.

SOME CONCLUSIONS

From this study of spiritual gifts among early believers in the church, we can draw certain conclusions. First, God through Christ and the Holy Spirit gave the "greater gifts" to launch and establish local churches throughout the New Testament world. In 1 Corinthians, Paul stated that *"God has appointed"* these gifted individuals (12:28) and in Ephesians, he wrote that it was *Christ* Himself *who gave* these "greater gifts" (see Eph. 4:7, 11).

Second, the "greater gifts" were given only to a selected few among the thousands who became believers. They definitely stood out as leaders who had experienced a supernatural empowerment by the Holy Spirit. However, once the churches were founded, the greater gifts introduced a second phase—permanent leadership roles in these churches. As we've seen in this study of *Elders and Leaders,* the first men to be appointed were elders/overseers, and this role *was open to any man* who desired the position and who had developed certain Christian qualities in his life. Consequently, there is no reference to having or being the "greater gifts" in the list of qualifications. This was not so much a "divine appointment" and a "direct endorsement" from heaven, but an appointment based on discernment regarding personal Christian maturity and a good reputation both within and outside the church.

Third, in addition to elders/overseers who were to manage and shepherd local communities of faith, when necessary deacons were to be appointed to assist these spiritual leaders. As with elders/overseers, this position was open to any mature man or woman who qualified. Again, there are no references to supernatural gifts in this list of qualifications.

Fourth, these leadership phases at times created confusion. It's apparent from both the New Testament letters and the writings of the early church fathers that confusion developed. Obviously, there was functional overlap. We see this clearly in the Corinthian church, primarily because there were no men mature enough to become elders. Evidently, this condition existed for a number of years.

We also see confusion when immature individuals wanted to become leaders in the church. Both Timothy and Titus faced this challenge to appoint qualified elders/overseers (1 Timothy 1:3–4; Titus 1:10–11).

THE DIDACHE

As the original "greater gifts" began to pass off the scene, we see the challenge leaders faced in discerning between authentic and false leaders who traveled throughout the New Testament landscape. For example, consider the following quotation from *The Didache*[14]: "Whosoever then comes and *teaches* you all things aforesaid, receive him. But if the *teacher* himself be perverted and *teach* another *doctrine* to *destroy these things, do not listen to him, but if his* teaching *be for the increase of righteousness and knowledge of the Lord, receive him as the Lord.*"[15]

Note how this quotation from *The Didache* correlates with the apostle John's concern in his second epistle when he wrote: "If anyone comes to you and does not bring this *teaching* [*didache*] do not take him into your house or welcome him" (2 John 10). Here John was referring to a person who claimed to be a "pastor-teacher" but who at the same time brought a message that denied the deity of Jesus Christ. Obviously, he would be a false teacher.

Consider the following quotations from *The Didache:*

☐ And concerning the *Apostles* and *Prophets*, act thus according to the ordinance of the gospel. Let every *Apostle* who comes to you be received as the Lord, but let him not stay more than one day, or if need be a second as well; but if he stay three days, he is a *false prophet*. And when an *Apostle* goes forth let him accept nothing but bread till he reach his night's lodging; but if he ask for money, he is a *false prophet*.[16]

☐ But every true *prophet* who wishes to settle among you is "worthy of his food." Likewise a true *teacher* is himself worthy, like the workman, of his food.[17]

☐ Appoint therefore for yourselves *bishops* and *deacons* worthy of the Lord, meek men, and not lovers of money, and truthful and approved, for they also minister to you the ministry of the *prophets* and *teachers*. Therefore do not despise them, for they are your honourable men together with the *prophets* and *teachers*.[18]

These quotations demonstrate several things that we have also noted in the biblical story. First, there were definitely two categories of leaders in the New Testament churches—those with the "greater gifts," who traveled and ministered at large, and those who were permanent leaders in local churches—elders/overseers/bishops and deacons.

Second, there were those who claimed to be the "greater gifts" but who were not truly gifted by the Holy Spirit and who were motivated by greed.

Third, there were those who were the "greater gifts" who were truly inspired and gifted by the Holy Spirit with special abilities and who at times worked alongside qualified elders/overseers/bishops and deacons.

Fourth, qualified elders/overseers were able to do much of the same work as those with the "greater gifts," not because of a special divine calling and "giftedness" but because of their position in Christ, the presence of the Holy Spirit in their lives, the character qualities outlined by Paul in the Pastoral epistles, and because of what they had learned from those who were and had the "greater gifts."

SOME FINAL WORDS

It's my personal opinion and experience that we need not be confused about these two leadership phases. The biblical story plainly defines who should serve as permanent leaders in the local church. These roles are open to any man and woman who measures up to the stature of Jesus Christ as reflected in the qualifications outlined by Paul in his letters to Timothy and Titus. On the other hand, when we do not distinguish the "greater gifts" from the very clear mandate regarding qualifications for local church leaders in the pastoral epistles, we will indeed experience confusion. This is predictable. When we emphasize what the Scriptures emphasize, it leads to unity. When we emphasize what the Bible doesn't emphasize, it invariably leads to confusion.

NOTES

1. When interpreting the exhortation to "eagerly desire the greater gifts," it's important to note that in the Greek text, Paul used the second person plural indicating that the Corinthians *collectively* were to "desire" that those who had and were the "greater gifts" should be given priority in terms of giving authoritative exhortations and directives to the church.

2. Greek scholars acknowledge that it is difficult to literally translate *tous men* and *tous de* in Ephesians 4:11. Most have chosen the English word "some," which certainly conveys the correct idea that not all had certain gifts (see 1 Corinthians 12:29). However, perhaps those scholars who have reworked the *Revised Standard Version*, now called the *English Standard Version*, have captured more adequately what Paul had in mind when they translated: "And he gave the apostles, the prophets, the evangelists, the pastors and teachers [or the pastor-teachers] to equip the saints for the work of the ministry" (Ephesians 4:11–12). This translation helps us avoid the tendency when we read the word "some" to over-categorize these gifted individuals. As we'll see, Paul was a multigifted man, whereas Agabus may have only been a "prophet."

3. George W. Peters, *A Theology of Church Growth* (Grand Rapids: Eerdmans, 1982), 17.

4. Merrill F. Unger, *Unger's Bible Dictionary* (Chicago: Moody, 1957), 892.

5. For example, see Acts 2:29–31; 7:37; 8:34–35; 13:27.

6. For example, see Revelation 11:3,10; 16:6; 18:24.

7. Paul's exhortation to Timothy regarding a ministry of evangelism raises a very interesting question. Was Timothy's gift (2 Timothy 1:6) that of evangelist, or was he simply to "do the work of an evangelist"? Based on the total biblical story, I believe it was the latter.

8. For example, see Acts 5:42; 8:12, 25; 14:7; 16:10; Galatians 1:11.

9. The word *kerugma* is also used several times to refer to the content of the Gospel. For example, Paul wrote to the Corinthians: "God was pleased with the foolishness of what was preached (*kerugma*) to save those who believe."

10. For example, see Acts 2:40; 8:25; 10:42; 18:5; 20:21, 24; 23:11; 28:23.

11. For example, see Acts 8:1; 11:18–21; see also page 54.

12. It should be noted that at least on one occasion Jesus used the term a couple of times to describe Himself as "the good shepherd" (John 11:1, 14, 16; see also Hebrews 13:20; 1 Peter 2:25).

13. See also 1 Timothy 4:11–12; 6:2; Hebrews 5:12. Paul's exhortation to Timothy to pass on to others what he had learned from Paul raises another very interesting question. Did Timothy receive any biblical truth (*didache*) directly from God or did he learn it primarily from Paul? We do know that Timothy had a special gift from the Holy Spirit (2 Timothy 1:6), but because of limited biblical data, it's difficult to pinpoint specifically the nature of this gift. Though I cannot prove it conclusively, it's my personal opinion that Timothy's scriptural knowledge came from the same basic source as my own—primarily from the apostles who had the revelatory gift of "pastor-teacher."

14. *The Didache* is an important document compiled near the end of the first century or the beginning of the second century. It is definitely not inspired Scripture, but it certainly reflects historical events. Scholars agree that this document was "one of the most important discoveries in the second half of the nineteenth century." T*he Didache or Teaching of the Twelve Apostles: The Apostolic Fathers with an English Translation*, Kirsopp Lake, trans. (Cambridge, Mass.: Harvard University Press. 1912), 305.

15. *The Didache or Teaching of the Twelve Apostles: The Apostolic Fathers with an English Translation*. Kirsopp Lake, trans., XI,(Cambridge, Mass.: Harvard University Press. 1912), 325. All emphasis is added.

16. *The Didache*, IX, 3–6, 327.

17. *The Didache*, XIII, 1–2, 329.

18. *The Didache*, XV, 1-2, op.cit; 331.

The Companion
Elders and Leaders Field Guide

The **Field Guide** provides a framework for governing boards to navigate through issues concerning managing and shepherding a local body of believers. Including contributions from senior pastors and governing boards and from several denominational structures, the Field Guide will assist governing boards to effectively lead the church entrusted to their care.

ELDERS
and
LEADERS

FIELD GUIDE

Governing Boards Learning Together in Community

The Center for Church Based Training

Now available through
The Center for Church Based Training
888-422-2896   www.ccbt.org